TRANSFORMING SELF AND WORLD

•

SANGHARAKSHITA

•

TRANSFORMING SELF AND WORLD

•

THEMES FROM THE SŪTRA OF GOLDEN LIGHT

•

WINDHORSE PUBLICATIONS

Published by Windhorse Publications
Unit 1-316 The Custard Factory
Gibb Street
Birmingham
B9 4AA

Printed by Biddles Ltd, Guildford, Surrey.

Design   Lisa Dedman
Cover design   Dhammarati
Text illustrations   Varaprabha

British Library Cataloguing in Publication Data
A catalogue record for this book is available from the British Library

ISBN 0 904766 73 X

CONTENTS

·

About the Author

SANGHARAKSHITA WAS BORN DENNIS LINGWOOD in South London, in 1925. Largely self-educated, he developed an interest in the cultures and philosophies of the East early on, and realized that he was a Buddhist at the age of sixteen.

The Second World War took him, as a conscript, to India, where he stayed on to become the Buddhist monk Sangharakshita ('protected by the spiritual community'). After studying for some years under leading teachers from the major Buddhist traditions, he went on to teach and write extensively. He also played a key part in the revival of Buddhism in India, particularly through his work among the ex-Untouchables.

After twenty years in India, he returned to England to establish the Friends of the Western Buddhist Order (FWBO) in 1967, and the Western Buddhist Order (called Trailokya Bauddha Mahasangha in India) in 1968. A translator between East and West, between the traditional world and the modern, between principles and practices, Sangharakshita's depth of experience and clear thinking have been appreciated throughout the world. He has always particularly emphasized the decisive significance of commitment in the spiritual life, the paramount value of spiritual friendship and community, the link between religion and art, and the need for a 'new society' supportive of spiritual aspirations and ideals.

The FWBO is now an international Buddhist movement with centres in sixteen countries world-wide. In recent years Sangharakshita has been handing over most of his responsibilities to his senior disciples in the Order. From his base in London, he is now focusing on personal contact with people, and on his writing.

•

Editor's Preface

I LIVE ON A HILL OVERLOOKING A CITY. In winter, the sheer mass of brick and stone is overwhelming. Now, in summer, the view is softened by the leaves of the trees, and a pale blue sky through which swifts dart and skim.

Yesterday evening the sunset was a deep, rich gold. Golden light suffused the atmosphere, filtered through the trees, cast a soft glow over the whole city, a kindly touch, as though the city were somehow blessed, purified.

It was, I know, an illusion. Somewhere in the depths of the city, no doubt, crooked business deals were being struck, drugs were being pushed, children were being abused. The mass of brick and stone hides loneliness, grief, despair, greed, and ugliness in every form.

But that brilliant sunset, which lent such splendour to dingy city streets, brought to mind the aptness of the central image of the *Sūtra of Golden Light*, the golden light of the Buddha's teaching which shines upon and transforms the life of an individual Bodhisattva, Ruciraketu, and – as a consequence – the whole world. This is not just a change of outward appearance, but a purifying, liberating transformation deep in the heart of the individual and of the world.

The sūtra contains some very beautiful passages, especially those in praise of the Buddha, who 'stands amid the darkness like the sun in the three worlds'. But frankly, if I had come across an English translation of the work and read it without guidance, I'm sure I would have made neither head nor tail of it. As Sangharakshita points out in his introduction to the text, it is rather a rag-bag – 'a transcendental rag-bag, to be sure, a rag-bag full of bits and pieces of wonderful, jewelled brocade – but still a rag-bag.' At first sight it is no more than a miscellany of bizarre events.

In speaking of his work Sangharakshita has sometimes chosen to see himself – in a broad, almost an archetypal sense – as a translator. He once explained his affinity for the figure of St Jerome (who translated the Bible from Hebrew and Greek into Latin): 'I was trying to teach Buddhism in the West, which meant I was trying to communicate the spirit of the Dharma in terms of Western rather than in terms of Eastern culture. I was thus a translator, with all that that implies in the way of seeking to fathom the uttermost depths of what one is trying to translate so that one may translate it faithfully, i.e. bring its meaning to the surface, or from darkness into the light. Thus I was drawn to the image of St Jerome....'

In this commentary, Sangharakshita translates the cultural language of ancient Indian symbolism into the language of the modern West. Before our very eyes, this beautiful but strange text becomes a compelling spiritual manifesto with urgent implications for the way we lead our lives.

The book, which is based on a series of lectures given by Sangharakshita in 1976, is divided, after the introduction to the sūtra, into two parts. The first, 'Transforming Self', focuses on the theme at the heart of the *Sūtra of Golden Light*, confession – which, in the context of Buddhist practice, is not a sorry, guilt-ridden affair, but a liberating, positive step towards freedom and happiness. In this part of the book the lecture material is augmented to become a detailed, almost line-by-line commentary on the text, with the help of material drawn from a seminar conducted by Sangharakshita – also in 1976 – at Sukhavati community in London.

The second part of the book, 'Transforming World', applies the text to our own society, exploring its implications for our relationship to our culture, the way we live in relation to nature, how we can bring the practice of Buddhism to the work-place and the world of business, and the nature of ethical government. In both parts of the book extra points are added from a question-and-answer session held at Padmaloka retreat centre in 1987, in the course of which Sangharakshita answered questions on the original lecture series.

Although I have been drawing attention to the very pragmatic nature of Sangharakshita's exposition of this text, I should add that this pragmatism is in no sense at the expense of the magical and fervently devotional atmosphere of the original sūtra. It is one of Sangharakshita's strengths as a teacher that because he practises Buddhism so wholeheartedly himself, his approach could never be academic or theoretical. With him, clarity of thought is never separate from depth of feeling.

In preparing this book for publication, I couldn't have managed without the help and criticism, so cheerfully (and firmly!) offered, of my colleague Jinananda. Thanks also to Varaprabha for her illustrations and to Lottie Berthoud and all at Windhorse for their careful work on this publication. And thanks, of course, to Urgyen Sangharakshita, who has been closely involved with all stages of production, including reading and amending the final text. He once told me that this teaching is particularly special to him; I know he will be very glad to see it at last in print.

Editing is a solitary business. I have sat in my room on the hill these many months, surrounded by drifts of scribbled-on typescript, and tried to imagine you, the reader of this book. For me too, working on this text has been no academic enterprise. As I have looked out over the great city, watching the light shift across its roofs and walls, I have not felt separate from it, but have imagined the golden light of this text filtering through the haze of contemporary opinion and ideology to touch and transfigure other hearts and minds, as my own heart has been touched. May it be so.

Vidyadevi
Spoken Word Project
Norwich
August 1995

INTRODUCTION:
THE GROWTH OF A MAHĀYĀNA SŪTRA

MOST OF US CARRY IN OUR MINDS what we might call a model of the spiritual life, some image that conjures up what it means for us. Quite possibly we will tend to think in terms of development, growth, opening. We may even see in our mind's eye the unfolding petals of a flower. Perhaps for many of us this is the most helpful way of thinking about the spiritual life. But it is not the only way. We can also see the spiritual life, for example, in terms of transformation.

The word transformation suggests something radical, some fundamental change. Literally it means a change of form. But as a model for the spiritual life it means something much deeper and more thoroughgoing. It signifies a change of consciousness, a total shift in our being, a revolution that affects us from the depths to the heights of our individuality. It describes a *transition* from what is worldly to what is transcendental. It also means a death and a rebirth.

If we are honest with ourselves, if we allow ourselves to think and feel deeply, this is surely what we are looking for: to die and be reborn – but not necessarily in the flesh. What we seek is a withering of the roots of our being and a truly radical rebirth. We are fed up with ourselves as we are, with the self we have been stuck with for so long, perhaps for years upon years. We would like to trade it in for a pristine, brand new self, to emerge like a butterfly from the chrysalis of all our old conditions into an entirely new life of greater freedom and joy, greater awareness and spontaneity.

And not only are we tired of the old *self*. We are tired of the old *world* as well. We want to transform the world, so that it supports our spiritual growth and transformation at every step. We have had enough of political, social, and economic arrangements that do not allow people a decent human life, let alone a life that goes beyond this modest ideal. We are weary of the whole culture of consumerism and possessiveness. We are sometimes tired too of the arts within our civilization, when they express the sick mind and the diseased imagination. We want everything to be made new.

This transformation of the self and of the world is what the Buddhist way of life is about. It is also what the *Sūtra of Golden Light*[1] is about, for the golden light is what transforms the self and transforms the world. But where does this light come from? It is not enough to say that it is a spiritual light, for it is more than this. It is, we may say, a *transcendental* light. It is transcendental in the traditional Buddhist sense of the *lokuttara*: that which is beyond the world, beyond the mundane, beyond all that is conditioned. It is therefore without beginning and without end. It does not shine forth from anything – from any particular place, any particular direction – though it may appear to do so, or even be spoken of as doing so. We may call it the light of truth, the light of Reality, the light of the Buddha – but even that does not go far enough. It is the light which *is* the truth, *is* Reality, *is* the Buddha. And as we examine this text we shall be laying ourselves open to this golden light, for it suffuses the whole of this most popular of all Mahāyāna sūtras.

Being a Mahāyāna sūtra, the *Sūtra of Golden Light* exemplifies many of the characteristics of Mahāyāna Buddhism – as well as possessing certain special features of its own. The Mahāyāna, which is one of the three major historical forms of Indian Buddhism, is not a particular sect or school of Buddhism, but rather a particular attitude to Buddhism. It arose as a movement of reaction against a narrow interpretation of the letter of the Buddha's teachings, seeking to reconnect with the original spirit of those teachings. This movement has swept through Buddhist history, affecting all aspects of religious, artistic, and even social life. Transcending the immediate historical context, going beyond the reaction which led to its arising, the Mahāyāna has developed a positive spiritual character of its own. Lama Anagarika Govinda captures this distinctive character in a single phrase: universal perspective.

It is its universal perspective which gives the Mahāyāna its name. Mahāyāna literally means 'great way', and it is so called because it is the way to Enlightenment for a great number of people, in fact for all sentient beings. So the Mahāyāna Buddhist doesn't think only in terms of his or her own personal spiritual development. There is no question of gaining Enlightenment for oneself and leaving everybody else to fend for themselves. The Mahāyāna vision is that all men and women can develop spiritually, and that helping them to do so is an intrinsic part of the spiritual life. For this reason, the Mahāyāna stresses the ideal of the Bodhisattva. As the word implies (it literally means 'one who is bent on Enlightenment'), the Bodhisattva is one who has dedicated himself to the highest spiritual realization. But he is dedicated to it not for his own sake alone, but for that of all living beings whatsoever. He expresses this dedication and determination by taking four great vows:

However innumerable beings are, I vow to deliver them.
However inexhaustible the passions are, I vow to extinguish them.
However immeasurable the Dharmas are, I vow to master them.
However incomparable the Buddha's Truth is, I vow to attain it.

It may be traditional to speak of the Bodhisattva as a person, but if we really try to get a feeling for these vows, we will realize that we cannot think of a Bodhisattva in the same sort of way as we think of an ordinary man or woman. We cannot think of a Bodhisattva as simply an extraordinary individual. The Bodhisattva is not literally a person at all. At least in the more advanced stages of his spiritual career, he transcends individual personality altogether to become what we might call a 'suprapersonal' stream of spiritual energy. But however lofty the spiritual attainment of the Bodhisattva may be, Mahāyāna Buddhism encourages absolutely everybody to make that their aim. That is to say, it encourages every single person to co-operate in what it describes as the great work of universal transformation. The Bodhisattva ideal is therefore universal in its aim, which is nothing less than supreme Buddhahood; it is universal in its scope, which encompasses all sentient beings; and it is universal in its frame of reference, which is infinite space and boundless time. It is a supremely heroic aspiration.[2]

But, of course, not everybody wants to be a hero. Even among the followers of the Mahāyāna, not everybody wants to be a Bodhisattva. Strange to say, some people are quite reluctant to gain supreme

Buddhahood! It is therefore part of the task of the Bodhisattva to offer them a helping hand – not to say a crutch or two. To do this the Bodhisattva has to assemble a toolkit of what are technically called 'skilful means': an array of methods of helping people spiritually in a way appropriate to their present stage of development, to their temperament, and to their position in life. If the Bodhisattva is skilful enough, the recipients of his help may not even notice that they are being helped. In other words, the Bodhisattva meets people half way. He tries to meet them on their own ground, to learn their language. In short, he makes things easy for them – as easy, that is, as is compatible with the objective demands of the spiritual life.

However willing and helpful a Bodhisattva may be, he can't magically produce spiritual transformation in you; you have to do it yourself. Whatever the Bodhisattva gives you in the way of guidance, encouragement, and inspiration, you need to supply your own active co-operation, even if what you are doing is simply being receptive to his influence.

The Bodhisattva does not necessarily do very much – sometimes he helps simply by being around. Nor does he necessarily turn up dressed for the part (as it were), with jewelled headdress and resplendent lotus throne. He may sometimes leave all that behind and appear as just a positive, friendly, sympathetic, warm-hearted, encouraging human being. In the spiritual life we need plenty of encouragement: encouragement not to be afraid of behaving ethically, whatever anyone else may think; encouragement to be generous with our money, our time, and our energy; encouragement to express our feelings of faith and devotion.

In this way, as the Bodhisattva learns to meet people half way, there comes into existence the more popular, even the more ethnic side of Mahāyāna Buddhism. In the Mahāyāna Buddhist countries of the East, people are encouraged to co-operate in the building of temples and monasteries, to give offerings of food to wandering monks, and to perform simple devotional acts – acts which are simple in form but so meaningful in content – like offering flowers to the Buddha, reciting mantras, and going on pilgrimage to holy places.

Such popular Buddhism is not to be disparaged as a degeneration of the teaching. We can think of it as a kind of bridge: a bridge between ordinary worldly existence and purely spiritual, even transcendental, life. As Buddhism is becoming established in the West, this 'bridge' is taking new forms.[3] Buddhist centres are running arts events which draw on the Western cultural tradition, and putting on activities such as T'ai Chi Ch'uan, Alexander Technique, and yoga classes, as well as establishing businesses such as vegetarian restaurants, all of which give people a means of approach to the Buddhist way of life.

Where popular Mahāyāna Buddhism represents a degeneration of the teaching it does so only because it has become an end in itself, because there have been no Bodhisattvas around to remind people what it is all for, and the ultimate goal of supreme Buddhahood has been forgotten. With no one around to remind them of why they are doing what they are doing, people tend to start building houses on the bridge instead of using it to cross over to the other side.

This is the moral of a little Japanese story about the career of a young monk. Looking ahead to the future, this novice monk thought 'One day I'm going to be in charge of a temple, and people are going to come along for instruction. So it is very important that I should be on good terms with them. Now what would I be able to do to please them and put them at their ease?' He decided that the best thing to do would be to learn to play the flute. If he could perform some nice music when people came to the temple, it would create a good impression and lead to friendly relations. So he started practising on the flute and – to cut a long story short – in the end he became so engrossed in his music that he forgot all about being a monk. Prematurely adopting 'skilful means' proved his own undoing: he got sidetracked.

So in our Western context, to take the example of a vegetarian restaurant, people might start forgetting that the reason they started running the restaurant in the first place was to offer newcomers a stepping-stone to a Buddhist way of life. They might just settle down into trying to get into the *Good Food Guide*. The only real safeguard against such degeneration is to make sure that all such activities are run by people who are deeply committed to the spiritual life.

While negotiating such pitfalls, Mahāyāna Buddhism has spread very widely indeed, from India to Tibet, China, Japan, and now the West; and as it has done so it has taken in elements from each indigenous culture. We could think of this as an aspect of the Bodhisattva's learning to speak the language of the people he tries to help. This integration with popular culture has developed so abundantly in the East that some modern scholars have been fooled into thinking of the Mahāyāna as an essentially popular movement. But in fact, though the Mahāyāna may be popular, it is also very profound, not just intellectually but spiritually.

For evidence of this, we need only turn to the teachings that centre upon Perfect Wisdom, or – as it is sometimes called – 'the wisdom that has gone beyond', that is to say, gone beyond the mundane, gone to ultimate reality. And this ultimate reality to which Perfect Wisdom has gone is known technically in the Mahāyāna as *śūnyatā*, which literally means 'voidness' or 'emptiness'. We should not, however, be misled into imagining some sort of blankness or black hole. Śūnyatā is not voidness in the sense of vacuity; it is voidness in the sense of being beyond all concepts, beyond thought, beyond the reach of the rational mind. From the standpoint of ultimate reality, we may say that Perfect Wisdom is the spiritual faculty that intuits śūnyatā, and śūnyatā is what is intuited by Perfect Wisdom – the one being the subject and the other the object. But from the standpoint of śūnyatā – if we can really think of śūnyatā as having a standpoint – there is no such distinction. In absolute or ultimate reality there is just one unbroken awareness, undivided by the polarity of subject and object.

It is Perfect Wisdom that makes the Bodhisattva a Bodhisattva. In realizing śūnyatā, he transcends completely the distinction between self and other. Only then, paradoxically, can he help others. The Bodhisattva ideal is not a kind of humanitarianism, not even a religious humanitarianism. It is nothing less than the wisdom of the voidness breaking through into the world and functioning in the midst of the affairs of everyday life.

All this emphasis on wisdom does not mean that the Mahāyāna neglects faith and devotion. On the contrary, in Mahāyāna Buddhism devotion is particularly intense, and directed not only to the historical Buddha, Śākyamuni, but also to the ideal Buddha, the universal Buddha, the Buddha who occupies the centre of the Mahāyāna's spiritual universe and appears in a number of different forms or aspects: for instance, Amitābha, the Buddha of Infinite Light, and Vairocana, the Buddha of Sun-like Splendour. Devotees of the Mahāyāna venerate as well the archetypal Bodhisattvas: Avalokiteśvara, the Lord who looks down in Compassion; Mañjuśrī, the gentle-voiced one, the Lord of Wisdom; Samantabhadra, the universally beneficent; Kṣitigarbha, the Earth Womb, who descends into the depths of the states of suffering; and many more. The devotion of the Mahāyāna is directed towards all these great beings.

The *Sūtra of Golden Light* exemplifies many of these characteristics of the Mahāyāna: its universality, its emphasis on the Bodhisattva ideal, its spirit of intense devotion, its worship of a plurality of Buddhas and Bodhisattvas. It is also, in some ways, a typical sūtra (or at least a typical Mahāyāna sūtra) – that is, a particular kind of Buddhist scripture. But before we consider what kind of scripture a sūtra is, we need to ask a more basic question. What is a scripture? The word literally means simply 'something written down'. But although these days we can go to the bookshop and take our pick of a whole shelf full of Buddhist sūtras, it is important to remember that these texts did not start out as written documents at all.

The Buddha himself, the historical Śākyamuni, never wrote anything. It's not even certain that he *could* read and write at all. In his day, writing was not a very respectable occupation. Businessmen used it for keeping their accounts, but the idea of committing anything as sacred as spiritual teachings to writing was simply unthinkable. The Buddha taught, therefore, not by writing spiritual best-sellers, but by talking to people, passing on his teachings through conversation, discussions, and discourses. For their part, his disciples made a point of remembering what he said. Sometimes, indeed, his words were so memorable that no one within earshot could possibly forget them. But even if some disciples did forget, there were others who remembered, and in due course passed on the teachings they had heard to their own disciples. In this way the Buddha's teaching was orally transmitted in India for many, many generations, spanning hundreds of years.

Not only did the early disciples remember hundreds and thousands of teachings, they also managed to arrange, edit, and even index them orally, without even beginning to put pen to paper – or rather stylus to palm leaf: surely a tremendous feat. The key figure in this whole extraordinary process was Ānanda, who was the Buddha's cousin and his constant companion for the last twenty years of his life. Wherever the Buddha went, Ānanda went. If the Buddha went for alms, Ānanda would be just a few paces behind him. If the Buddha accepted an invitation, Ānanda was naturally included. And if the Buddha gave a discourse, Ānanda was present in the audience. For twenty years the Buddha was very rarely to be seen without Ānanda in tow, committing everything his master said to a prodigiously retentive memory.

I must confess to having harboured doubts about Ānanda's superhuman memory, until I actually met someone with comparable powers of recollection, a man who could remember everything he had ever heard me say word for word – together with where I had said it, when, and even why I had said it. This was enough to satisfy me that such an individual as Ānanda is unusual, but no chimera.

It was shortly after the Buddha's death – his *parinirvāṇa* – that Ānanda's gift really came into its own. This was when the Buddha's followers gathered together in a great cave near Rājagṛha in modern Bihar for the purpose of what has since become known as the First Council. But this name for it comes nowhere near evoking the true nature of the occasion. The Sanskrit word used to described this gathering is *saṅgīti*, which literally means 'a chanting together' or even 'a singing together'. The monks – and there are supposed to have been five hundred of them – chanted or sang together whatever they could remember of the Buddha's teaching. The *saṅgīti* was dominated, however, by Ānanda's contribution to what might be called the collective memory of the spiritual community.

So the words 'Thus have I heard', with which almost every Buddhist scripture begins, represent Ānanda's personal testimony that what follows is a reliable account of what the Enlightened One actually said. They mean that Ānanda had been there, or that if he had not been present the Buddha had repeated it all to him afterwards. They are believed to guarantee the authenticity of that text. 'Thus have I heard at one time' is used like a general imprimatur, so to speak, for the content of any scripture.

The sūtra is not, of course, the only kind of Buddhist scripture, although it is perhaps the most important and representative kind. Even during the period of oral transmission, the monks drew up a list of nine forms – increased in the Sarvastivādin School to twelve – that the Dharma as oral communication assumed.[4] These forms appeared later as subdivisions of the canonical literature, but to begin with they were simply different ways in which the Buddha had chosen to speak.

Sometimes, for example – and this may come as a surprise – he chose to speak in verse. This wasn't as difficult as it might sound, because the ancient Indian languages slide much more easily into metre than does modern English. Usually in fact the Buddha would break into impromptu verse or *gātha* in response to a question. Occasionally the question would be put in verse, and the Buddha would reply in kind, but sometimes he would even answer a prose question in verse, perhaps because the verse format would make what he had to say easier to memorize. So he would just produce on the spot a little stanza or series of stanzas. This is the origin of one of the best-known of Buddhist scriptures, the *Dhammapada*, as well as of many other texts.

The Buddha didn't always need to be prompted by a question before he would give a teaching. Sometimes he would speak without any prompting at all – or even when there was no one else present. This spontaneous utterance on the part of the Buddha, usually in verse, is known as the *udāna*, meaning literally 'the outward-going breath'. According to ancient Indian tradition there are five different kinds of breath, and the 'outward-going breath', a forcible exhalation, is just one of these.

So the Buddha is not being asked a question. No one puts anything to him. He may even be alone. But suddenly there comes the *udāna*. It represents an utterance of the Buddha under tremendous pressure of spiritual emotion. We may say that the Buddha explodes into utterance. He can't keep it to himself – it forces its way out.

Among the other forms of scripture there are the *geya* – teachings given in prose interspersed with verses. Also included in this category are those occasions when the Buddha gave his teaching first in prose, and then repeated it all, sometimes with variations, in verse. There are also the *jātaka* or 'birth stories', in which the Buddha relates incidents from one or another of his previous existences.[5] And there are the *abhūtadharma*, the 'marvellous events', which describe extraordinary occurrences in the Buddha's present life, occurrences which we would regard as magical.

And yet another of these forms of teaching, like *gātha, udāna, geya, jātaka*, and the rest, is *sūtra*. *Sūtra* literally means 'a thread'. When we have lost track of what someone is saying, we say 'I've lost the thread'. The 'thread', in other words, is what connects a discourse. A sūtra, then, is a connected discourse given by the Buddha – or even a 'lecture' perhaps, if this meant something inspirational rather than dry as dust.

When it comes to content, sūtras are broadly of two kinds: Hīnayāna sūtras and Mahāyāna sūtras. The Hīnayāna is the first of the three major historical forms of Buddhism,[6] and it literally means 'little way'. It is not a particular sect or school. The Mahāyāna identified and designated the Hīnayāna as a broad spiritual movement in contradistinction to itself, and coined the term to describe those who in their view were concerned predominantly with their own spiritual development, and did not share the Mahāyāna's universal perspective. Just to complete the picture, the third historical form of Buddhism is the Vajrayāna, the way of the diamond or thunderbolt, but the Vajrayāna tradition finds its characteristic expression in what are known as tantras and sādhanas, and has produced only two major sūtras.

Hīnayāna and Mahāyāna sūtras could hardly be more different in character. In the Hīnayāna sūtras, or *suttas*, the Buddha's teaching is firmly embedded, not to say embodied, in a specific historical and geographical context: the north-eastern India of the sixth century BCE – the context of the Buddha's own life and times.[7] These sūtras are full of references to the contemporary political situation and economic conditions. They also contain details about social customs, currents of religious belief, and philosophical speculations, as well as information about what people wore and what they ate, the crops they grew, the kind of houses they built, their trades and occupations. One of the sūtras even lists thirty or forty different games that people played in those days – and there are also references to all sorts of trades and professions. As well as all this social history there is plenty of natural history. The Hīnayāna sūtras take place against a backdrop of the great impenetrable forests and the majestic mountain ranges of India, against the rhythm of her various seasons – the hot season, the cold season, the rainy season – and amidst her flora and fauna, amidst all sorts of animals, birds and trees, flowers and insects.

So in the Hīnayāna sūtras we are given a detailed and vivid picture of the India that was contemporaneous with Athens under Solon, with the Italy that Pythagoras knew, with the Persia of Zoroaster, and the China of Confucius. We also get a good idea of the kind of people the Buddha taught. Indeed, as the scriptures make clear, there was hardly any kind of person that he didn't teach. We find him addressing wandering monks and ascetics, kings, princes, and ministers, businessmen and farmers, philosophers and robbers, prostitutes and outcasts. He exerted his wise and compassionate influence throughout the northern Indian society of his time.

The Mahāyāna sūtras, on the other hand, present us with a very different picture. In many of them we may still be in India – but only just. We could also say that at least in some of them we're still on *earth* – but only just. Indeed, in some of them we have left the earth altogether, for some other, higher, heavenly world – we hardly know where, and we hardly care, because it is so beautiful and entrancing. In most of the Mahāyāna sūtras, however, the main features of the Indian landscape are still dimly visible. We can still see houses and trees – we can at least see, as though through a radiant mist, a solitary mountain peak. But although we can make out these familiar landmarks, they are all transformed, transfigured, bathed in a supernatural light.

Not only that. As we read or listen to the Mahāyāna scriptures, or rather as we *participate* in them – for that's what it feels like – we become aware of all kinds of extraordinary sensations. Celestial music sounds. Delicate fragrances waft through the air. Sometimes showers of golden blossoms rain down from the sky. And sometimes the scene expands even beyond the transformed landscape to include not just this world, not even just this universe, but thousands upon thousands of worlds, and thousands upon thousands of universes, all with their own Buddhas and Bodhisattvas teaching the Dharma.

And in the midst of it all, right at the centre of the Mahāyāna sūtra, sits the Buddha. He sits on a many-petalled lotus throne supported by a pair of lions, under trees made of all kinds of glittering and resplendent jewels. He is surrounded not just by a few beggarly-looking monks, but by a great host of beings, including many Bodhisattvas. From the assembly, and especially from the Buddha, there radiates a great blaze of light. It is this Buddha, seated in the midst of this great blaze of light, who teaches the Mahāyāna sūtras. While he teaches, all sorts of marvels occur. The earth shakes in various ways, flowers rain from the sky, and those listening experience all kinds of spiritual and transcendental insights. The world of the Mahāyāna is a world of light, a world of colour, a world of indescribable beauty and inexpressible joy.

At the same time, it's a very mysterious world. There is something about it that eludes the mind, something awe-inspiring and unfathomable. It is baffling, and yet to experience it gives a feeling of deep happiness and serenity. In the entire spiritual literature of the world there is nothing quite like the atmosphere of the Mahāyāna sūtras – they read almost like transcendental science fiction. Probably the nearest Western parallel is to be found in the gnostic sacred books, such as the *Pistis Sophia*;[8] they too are suffused with light and pervaded with a sense of mystery.

In his essay 'Buddhism and Gnosticism' Dr Conze has suggested that this parallel may not be coincidental and that Gnosticism may be historically connected with Mahāyāna Buddhism. His arguments are not quite convincing, however; in particular the connection he makes between gnosis and prajñā, between the wisdom of Gnosticism and that of Buddhism, seems doubtful. In fact, the distinct differences between gnosis and prajñā are quite instructive.[9] Whilst it is difficult to generalize, because Gnosticism is such a broad phenomenon, it would be safe to say that the Gnostics almost always thought of wisdom as the acquisition of knowledge about certain occult mysteries and mythological details. They seem to have had the idea that there were certain great mysteries about the cosmos – so many spheres of existence, so many aeons, and so on – and if you understood all those mysteries, if you had all the right passwords and key words, you had gnosis. For Buddhism, by contrast, wisdom is essentially a metaphysical insight into something which far transcends the myths and occult mysteries with which the Gnostics were concerned.

For example, the Gnostics believed that man was a prisoner – a reasonable enough metaphor for the human condition. But then they believed that the various spheres – the sun, the moon, and the planets – constituted prisons within prisons, each presided over by a particular divinity whose name or password you had to learn in order to become free. Gnostic 'knowledge' was thus a knowledge of certain occult facts, rather than of ultimate reality – śūnyatā – in the metaphysical sense.

This suggests that in the Gnostic view the acquisition of knowledge was not a matter of personal spiritual development in the way that Buddhists would see it. For Gnosticism, knowledge simply depends upon approaching someone in the right way, becoming his disciple, and getting him to impart to you certain facts. It involves taking certain mythological structures for literal, or if you like scientific, fact. It would be like saying that prajñā in Buddhism means understanding all the different planes of existence and knowing the names of all the deities who inhabited those planes. But no Buddhist would ever say that. Such knowledge may be part of the Buddhist tradition, but you cannot really develop wisdom until you have realized the true nature of those realms, considered from the highest point of view.

It therefore seems that there is a tremendous difference between what Gnosticism understands by wisdom and what Buddhism understands by it, a difference which is concealed by using the one word 'wisdom' for these two different concepts. However, although Mahāyāna Buddhism and Gnosticism differ in this way, I have felt for a long time that there must be some connection between them – not necessarily a historical one. There is certainly a slight but definite resemblance of spirit. Furthermore, it seems possible to detect the same spirit faintly reflected in later Western literature, in the Arthurian cycle (the earlier pagan-based material, not the later Christian incorporations) and particularly the legend of the Holy Grail – but this is pure conjecture.

The Mahāyāna sūtras are classified as either 'early' or 'late', according to whether they were written down and circulated before or after the time of Nāgārjuna. Nāgārjuna was responsible for promulgating on a wide scale the distinctively Mahāyāna teachings, particularly those on the Perfection of Wisdom, and it is fair to say that he is the greatest figure in Mahāyāna Buddhism. He 'flourished' (as scholars usually put it) probably in the second century CE (it is difficult to be certain of dates from this period) and he wrote a number of important works which are still widely and deeply studied today, including the celebrated Verses on the Middle Way', the *Mādhyamaka-kārikā*. And it is because Nāgārjuna quotes from various Mahāyāna sūtras that we can be certain that they were in circulation as literary documents by his time. This early group of sūtras includes the *Saddharma-puṇḍarika* or *White Lotus Sūtra*,[10] the *Aṣṭasāhasrikā Prajñāpāramitā* or *Perfection of Wisdom in 8000 Lines*,[11] the *Vimalakīrti-nirdeśa* or exposition of Vimalakīrti,[12] the two *Sukhāvatī-vyūha Sūtras*, the sūtras on the Array of the Happy Land, and the *Daśabhūmika* or 'Ten Stages of the Bodhisattva's Progress'. The later group of sūtras includes works that are just as well known: the large sūtra on Perfect Wisdom, the *Diamond Sūtra*, and the *Laṅkāvatāra Sūtra*, as well as the *Nirvāṇa Sūtra* and many others – including the *Sūtra of Golden Light*.

The *Sūtra of Golden Light* appeared in India during the period from the fifth to the eighth century CE, set down in the language known to Western scholars as Buddhist Hybrid Sanskrit. It did not appear all at once, fully formed and complete, at some particular point during those three hundred years. Rather, it emerged as a literary document gradually over that long period – not at all an unusual process of composition for sūtras, especially Mahāyāna sūtras.

How long the sūtra may have existed as an oral teaching before being written down there is no way of knowing, but in spirit at least it goes back to the time of the historical Buddha. He of course wrote nothing at all, and the great accumulation of oral teachings left after his death was arranged, edited, and even elaborated upon by the monks over a period of some four hundred years before so much as one word of it was written down. Even then, the teachings didn't get written down all at once. The whole process of committing the oral tradition to writing went on for a thousand years, from the first century BCE to the tenth century CE. Broadly speaking, the more exoteric teachings were the first to find form as scriptures, while the more esoteric ones remained hidden in the minds of the guardians of the oral tradition for longer, and emerged as scriptures rather later.

So the Buddhist scriptures cannot truthfully be described or judged as literature. They are more like successive literary deposits from the oral tradition. But what is the proof that they really are *Buddhavacana*, the authentic word of the Buddha? How do we know that they weren't just made up? In the case of the Theravāda or Hīnayāna scriptures – which were, incidentally, written down at around the same time as the Mahāyāna ones – we can point to repetitions and stock formulae that suggest a mnemonic element. It is not surprising, though, that the Mahāyāna sūtras are not characterized by such elements. The Theravāda has always been concerned with the letter, with verbal accuracy, hence the many repeated passages and formulae of the Pāli Canon. By the same token, it is only to be expected that such repetitions are not to be found in the Mahāyāna scriptures, the Mahāyāna tradition being much more concerned to transmit the *spirit* of the Buddha's teachings.

Although the *Sūtra of Golden Light* is a collection of deposits from the oral tradition, those deposits were not necessarily a literal word-for-word record of an oral teaching that already existed in exactly that form. It is much more likely that certain ideas were in circulation in a number of alternative versions, and that when they were written down they were given a 'literary' form. That would be more in accordance with the nature of the Mahāyāna. There is very little direct evidence that this was the case, but that does not really matter. The important point is whether or not one accepts some kind of spiritual continuity between the teaching of the Buddha and the Mahāyāna sūtras as we have them today. *Someone* must have produced them. If you maintain that the *Sūtra of Golden Light*, the *White Lotus Sūtra*, the *Perfection of Wisdom* sūtras, and all the others have no connection with the Buddha, then you have to posit a whole galaxy of remarkable spiritual personalities who were responsible for producing those sūtras – personalities who left no trace, no record of themselves. If the thought, or at least the essential spiritual inspiration, of an extra-ordinary work like the *Avataṁsaka Sūtra* doesn't go back to the Buddha, then who did produce it?

As we have seen, in the sūtras themselves it is the 'eternal Buddha', a glorious mythical figure, who teaches. But the Mahāyāna tradition is, or seems to be, that these sūtras were given by the historical Buddha himself. Indeed, some Mahāyāna sūtras begin with the Buddha seated on the Vulture's Peak, which was – and is – an actual place in northern India, near Rājagṛha, where the historical Buddha often used to teach. So we have what begins to look like a contradiction here. However, this kind of question – whether the Buddha who taught the sūtras was historical or mythological – would not have exercised the ancient Buddhists, whether Theravāda or Mahāyāna, because they did not distinguish between the historical and the mythological in the way we do. It is open to us to believe that the Mahāyāna sūtras were not preached by the historical Buddha in the literal sense: that is, in the sense in which if we had been around in India in 500BCE, we would have heard the Buddha preaching those sūtras in exactly those words. We are at liberty to believe that the sūtras were written down after the parinirvāṇa of the Buddha by yogis or mystics or meditators who, in their meditation, had heard the archetypal Buddha (the *sambhogakaya*) preaching in that way. But that is not the Mahāyāna tradition.

The scriptures which have come down to us, and which are so widely varying in character, represent different strands of the oral tradition. We could say that the Pāli Canon, for example, represents certain elements in the total oral tradition that the Theravādins chose to preserve. There were other elements that they chose to ignore, and this is where the Mahāsaṅghikas come in, because they seem to have preserved traditions which did go back to the Buddha, but which were ignored by or unknown to the Theravādins.[13] So it is not that different schools preserved different versions of the same tradition; it is more that each school preserved certain teachings that it regarded as important, and didn't preserve others.

There is an ancient account that says that the canon of the Mahāsaṅghikas was preserved by both monks and lay people, whilst that of the Theravāda was the preserve of the monastic community. This perhaps explains the somewhat monastic slant of the whole Pāli Tipiṭaka,[14] a slant which is probably not justified by the total tradition. The fact that the Mahāsaṅghikas preserved more of the non-monastic elements was partly responsible for the more universal teaching of the Mahāyāna.

The literary history of the Mahāyāna sūtras in China is quite different from the Indian tradition. The Chinese had a literary culture from the time of Confucius, and they were very critical students of texts. They were well aware of the existence of different readings, and even at an early period made studies of the authenticity of ancient texts. For example, about five hundred years after the time of the Buddha there was a certain Chinese emperor who wanted history to begin with his reign, and ordered a burning of the books. An enormous amount of literature was burned, but some years later, when he was dead, scholars started taking old books out of their hiding places. At that time a lot of forgeries were produced, but Chinese scholars were quite able to deal with the situation, because they were well aware, for instance, that certain words didn't come into existence before certain periods. If they found a text that was ascribed to a writer or teacher of 300BCE, but which contained a word that wasn't in circulation until 100BCE, they would know that it couldn't be genuine. They understood the principles of textual criticism, which means that the sūtras produced in China but purporting to have come from India were deliberate literary forgeries.

But the Indians knew nothing about textual criticism. We can therefore take it that sūtras produced in India which did not actually go back to the time of the Buddha were written by people who were in touch with some kind of existing tradition, and who did believe that what they were putting into writing was the teaching of the Buddha. They didn't have the literary sophistication of the Chinese.

So, gradually, over the centuries, one sūtra after another was committed to writing. Many of them, especially the longer Mahāyāna sūtras, were written down not all at once, but in instalments. This is why we may fairly speak of the *growth* of a Mahāyāna sūtra. The idea of instalments, however, should in no way be thought to suggest a logical sequence to the sūtra, or any purely artistic structure or unity – because, as we have seen, a sūtra cannot be approached in the first instance as a work of literature.

More usefully we may, in most Mahāyāna sūtras, look for a nucleus – a centre of spiritual energy – which if sufficiently powerful will have attracted to itself fragments from the vast memory bank of floating oral tradition. In the case of the *Sūtra of Golden Light*, this centre of spiritual energy is the famous chapter of Confession (chapter 3 of the text). As Nobel has demonstrated in detail in the introduction to his edition of the sūtra, the whole work was built up around this nucleus – or perhaps it would be more accurate to speak of the nucleus as *attracting* other materials from the oral tradition.

There is something very strange about this pivotal chapter of the *Sūtra of Golden Light*. As we have seen, a sūtra is meant to be a connected discourse by the Buddha – there are many exceptions to this principle, but it holds good in the main – and yet this most important part of the sūtra is not spoken by the Buddha at all. It is not even spoken by a Bodhisattva. It is spoken by a drum – a golden drum. And it is spoken in somebody's dream. And as you continue to read the sūtra, or hear it read, you discover something even more mysterious. Not at first, but gradually, after a while, you realize that there is no question of just sitting back and listening to a definite, specific discourse given by the Buddha – or whoever is speaking. The Buddha, and others in the sūtra, are talking *about* the sūtra. All manner of marvellous things are happening in it. But then if you start to ask yourself where or what the sūtra is, you find there is no locating or identifying it. You are listening to it, people in it are referring to it, praising it ... but *where is the sūtra*? What is it? There seems to be no sūtra at all.

It gradually dawns on you that the sūtra can only be what is happening in it. And it also dawns on you that you are yourself involved in what is happening in it. The *Sūtra of Golden Light* refers to itself not as a particular kind of text or scripture but as 'the profound Buddha region'. What this means is that the sūtra is not an item in our own world, but a whole world in itself, a whole spiritual world. In short, it is a *vaipulya* sūtra.

There are in existence several hundred Mahāyāna sūtras, some of them in the original Sanskrit, others in both Sanskrit and in Chinese or Tibetan translations, and some only in translation. And a number of the most important of these texts are known as vaipulya sūtras. Vaipulya means 'broad, vast, extensive', and the vaipulya sūtras are certainly of a very considerable length, amounting sometimes to a whole thick volume in the English translation. But this is not really what is meant by the term. They are called vaipulya because they are broad, vast, and extensive in their scope. Their scope, in fact, is not just one subdivision of the teaching, or one section, or even one aspect, but the total Dharma, although each of the vaipulya sūtras sees that total all-inclusive Dharma from its own distinctive angle of vision, and perhaps in terms of the special spiritual needs of a particular kind of spiritual aspirant.

Each of the vaipulya sūtras is therefore complete in itself. It can be studied and reflected upon, even practised, without reference to any other formulation of the Dharma, at least so far as the spiritual needs of the student are concerned. If you want to study the sūtra from a linguistic or scholastic point of view, that's another matter, but from the spiritual point of view one can confine oneself quite satisfactorily to just that one vaipulya sūtra.

The *Sūtra of Golden Light* does not style itself a vaipulya sūtra in so many words – the expression 'vaipulya sūtra' is not part of its official title, as it were – but there is no doubt that this is what it is. To begin with, it is fairly extensive in size, and very extensive indeed in content. Like the other vaipulya sūtras, the *Sūtra of Golden Light* is a whole world in itself. And as we have just seen, the sūtra itself, so to speak, knows this. In the introductory chapter the Buddha says: 'I will make known this sūtra, the profound Buddha region, the marvellous mystery of all the Buddhas, for millions of aeons.' In much the same way, in chapter 13, the sūtra is spoken of as 'the profound sphere of activity of the Buddha'.

Let us begin this exploration of this profound Buddha region by charting its main outlines, its nineteen chapters:

Chapter 1: An introductory chapter. The Buddha is on the Vulture's Peak (where a great many of the Mahāyāna sūtras are delivered) not far from the city of Rājagṛha. Ānanda is also present, not just listening and memorizing, but asking questions to which the Buddha replies, praising the *Sūtra of Golden Light*.

Chapter 2: In Rājagṛha, a Bodhisattva called Ruciraketu (which means 'beautiful comet') is worried. He is a Bodhisattva, but he has a problem – not a psychological problem, but a spiritual, metaphysical one. He is puzzled as to why the Buddha has such a short life – only eighty years. In answer to his question, four Buddhas appear to him, and as a result of their appearance he comes to understand that the Buddha's life is in fact immeasurable.

Chapter 3: The Bodhisattva's dream. Ruciraketu has a dream in which a brahmin beats a golden drum, and the drum sounds forth a series of beautiful verses of confession. It is these verses that form the nucleus of the whole sūtra.

Chapter 4: The abundance of lotuses. The Buddha tells of a king who once praised the Buddhas of the past, present, and future. Although we are not explicitly told so, this king is apparently the Bodhisattva Ruciraketu in a previous existence.

Chapter 5: 'On Emptiness.' This chapter deals with the subject of śūnyatā.

Chapter 6: The longest chapter of the whole sūtra, taking up a fifth of its total length. In it the four great kings, the protectors of the four quarters of the world, promise to protect the sūtra, as well as the monks who proclaim it and the kings who promote it.

Chapters 7, 8, and 10: In these chapters three goddesses appear: Sarasvatī, the goddess of learning, Śrī, the goddess of wealth, and Dṛḍhā, the earth goddess. Each goddess also promises to protect the sūtra.

Chapter 9: This deals with the maintenance of the names of Buddhas and Bodhisattvas, and in it various Buddhas and Bodhisattvas are enumerated and saluted, among them several that play a prominent part in other Mahāyāna sūtras.

Chapter 11: Saṁjñāya, the general of a class of deities known as yakṣas, comes forward and promises to protect the sūtra.

Chapter 12: 'On Instruction concerning Divine Kings.' This deals with the ethical, even spiritual, basis of kingship.

Chapter 13: The Buddha describes one of his previous lives, in which, as a king called Susaṁbhava, he invited a monk called Ratnoccaya to expound the *Sūtra of Golden Light*, and also made offerings to the sūtra on a rather lavish scale.

Chapter 14: 'On the Refuge of the Yakṣas.' The Buddha addresses Śrī, the goddess of wealth, and explains that those who want to worship the Buddhas of the past, present, and future should listen to the *Sūtra of Golden Light*. He also enumerates a long list of deities who will protect the sūtra.

Chapter 15: A chapter of prophecy and prediction. Ten thousand gods come down from heaven into the presence of the Buddha to hear the Dharma. The Buddha predicts that in the infinitely remote future they will all attain Buddhahood through their faith in the *Sūtra of Golden Light*.

Chapter 16: 'On Healing Illness.' This describes how Jalavāhana the merchant's son learned the medical art from his father, and how he travelled throughout India curing people of their illnesses. This chapter gives a lot of information about ancient Indian ideas concerning the origin and treatment of disease, and makes particular reference to the influence on health of food, drink, and the seasons of the year.

Chapter 17: A Jātaka story. Jalavāhana saves ten thousand fish from dying of drought. These fish are eventually reborn as gods, and out of gratitude to Jalavāhana, one night while he is lying asleep they come and shower him with 40,000 pearl necklaces. This chapter also contains a statement of the law of conditioned co-production.

Chapter 18: Another Jātaka story. In this one, the Buddha, in a previous existence, sacrifices his life to save that of a starving tigress and her five cubs. This is one of the best known of all the Jātaka stories, and here it is related at some length.

Chapter 19: The last chapter, 'On the Praise of all the Tathāgatas'. In this chapter innumerable Bodhisattvas sing the praises of a certain Buddha whose name is so long that it takes up almost a whole line of text. The Bodhisattva Ruciraketu also praises that same Buddha, as does a goddess who also has a very long name. Then, amid general rejoicing, the sūtra concludes.

This, in outline, is the *Sūtra of Golden Light*. Of course, such a swift survey of the 'profound Buddha region' is terribly inadequate. No summary could possibly do justice to the sūtra's spirit of fervent devotion. Every page positively thrills with reverence for the Buddha – and for the *Sūtra of Golden Light* itself. And no summary could capture the sūtra's moments of great literary beauty, including hymns of praise to the Buddha as beautiful as we will find in any Buddhist literature anywhere. But the summary does perhaps do justice to one thing – to the highly composite, not to say miscellaneous, nature of the sūtra. When you read the text for the first time, you could be forgiven for thinking that it was a sort of rag-bag – a transcendental rag-bag, to be sure, a rag-bag full of bits and pieces of wonderful, jewelled brocade – but still a rag-bag.

But, despite appearances, the sūtra does hang together. It does possess a spiritual unity. Broadly speaking, the nineteen chapters can be classified into three groups. The first 'group' consists of one chapter on its own, the chapter on confession, the original nucleus of the sūtra. A second group is formed out of all those chapters in which gods and goddesses come forward and promise to protect the sūtra. And the third group contains all the remaining chapters, most of which can be regarded as attempts on the part of the sūtra to draw into its orbit all the principal Mahāyāna teachings, and all the different kinds of Buddhist scriptures. Chapter 2, for instance, deals with the measure of life of the Tathāgata, which is one of the two major themes of the *White Lotus Sūtra*; and chapter 5 is concerned with śūnyatā, which is treated at length in the many sūtras of Perfect Wisdom.

In this book we shall be concerned mainly with the material contained in the first and second groups, because these chapters contain the sūtra's special, distinctive teaching: transformation of self and transformation of world. The first group, the chapter on confession, involves the transformation of one's individual life through confession and purification. But transformation of self inevitably comes to involve transformation of world, and this is represented by the chapters in which the gods and goddesses promise to protect the sūtra. Who these gods and goddesses are, and how their promises represent a transformation of the world, are questions we must leave to be answered in chapters 5, 6, and 7.

Meanwhile, we are still left with the question of what principle of attraction it is that holds the sūtra together. What is it that holds transformation of self and transformation of world together? The answer is very simple. This apparently miscellaneous collection of material is held together by the spiritual needs of the individual who wants to transform himself. It is this factor that gives the sūtra its spiritual unity.

This principle of attraction is mirrored in the situation in which we find ourselves as Western Buddhists. There are now a great number of Buddhist scriptures available to us, but they do not all hold an equal appeal for serious practitioners of the Dharma in the West. Some are much more appealing than others, because they seem much more relevant to our real spiritual needs. It is these that we draw on, these in which we find spiritual nourishment and inspiration, these that we read and study and discuss. In other words, we draw them into our orbit. And simply by virtue of the fact that these texts are drawn into our orbit, they have something in common: us. Each of them in some way meets our spiritual needs. So now we can draw the *Sūtra of Golden Light* into our orbit – or perhaps we could think in terms of allowing ourselves to be drawn into the orbit of the sūtra, allowing ourselves to plunge into the heart of the light that transforms both self and world.

Part One

TRANSFORMING SELF

1

The Bodhisattva's Dream

THESE DAYS MOST OF US IMAGINE we have so many things to do that we can't afford to spend much of our precious time sitting about reflecting on life. But if we do happen to find time to turn things over in our minds a little more seriously then usual, we may well have to acknowledge certain things about ourselves, things that we may not find altogether pleasant or creditable to accept. And one of the things that on reflection we may be forced to acknowledge is that as human beings we take quite a lot for granted. There are certain things which we know we possess, we know we experience, but of the value and significance of which we are totally unaware – so unaware, indeed, that we might as well not possess them at all.

Suppose that when you were a baby, you had been given a pebble to play with. And suppose you kept that pebble and played with it every day, every hour, so that it became as familiar to you as your own hand. You would gradually become so used to the pebble that you would probably not take any particular care of it or attach any particular value to it. You might never realize, in fact, that the 'pebble' was not a pebble at all, but a priceless precious stone.

One of the things we tend to treat as a pebble, instead of the precious stone it really is, is life itself. We fail to understand the significance of the bare fact that we are alive. But it *is* significant. After all, we might just as easily be dead, or never have existed at all. But we do exist. There was, we could say, some unique, unrepeatable combination of circumstances, and here we are. It may have been a billion to one chance, but it has come off. Marvellous to relate, we are alive. We are sitting here. How wonderful!

This is surely what the old Zen monk was celebrating when he cried out 'How wonderful! How miraculous! I draw water and I carry fuel.' He had realized that until then he had taken his ordinary, everyday life for granted, utterly failing to realize its value and significance. Of course, drawing water and carrying fuel are simple, basic human activities. One could hardly imagine even a Zen master being able to say 'How wonderful! How miraculous! I catch the train to the office in the morning, I watch the television at night.'

Another thing that we take for granted is our 'ordinary' human consciousness, the normal waking state. We take it for granted that we can see and hear. We take it for granted that we can think – those of us who do think. We take it for granted that we can be aware. More often than not, we simply fail to realize the unaccountable singularity of it all.

And in the same way we take sleep for granted – such a wonderful, such a refreshing thing as sleep – unless of course we are unfortunate enough to have to resort to sleeping tablets. We even, most of us, take our dreams for granted. You get bad dreams – this is what our grandmothers used to tell us – if you eat too much cheese at night, and that's all there is to it. Or else – this is another popular theory – dreams are just a jumbled reminiscence of the events of the previous day.

But if you think about it, the dream state is a rather strange thing. In the dream state, the physical sense organs are not functioning, but none the less we see, we hear, we even smell and taste. In the dream state we're oblivious to the physical body, but we do seem to have a sort of body. We are free to move about, free to go places – in fact, we have more freedom than we do when we are awake. We can go anywhere, by any method. Sometimes we can even fly.

And in dreams we experience a different kind of time, a different kind of space – even a different kind of world. Usually the dream world is a recognizable extension of the world of everyday waking consciousness, but not always. Sometimes it's a completely different world, a world of which we have had no previous experience in any form. It's almost as though we have passed through the dream state into quite another state of consciousness, quite another mode of being – even into a higher state of consciousness, a higher mode of being. To suppose that higher states of consciousness are accessible only from the waking state is pure assumption. It's just another of those things that we take for granted. The fact is that we certainly can have access to these higher states from or through the dream state.

In Buddhism, especially in the Mahāyāna and the Vajrayāna, the value of the dream state is recognized as being twofold. In the first place, it shows us that it is possible to experience a state of consciousness other than the waking state. This is quite an obvious point, but no less profound for that. And secondly, certain dreams show us that we can experience states of consciousness which are not only different from the waking state but higher than it. For this reason, dreams play an important role, sometimes even a crucial role, in the transformation of the individual.

It is a dream that leads directly to the heart of the *Sūtra of Golden Light*, the chapter on confession. At the beginning of the chapter (which is the third one of the sūtra) we find the Bodhisattva Ruciraketu falling asleep. And while he is asleep he has a wonderful dream. It's what the American Indians call a 'big dream', a dream of vast archetypal significance. More than that, the dream is a spiritual experience, even a transcendental experience.

In order to begin to understand something of this dream, we need to know at least a little of the dreamer. We need to go back to the previous chapter of the sūtra, the chapter at the beginning of which we meet Ruciraketu – his name means 'Beautiful Comet' – for the first time. The scene is set in the time of the Buddha, in the city of Rājagṛha, which in the Buddha's day was the capital of the kingdom of Māgadha. It is here that Ruciraketu lives and practises Buddhism, for he is a follower of the Mahāyāna. Indeed, he is a very advanced follower, because he is a Bodhisattva, which means he has dedicated himself to the attainment of supreme Enlightenment for the sake of all living beings. Not only is he a Bodhisattva; according to the text he is quite an advanced Bodhisattva. The sūtra tells us, for instance, that in previous times he has rendered great service to a previous Buddha, planted great roots of merit (that is to say, performed innumerable skilful actions), and is highly respected, even revered, by hundreds of thousands of millions of Buddhas (such is the cosmic scale of events in Mahāyāna sūtras).

But although Ruciraketu is a Bodhisattva, and an advanced one at that, although he is revered by all these Buddhas, he has a problem. It isn't a personal problem or a psychological problem. It's a problem about the

Buddha. He simply cannot understand why the Buddha had such a short life. Why did the Buddha live for only eighty years?

We would probably not find this a problem. After all, surely eighty years is a very natural life-span, even for a Buddha. If he had lived to be very much older than that, we might consider that to be a bit of a problem. But not so Ruciraketu. For him, the fact that the Buddha only lived for eighty years is a problem. His reasoning is as follows. In his discourses, the Buddha says that there are certain factors which determine whether one has a long or a short life. In particular, there are two main causes of long life: refraining from killing living beings – that's the first precept,[15] of course – and giving away great quantities of food. If you want to live for a long time in your next life, these are the courses of action you must pursue.

We cannot, of course, claim that Ruciraketu's reference point for this information is in the Pāli Canon, but that is where several assertions of this kind are to be found. For example, in the *Majjhima-Nikāya* several suttas describe the different kinds of karma, and the nature of their effects, in some detail. One of the points made is that the results of karma are in keeping with the particular karma or action you have performed. If you are very greedy or selfish, for example, and you are always misappropriating other people's property, you will be poor. In the same way, if you continually take the lives of others, your own life will be taken, or at least shortened. These examples are typical of the Pāli Canon, in which the principle is formulated in negative terms rather than in the positive terms which Ruciraketu recalls. None the less, although this is more of a general tendency than something that can be scientifically justified, we are left in no doubt that the karmic effect is in keeping with the nature of the karmic cause.

So Ruciraketu's problem begins with the knowledge that the Buddha refrained from killing living beings for innumerable lifetimes – for many incalculable hundreds of thousands of millions of aeons, according to the text. In all these previous existences the Buddha adhered to the ten skilful actions. Not only that – he also gave away food and all manner of good things. In some of his previous existences he is even said to have gone so far as to sacrifice his own body – his own blood, bones, and marrow – to feed other beings, as when, according to the famous Jātaka story, he fed the starving tigress and her cubs with his own flesh.

Ruciraketu knows that on the basis of his previous actions, the Buddha should have an immeasurably long life. He should live for at least a few million years. But no, the Buddha's measure of life is only a miserable eighty years. So Ruciraketu has a problem, and he's very worried about it, as people usually are when they have a problem. As I have said, we probably wouldn't be bothered by this particular problem – we don't have that sort of faith – but we do have problems of our own. We could even say that there is no spiritual life without problems. Problems, we could say, are a means of development, even a means of transformation.

Problems are not, however, the same as difficulties. Difficulties may seem very big and important when we are assailed by them, but we can settle them simply by using our intelligence and making an effort. Problems, real problems, have to be solved in quite a different way. A problem as distinct from a difficulty is something that cannot be solved on its own terms – even while the terms themselves cannot be changed. Strictly speaking, a real problem cannot be solved at all – that's the beauty of it. At the same time, it *must* be solved.

This is quite obviously the case with Ruciraketu's problem. He believes that under the law of karma the performance of certain skilful actions will result in long life. He also believes that the Buddha has performed those actions to an immeasurable extent. At the same time, he knows that the Buddha has only a very short life. So it is impossible for him to change the terms of the problem. He cannot doubt the law of karma, or that the Buddha has performed the appropriate skilful actions; he also cannot deny that the Buddha's life is short. The situation in which he finds himself is both logically absurd and, from a spiritual and psychological point of view, intensely unsatisfactory, uncomfortable, and distressing.

This is the kind of situation we find reflected in the Zen koan; Zen stories are full of these impossible problems. You come into the master's room empty-handed, and the master says 'What are you carrying?' You say, of course, 'Nothing' – and the master replies 'Well, put it down, then!' If you have no satisfactory response to this, you apparently get thirty blows. There are very famous koans, like 'What is the sound of one hand clapping?' and – arguably the most famous of all, at least in the West – the koan of the goose and the bottle. There is a goose, we are told, in a bottle. Naturally we are never told how it got there. The goose is fully grown; the neck of the bottle is very narrow. The problem is that you have to get the goose out of the bottle without damaging the bird or breaking the glass. In other words, you can't change the terms of the problem.

In Zen monasteries students sweat over these koans for years. But for us here in the West such koans aren't really koans at all. We may read about them in books or hear about them in lectures, but they're not problems for us. We certainly don't lose any sleep over them. A real koan is something that springs up quite naturally from your own life, your own experience. It's something you can't get rid of, something you're stuck with, something inseparable from your own personality, something that is, in a sense, you – impossible, contradictory you, problematic you. That's the real koan.

This is in fact how koans, or what were later called koans, seem to have originated in the East. They crystallized actual problems arising in the lives of the Zen masters and their disciples. Having found that certain problems focused attention on particular aspects of Reality, or constituted points at which it was possible to break through into Reality, the masters naturally tended to think that those particular koans, to call them that, might well be useful to their disciples. The master would give his disciple a koan not in an external or mechanical way, but to draw his attention to the particular existential dilemma that the koan represented.

Usually koans involve a contradiction in logic. They are not just pondering on some deep teaching like 'All things are void'; they involve an element of contradiction and dilemma which you cannot resolve. You are strongly convinced of two different things, but you see that they are inconsistent: if one is true, the other can't be.

An exception to the rule of contradiction is the well-known koan 'mu', which simply means 'not'. This has a certain universality, because looking at it from a philosophical point of view 'mu' denies that anything can be predicated of ultimate reality, and this is what you have to realize. So you reflect on 'mu' in all sorts of ways, and usually all your reflections are rejected by the master, because they are all intellectual. But eventually, by trying to see that nothing can be predicated of ultimate reality, you do break through at the particular point represented by the 'mu'; this is what is meant by solving the koan. What you say to the master, although it may not seem to have any logical connection with 'mu', shows that you have broken through into that dimension.

Since 'mu' has a place in Zen tradition, somebody working within that tradition will be able to use it – if, that is, they have great faith in the master, so that even if he rejects all their solutions and explanations, they will be able to accept what he says. Apparently when Alan Watts spent a short time with a roshi, he ended up losing his temper with the teacher and saying he had got it all wrong.

These days the tradition of koans has become scarcely more than a matter of routine and formula. In modern Japan you get not only dictionaries of koans with as many as three thousand entries, but also books that provide you with the answers – clear evidence of the degeneration of the koan system. But originally koans did embody life experiences of the kind that I have mentioned, and they can still be useful, if they are used in the traditional way, not just mechanically. It's as though the master needs to manoeuvre the disciple into a position where the koan naturally arises.

This raises the question of the general usefulness to spiritual development of formal structures. There is a pattern to the development of such structures. Someone has a certain spiritual experience which apparently resulted from certain conditions, and on this basis a system is set up that reproduces those conditions, in the hope that this will make it easier for other people to have the same experience. Sometimes this works, and sometimes it doesn't. You have to be careful not to reduce the experience to the conditions under which it took place. Just reproducing the conditions faithfully will not make the experience happen automatically.

So yes, koans have their value if they are used well. We could even reflect on koans that have arisen from Western culture. For instance, we might ponder on Keats's words: 'Beauty is truth, truth beauty.'[16] How can beauty be truth and truth beauty? They are surely quite different things. Surely Keats was talking nonsense! But if you keep on reflecting, you may eventually 'solve' the koan. But how? How do you solve the insoluble? How do you resolve the absurdity, the discomfort of it all? What happens? Let's return to the *Sūtra of Golden Light* to see what happens in Ruciraketu's case.

As Ruciraketu is sitting in his house – because after all he is a householder as well as a Bodhisattva – thinking about his problem, something happens. All of a sudden, the house starts to grow. It expands and expands until it is unutterably vast. Not only that – the entire house is transformed into beryl (beryl being a kind of precious stone) and becomes adorned with numerous divine jewels and filled with perfumes. All this, the sūtra tells us, is a transformation due to the Tathāgata, the Buddha.[17]

And then something even more wonderful happens. In the house there appear in the four directions four thrones made of divine jewels. On these thrones appear mats made of jewels and fine cotton cloth; and on the mats appear jewel-adorned lotuses. Then on the lotuses appear four Buddhas: Akṣobhya in the east, Ratnaketu in the south, Amitāyus in the west, and Dundubhīśvara in the north. At the same time, the whole city of Rājagṛha, and indeed the whole universe, is filled with light, and all beings in the universe 'become possessed of divine happiness'. The blind can see; the deaf can hear. The mentally disturbed are restored to their senses, the naked are clothed, and the hungry are fed. Disease and deformity disappear. And, the sūtra says, on a large scale in the world there is an appearance of miraculous things.

When Ruciraketu sees these four Buddhas, naturally enough he can hardly believe his eyes. Joyful and delighted, he pays homage to them – and in the act of doing so bumps straight into his problem again. He is prompted to recollect the virtues of the historical Buddha, Śākyamuni, and that in turn reminds him of the fact of the Buddha's short life. Once again he is obsessed with his problem.

The four Buddhas seated in the four directions immediately become aware that Ruciraketu's mind is troubled, and, being Buddhas, they also realize what he is thinking. And they all simply tell him that he should not think in this way. The Buddha's life is not limited to eighty years, but is immeasurable, they say. In effect they tell him not to identify the Buddha with his physical body. In effect they tell him that the Buddha is Buddhahood, and that Buddhahood transcends time – hence cannot be measured in terms of time. The Buddha's life is immeasurable not because he lives for an inconceivably long time, but because in the depths of his being he does not live in time at all.

And now, innumerable gods and Bodhisattvas come together in Ruciraketu's house, and the four Buddhas proclaim the truth of this teaching to them all in a series of verses. There then follows an episode involving a brahmin called Kaundinya which also demonstrates the Buddha's length of life. Having had his problem solved, Ruciraketu is extremely happy; the sūtra says that he becomes filled with noble bliss. At the same time, innumerable beings develop the will to Enlightenment. The four Buddhas then disappear, and the chapter comes to an end.

So what on earth does all this mean? Well, in a sense it speaks for itself. Above or below or even beyond our rational mind, the sūtra does get through; it does manage to speak to us and produce an impression. But it may be difficult for us just to absorb the meaning in this way; our rational mind is also going to want an explanation. Just a few pointers, then, for the rational mind to chew over.

To begin with, Ruciraketu's house and its expansion. The house is everything that belongs to us. It represents our personal framework, our habitual state of consciousness, and its expansion means that when we have a problem, we cannot solve it with our present state of consciousness. The problem, indeed, is in a sense an expression of that state of consciousness. So there must be an expansion of consciousness beyond the problem: not just horizontal expansion into different states of consciousness, but vertical expansion into higher states of consciousness.

The house is therefore transformed from wood and stone or brick and plasterwork – or whatever mundane things it's made of – into beryl and other precious stones. Before the transformation it was opaque; now it's translucent, or at least semi-translucent.

In other words, there has been a transformation from ordinary waking consciousness to meditative consciousness. Ruciraketu is now in fact in a state of *dhyāna*.[18] In Buddhism, as in all spiritual traditions, higher states of consciousness are associated with and symbolized by light and jewels. Jewels are colourful, glittering, dazzling, and beautiful, and they therefore fittingly represent a consciousness that is not only higher than the ordinary, but more fascinating and attractive, more beautiful and valuable. It is for the same kind of reason that whilst ordinary dreams are in black and white, 'big dreams' are in vivid colour. Likewise, in the visualization practices of the Tibetan Buddhist tradition, great importance is attached to the visualization of colour. You visualize not just a Buddha, but a vivid emerald green Buddha, say, or a brilliant red Bodhisattva. The colours visualized in this way should be rich and glowing, like those of a stained glass window through which the sun is streaming, only softer and more diaphanous. To employ a more traditional simile, they should be like the colours of the rainbow.

The fact that Ruciraketu is sitting inside his expanded house signifies that he is completely within the higher state of consciousness. His state is reminiscent of the Buddha's simile for the fourth dhyāna: a man who has taken a bath on a hot day and sits completely wrapped in a pure white sheet. We also find a parallel in Tibetan Buddhist iconography, in the haloes of coloured light with which Buddhas and Bodhisattvas are surrounded. Of course, because paintings are two-dimensional, it appears that the figure is surrounded by a circle of light rather like a rainbow, but in fact the 'halo' is a cross-section of a three-dimensional 'shell' of light. Sometimes the deity is shown sitting not within a series of shells of coloured light, but within tents – tents made of silk of different colours. The general significance is the same, and it comes quite close to that of Ruciraketu sitting inside his expanded and bejewelled house.

The transformation of Ruciraketu's house is said to be due to the power of the Tathāgata (that is, the Buddha) but this is not to be taken at face value. It is not just that the Buddha, the human historical Buddha, has worked a miracle, although on a factual plane a miracle has certainly taken place – as tends to happen in a Mahāyāna sūtra. But what is the meaning of the miracle? Remember the starting point of it all: Ruciraketu's painful, insoluble problem. When we're in this sort of situation –

assuming that the problem has arisen in the context of the spiritual life – what happens?

What happens is that a new factor comes into operation from a deeper level of our being – or a higher level – anyway, a level which we are not conscious of, at least not conscious of as being ours. This new factor is represented by the Buddha. Each of us has, however remotely, the potential to become – to transform ourselves into – a Buddha. Having reached the end of his conscious resources, Ruciraketu has had to call up, or call down, resources of which he is not conscious. The problem is resolved by the intervention of a higher factor, a factor that operates from the unrealized depths or heights of Ruciraketu's own being, and which enables him to rise to a higher level of consciousness.

We could say that the four Buddhas who appear in the house form a mandala, the centre of which Ruciraketu occupies, although he is not yet a Buddha. The appearance of this four-Buddha mandala in the *Sūtra of Golden Light*, prefiguring as it does the Vajrayāna's later development of the mandala of the five Buddhas, seems to suggest a slight Tantric development within the sūtra. This is quite possible in view of the fact that as a literary document the sūtra is quite a late work, though the original nucleus is a bit older. The names of some of the four Buddhas who appear in the sūtra were later standardized in the Vajrayāna tradition. The Buddha who appears in the east keeps the same name – Akṣobhya, the Imperturbable, as does the Buddha of the west, who has the familiar name Amitāyus (Immeasurable Life, a form of Amitābha, Immeasurable Light). But the name of the Buddha of the south, who in the *Sūtra of Golden Light* is called Ratnaketu (Precious Comet or Precious Streamer), was later standardized as Ratnasambhava, the Jewel-Born One. And as for the Buddha of the north, he is called Dundubhīśvara, Lord of the Drum, in the sūtra, but his name was later standardized as Amoghasiddhi, the Unobstructed Success.[19]

The appearance of the four-Buddha mandala within the expanded house signifies the appearance within an already heightened state of consciousness of a still higher state of consciousness. Within the meditative state appears the state of contemplation. Within the dhyāna or samādhi[20] state appears wisdom. Within the context of śamatha, calm, arises *vipaśyanā*, insight. Within the context of spiritual experience appears transcendental experience, experience directly connected with ultimate reality. Sparked off by his problem, Ruciraketu has undergone a profound transformation. And this transformation is very much an individual matter. It is Ruciraketu's own life that is transformed, his own self, his own consciousness.

So this part of the sūtra is mainly concerned with the transformation of self. But there is an objective counterpart to all this. Corresponding to transformation of self, there is transformation of world. This is why we find that the city of Rājagṛha is filled with a great light. The blind see, the deaf hear, and so on. These wonders all serve, as it were, to anticipate the other aspect of transformation: transformation of world.

Then we return to Ruciraketu. The four Buddhas speak to him. Representing different aspects of the higher transcendental awareness, they communicate with him. He is aware of them, as they are of him, and something passes between them – something of the Buddhas' awareness impinges on him. As he experiences flashes of their awareness, his problem is solved on this higher level.

All these miraculous happenings are simply a prelude to the chapter that follows. We may therefore expect something very astonishing indeed to happen next. If we do, we may be momentarily disappointed because the next chapter, chapter 3, opens with the following words: 'Then indeed the Bodhisattva Ruciraketu slept.' So Ruciraketu has had all these wonderful experiences. His house has expanded; he has seen the four Buddhas; and the Buddhas have spoken to him – and what does he do then but go to sleep?

But we must be on our guard. The dream that Ruciraketu is going to have in this chapter, 'The Bodhisattva's Dream', is no ordinary dream, and his sleep is no ordinary sleep. To understand why he must sleep this extraordinary sleep, we need to go back and have another brief look at the previous chapter. In chapter 2, however wonderful the experiences that Ruciraketu has undergone, his transformation is not complete, and there are various clues which point to this. First, Ruciraketu himself still occupies the centre of the mandala, although he is not yet a Buddha. He only sees the Buddhas. The innermost core of his being, what makes Ruciraketu Ruciraketu, is not yet transformed. Buddhahood, however lucidly he sees it, however sublimely he sees it, however truly he sees it, is still something external to himself. It's still something out there. So although his realization is genuine, it is still a mental realization, still in the realm of mundane consciousness; it has not yet permeated and transformed every aspect of his being. Moreover, even in the midst of the mandala of the four Buddhas, his problem is still with him. True, he now has the solution to it, but so long as you have the solution to a problem, you still have the problem. What you have to do is forget both problem and solution: only then have you really solved your problem. And this is what happens now.

'Then the Bodhisattva Ruciraketu slept.' As I have said, this is no ordinary sleep. It represents the complete erasure, the complete obliteration, the complete blotting out of the old self, of the old consciousness. In Shakespeare's phrase, it is the sleep of death. But it's not physical death; it's the sleep of spiritual death. It is not the death that comes when we have shuffled off this mortal coil, but the death that comes when we have abandoned all previous conditions. In other words, if we want to develop spiritually, if we want to be completely transformed, as opposed to peripherally transformed, we must die. The *Tibetan Book of the Dead* is famously associated with death, but we may say that the *Sūtra of Golden Light* is also a Book of the Dead. Indeed, every Buddhist scripture is a Book of the Dead, because the whole purpose of any Buddhist scripture is to act as the agent of transformation. That's what it's there for. If we're not prepared to die, we cannot become a Bodhisattva. We cannot, in fact, become a Buddhist. The *Tibetan Book of the Dead* is concerned with spiritual death in the context of physical death, but we have to be ready to experience spiritual death at any time. We have to be ready at any time to give up the old life, the old self, to forget the old problems and the old solutions. We have to be ready to make a completely fresh start. Otherwise, we cannot be totally transformed.

So the Bodhisattva Ruciraketu slept. And as he slept he had a dream. In his dream he saw, in all directions, innumerable Buddhas seated on thrones of beryl, under trees made of jewels, surrounded by assemblies numbering many hundreds of thousands. And in the midst of it all he saw a golden drum, a drum that shone just like the sun in the midday sky, a drum that radiated brilliant golden light throughout the whole of space. A man – a brahmin – was beating this drum, and as he struck it, it seemed to speak.

Ruciraketu's dream, then, is full of symbolism, symbolism which should give us at least a few hints as to what the dream is all about. On the level of the literal meaning of the sūtra, the dream is just a dream, a state of consciousness other than the waking state. But on the level of the real meaning of the sūtra, the dream is not just a different state but a higher one, which means that what happens in the dream is to be understood as pertaining to a higher order of reality.

Such dreams are of course the stuff of literary convention in Western culture. Bunyan's *Pilgrim's Progress*, for example, takes place in the context of a dream; so does Langland's *Piers Plowman*; so, come to that, does

Lewis Carroll's *Alice in Wonderland*. In these cases, as in the *Sūtra of Golden Light*, the dreamer falls asleep when they are not actually tired; they just fall asleep during a pleasant summer afternoon and start dreaming. The dream in these and many other works suggests an entry into some other level of reality.

Dreams in the ordinary sense are produced by the subconscious or the unconscious mind, that is, they represent an influence that operates below the threshold of consciousness. And though Ruciraketu's dream is no ordinary one it still functions in the same way. It represents the working out of his spiritual experiences at a deeper level of his being than the purely mental level. If seeing the mandala of the four Buddhas represents for Ruciraketu the path of vision, the dream represents the path of transformation.[21] His being is beginning to be completely transformed. And the symbol and centre of that total transformation is the drum, the golden drum which he sees at the beginning of his dream.

Why a drum of all things? We cannot be sure, for after all we are dealing with a dream, but it could be that the image of the drum was sparked off by an interesting detail to do with his vision of the four Buddhas, which is that the name of one of them, Dundubhīśvara, the Buddha of the north, means the Lord (*īśvara*) of the Drum (*dundubhi*). The drum is anyway a very ancient symbol in Buddhism. Shortly after his Enlightenment, when the Buddha declared that he would go to Benares and there proclaim the Dharma, the way he actually put it was that he would beat the drum of the deathless – the drum of nirvāṇa, the drum of the Absolute.

We may not know quite why the drum appears in Ruciraketu's dream, but we can be sure of one thing – that we cannot assign just one meaning to its appearance. Like all true symbols, it has many meanings, and at the same time it is more than all its meanings. The drum is the Absolute, the Truth, ultimate Reality. I think one has to imagine it as some kind of large suspended kettledrum. It is circular in shape, and in many spiritual traditions the circle or sphere symbolizes perfection (a round jewel, the pearl, for instance, has the same general significance). It is made of gold, and it radiates golden light, the colour gold being the colour of incorruptibility, immortality, eternity.

The drum is also the Buddha: the historical Buddha who proclaims the Dharma even as the drum shines with its golden light; and the eternal Buddha of the Mahāyāna, who is the sun of the spiritual universe. The drum is the Buddha who occupies the centre of the mandala, the missing Buddha, the fifth Buddha. It is also Ruciraketu, the Ruciraketu who is in the process of being completely transformed. And it is the sun, with all the accompanying rich solar imagery of the Indian tradition going back to Vedic times, imagery that is at times reminiscent of the hymns of the so-called heretic Egyptian pharaoh, Akhenaton. And finally the drum is the *Sūtra of Golden Light* itself, especially the nucleus of the sūtra, the verses of confession. All these are elements of the drum's significance, a significance that cannot be confined to words.

There are, of course, other symbols in Ruciraketu's dream. He sees innumerable Buddhas sitting on thrones of beryl underneath radiant jewel trees, and all teaching the Dharma to large assemblies. There is a parallel here with the episode in the previous chapter in which after Ruciraketu had seen the mandala of the four Buddhas, the great city of Rājagṛha became filled with light, and many miracles occurred; in other words, the world was transformed. In Ruciraketu's dream, the world is not just transformed, but totally transformed. It becomes a Pure Land, a land in which there are only Buddhas and their disciples, in which everybody is either teaching the Dharma, or listening to the Dharma, or sitting in silence thinking about the Dharma.

More than that, the world in Ruciraketu's dream has been so completely transformed that it is no longer 'world' out there at all. The golden light of the drum fills the whole of space; the innumerable Buddhas and their assemblies also fill the whole of space. The transformed self interpenetrates the transformed world so that there is no self, no world, no subject, no object. The two have become interfused. Indeed, there are several places in the confessional verses where we are unsure whether it is the drum or Ruciraketu speaking, or both or neither.

The third symbol that Ruciraketu sees in his dream is a man, a man with the appearance of a brahmin beating the drum and calling forth the confessional verses. But what is a brahmin doing in a Bodhisattva's dream? Surely this is rather odd. Well, he is not the kind of brahmin who may first spring to mind, the kind of zealous Hindu brahmin who is always cropping up in Buddhist scriptures to argue with the Buddha. In the early days of Buddhism the terms 'brahmin' and 'bhikkhu' were practically synonymous. Both, as used by the Buddha, represented the spiritual ideal. In the *Dhammapada*, for instance, we find a 'Brāhmaṇa-vagga', a chapter on the brahmin, and here the brahmin stands for the man devoted to the spiritual life, or even for the Enlightened man – just as the bhikkhu does. It must be admitted that the Buddha's attempt to 'upgrade' the word 'brahmin' and dissociate it from its caste significance did in fact fail. Indeed, in this context, as a drum of any size would have to be made of leather, a traditional brahmin would not touch it, let alone beat it.

But perhaps there is another reason for the presence of the brahmin in Ruciraketu's dream. Originally the brahmin was the priest or shaman of the invading Aryan tribes, and he is therefore a very ancient, arcane figure, a figure that goes right back to the beginning. In the literal sense, to go back to the beginning is to go back in time, but metaphorically, to go back to the beginning is to go out of time altogether. Taken in this sense, the figure of the brahmin suggests that whatever happens in the dream happens outside time, that the ultimate significance of the dream is transcendental.

It is in the nature of dreams that they conjure up archaic images. And the images they conjure up tend to reflect your cultural background. If as a Western Buddhist you have an archetypal dream, the chances are that you won't dream about a Buddhist temple. You will find yourself in the middle of some beautiful cathedral, because you have been brought up to associate cathedrals with all that is religious and spiritual. That is deeply ingrained in your unconscious mind, even though you are a Buddhist. Maybe your unconscious mind hasn't yet been converted, and still dwells on cathedrals and stained glass windows.

It is probably the same with Ruciraketu. He is a Buddhist, he is a Bodhisattva, but because he is an ex-Hindu he has residues of Hinduism and even Brahmanism in his consciousness, which means that his deeper psychological experience is in Hindu terms. As we will see, the sūtra exemplifies this throughout by bringing into the sphere of Buddhist teaching quite definitely Hindu figures. It's as though the sūtra, and in particular Ruciraketu's dream, represents an attempt to integrate these more archaic attitudes into the Buddhist vision.

The first time I read the *Sūtra of Golden Light*, I pictured the brahmin as a white-robed man, but when I re-read it, I was surprised to find that there is no mention of the brahmin as being white-robed. Perhaps I imagined him in white because in India that is the colour that brahmins traditionally wear, especially for religious ceremonies, and the white-robed figure therefore represents one devoted to spiritual development. I am also reminded of the man wrapped in the white sheet who illustrates the experience of the fourth dhyāna. These are purely personal associations, but perhaps they are of some significance.

The brahmin is not just present in Ruciraketu's dream; he is doing something – beating the drum. In other words, the spiritual devotee takes the initiative. He gathers up his strength, lifts the hammer, and strikes.

He beats on the drum, he beats on the Absolute. The drum is what in earlier Indian traditions was a solar symbol – that is, the sun as a golden door into a higher world: to open the door, you have to knock. It's rather like what Yeats said of William Blake: 'He beat upon the wall / Till Truth obeyed his call.' The brahmin beats on the drum, beats on the Absolute – and there's a response. The drum speaks. Reality speaks. The confessional verses come forth.

And the golden drum's response takes the form of the celebrated verses of confession which not only make up the greater part of this chapter, but also form the original nucleus of the entire sūtra. As one might expect, this being a dream, the verses don't seem to come forth in any particular order. There's no logical sequence. They just flow forth from the golden drum like a great stream of golden light. The golden light is the sound of the drum; the sound of the drum is the golden light. It's what Coleridge called 'a light in sound, a sound-like power in light'.[22] And because they are part of Ruciraketu's dream, both the drum and the golden light *are* Ruciraketu, are *in* Ruciraketu. So it is also Ruciraketu who is speaking – not the old Ruciraketu, but the new Ruciraketu.

Haphazardly as they flow forth, the verses can be divided into ten sections. The first is a prayer, a prayer that by the sound of the drum the world and all living beings may progress. In other words, it's a prayer for the complete transformation of self and world. In the second section we have the drum speaking as Ruciraketu – or Ruciraketu speaking as the drum – and making the Bodhisattva Vow. He vows to attain supreme Enlightenment for the benefit of all beings, to dedicate himself to the great task of the transformation of self and world. So the influence of the golden light is beginning to make itself felt.

The third section is a lengthy confession of faults. Ruciraketu acknowledges all the unskilful actions which have hitherto prevented him from realizing his ideal, from being a real Bodhisattva, from becoming a Buddha. This is followed in the fourth section by a promise to worship the Buddhas in the ten directions; in effect this is a more detailed statement of the Bodhisattva Vow. Among other things, Ruciraketu undertakes to expound the *Sūtra of Golden Light,* and in particular the confession.

Section five is a second confession of faults, rather shorter than the first, and the sixth is a brief rejoicing in the merits of all beings who perform skilful actions. In the seventh section there is a third confession of faults, the shortest one of all. Then section eight is taken up with praising the Buddhas; here solar imagery is very conspicuous. The Buddha is described as 'the Buddha-sun, removing the obscurity of darkness with his rays of Compassion' and 'a fully Enlightened sun'. 'With meshes of beams full of glory, merit, and splendour, he stands amid the darkness like the sun in the three worlds.' Section nine contains more aspirations, good wishes, and rejoicing in merits, and the last section declares the advantages of worshipping the Buddha by means of these verses of confession.

From this brief summary we can see that the main subject matter of the verses is the confession of faults, although this is balanced by the Bodhisattva Vow, verses of praise to the Buddha, and rejoicing in merits. So there is a resemblance between these verses and chapter 2 of Śāntideva's *Bodhicaryāvatāra*, 'Entering the Path of Enlightenment';[23] and what we really have here is a rudimentary and unsystematic but very beautiful sevenfold puja.[24]

2

The Spiritual Significance of Confession

Introduction: Confession in Religious Tradition

WHEN WE HEAR THE WORD 'CONFESSION', those of us with a background in Western culture may well see in our mind's eye the little wooden box with the grille and the hidden priest which is such a central feature of the Roman Catholic church. If we have come close enough to the undesirable aspects of the Catholic confessional, we may associate confession with sin and guilt, punishment and eternal damnation. It may therefore come as a surprise (and perhaps not altogether a welcome one) that confession also occupies a very important place in Buddhist spiritual life. I should hasten to make it clear, therefore, that confession as a Buddhist practice is radically different from Roman Catholic auricular confession, which plays so heavily upon irrational feelings of guilt. Buddhist confession is also very different from the kind of confession valued by modern psychoanalysis. Psychoanalysts may value confession, but they do so very much within a theoretic framework which is – with the possible exception of the Jungian school – secular and humanistic, not to say scientific and rationalistic. The value and significance of confession as understood by psychoanalysis is therefore strictly limited.

But in Buddhism confession has not just a psychological effect, but a profound spiritual significance – as we shall see when we study chapter 3 of the *Sūtra of Golden Light* in detail. But first, why stress that confession – or any other practice – has a *spiritual* significance? The point that some people have made to me in the past is that we should be better off without the word 'spiritual' altogether, because it fulfils no function that is not covered by the word 'psychological'. After all, they say, 'spiritual' experience pertains to the psyche, so we might just as well speak of 'psychological' experience. But to me it seems helpful to draw a sharp distinction between the psychological and the spiritual.

Strictly speaking 'psychological' means 'that which pertains to or belongs to the *science* of the mind', and when we want to refer to that which pertains to or belongs to the mind (or the psyche) itself, we should, again strictly speaking, use the word 'psychical'. Still, the usage of 'psychological' is well established, and not worth quarrelling with. There are some aspects of the word's use, however, that definitely are worth taking issue with. What we mean by psychological clearly depends on what we mean by psyche. Psyche is 'mind' (or even 'soul' in the popular sense of the term) – but what is 'mind'? As far as most people are concerned, mind is simply that which is different from the body, that which is the seat of thoughts, feelings, and impulses (whether conscious or subconscious): thoughts about work, home, money, politics; feelings of love, hate, jealousy, fear, anxiety; impulses to pursue what is pleasant and avoid what is unpleasant. And if you are going to take 'mind' to mean all these things, you are going to tend to take 'psychological' as indicating something belonging to the psyche or mind as you yourself know and experience it.

If we think of Enlightenment as a psychological experience, we are going to tend to think that it is a mental state of a type with which we are already more or less familiar. In other words, we will misunderstand it completely. If, on the other hand, we think of Enlightenment as a spiritual experience – in other words, as an experience of a type with which we are not familiar at all – there is then much less danger of misunderstanding. We will at least register that this is something that does not fall within our present range of experience, something that involves a shift to a higher level of consciousness. According to Buddhist tradition, there are many higher levels of consciousness accessible to us. Above and beyond our everyday consciousness there are, as we have seen, what are called the four dhyānas, the four superconscious states of the world of form, each succeeding one higher than the last; beyond them there are what are known as the four formless dhyānas; and beyond all of them, there is nirvāṇa or Enlightenment.

At this point a further distinction is called for. We can define 'spiritual' both in a broad general sense and in a narrow, more specific one. In the broad sense, it refers to all the eight dhyānas plus the state of Enlightenment; in the narrower sense it refers only to the dhyanic, not the nirvanic level. If we use the word in this narrower sense, we need a different word to refer to the state of Enlightenment. For this I would suggest the term 'transcendental', which I use as the equivalent of the Pāli and Sanskrit word *lokuttara* – literally, 'beyond the world'. So we have three words: psychological, which pertains to ordinary human consciousness; spiritual, which pertains to the higher, dhyanic levels of consciousness; and transcendental, which pertains to Enlightenment, to ultimate reality.

Having rectified our terms in this way, we can no longer use expressions like spiritual practice, spiritual life, spiritual path, and spiritual ideal in a vague, woolly way. Spiritual practice is specifically that practice which is conducive to a state of consciousness higher than that we usually experience, to a dhyanic state, or even, if the word is used in the broader sense, to the state of Enlightenment itself. Spiritual life is the life which is systematically organized to make possible the attainment of higher states of consciousness, and which expresses those higher states. And so on.

To say that confession has a spiritual significance is therefore to say that it has significance for the attainment of higher levels of consciousness, whether the dhyānas or the state of Enlightenment itself. Consequently, confession plays a crucial role in the transformation of the individual, in the shift of the centre of gravity from the psychological to the spiritual and from the spiritual to the transcendental. It is confession in this sense that is expounded in the *Sūtra of Golden Light*, especially in the celebrated verses of confession.

Just to set the scene before we explore the text of the sūtra in detail, we will take a look at the history of confession in Buddhism. The *Sūtra of Golden Light* illuminates our understanding of Buddhist confession in a particularly beautiful and comprehensive way, but it is not the first mention of confession as a practice to be found in the scriptures. Confession goes back much further in Buddhist history – back, in fact, to the time of the Buddha.

The history of confession in Buddhism is intimately connected with – believe it or not – the weather. In every country the pattern of life is shaped by the climate. It is the climate that determines when the crops will grow, what kind of housing is needed, what kind of transport will run. Some countries are dark and icebound for part of the year; others have to cope with intense heat and aridity all year round. Everywhere there is some kind of pattern to which life adapts itself.

An aspect of the climate in India that has had a formative effect on life there for thousands upon thousands of years is the rainy season. For three or four months of the year the rain falls solidly and continuously. If you go out in the rain it's like stepping into a warm shower fully clothed; you get completely soaked within minutes. And of course the ground gets so muddy that – if you live out in the countryside – it is difficult to walk very far.

As well as affecting the pattern of social and agricultural life, the rainy season has had its effect on Indian spiritual life, at least so far as its outward expression is concerned. In the Buddha's day, and for centuries afterwards, those of his followers who had given up the household life used to wander from place to place living on alms and teaching the Dharma. But in the rainy season it was impossible to wander about and sleep under trees, as you could do the rest of the year. You needed to find a place to shelter.

At first, the Buddha's followers used to stay in all kinds of places during the rainy season. They might stay in a cave or a wayside shrine devoted to local gods; they might find a shed in somebody's garden or park, or even spend the rainy season in a hollow tree. But as time went on simple buildings were put up for the use of the bhikkhus by the lay supporters who continued to live at home.[25] It was these rudimentary shelters that eventually became what we usually refer to as monasteries.

The rainy season increasingly became an opportunity for the monks to spend time together. Some of them remained absorbed in meditation for much of the time, but others took the chance to repeat to each other what they knew of the Buddha's teaching, to preserve the oral tradition. They also used to spend time on more homely tasks – if one can use the word 'homely' in connection with monks – mending and patching their robes, washing and dyeing them.

Come the end of the rainy season, though, they would set off on their wanderings again, either singly or in twos and threes, sometimes even in small bands. The monks wandered on foot from place to place all over north-eastern India. The area they covered was so vast – the Buddha himself is known to have wandered over an area the equivalent in extent to Great Britain – that they might well go for days and days without seeing any other monk. But twice a month, on the night of the full moon and the night of the new moon, wherever they might find themselves in the course of their wanderings, all the monks in a given area would gather together. There might be as many as a thousand of them, especially if the Buddha was going to be present. They would gather together in a forest clearing in the light of the full moon, and chant together verses in which the Buddha's teaching had been summarized, either by the Buddha himself or by one of his disciples who happened to be poetically gifted. Then, having refreshed their memory of the teaching, they would meditate and reflect on it.

This is what happened during the Buddha's lifetime, as far as we can reconstruct events. But after the Buddha's death, after the parinirvāṇa, it seems that a change took place. The bhikkhus continued to meet on the nights of the full moon and the new moon, but they no longer meditated or chanted together. Instead, they confessed any offences against the monastic code – by this time comparatively fully schematized – that they had committed since the last meeting.[26] Any transgressions were then dealt with by the assembled chapter of the Order.

Later still, another change took place. The monks confessed their offences not during the actual meeting but before it. They got together in pairs and took it in turns to confess, the senior going first. In the meeting itself the monastic code was simply recited by a single monk appointed for the purpose. The rest of the assembly, having already confessed in private, remained silent.

This kind of confessional meeting is still held in many parts of the Buddhist world today, especially those that follow the Theravādin tradition. Unfortunately the practice has degenerated considerably, at least in some circles, as I discovered for myself as a young monk in Nepal. The occasion was the ordination ceremony of two young novices. Before the ceremony could commence, all the monks present had to purify themselves, and that meant they had to confess. So we all paired off, each pair of monks squatting on their heels face to face and confessing to one another, first the senior monk confessing to the junior, then the junior to the senior. I was quite pleased to discover that we would be confessing to each other in this way, because although I had been ordained for about a year, I hadn't so far had an opportunity to confess any faults. I began to think 'What have I got to confess? Have I done anything I shouldn't have?' But before I could get very far in my thinking, the monk with whom I was paired started chanting something very rapidly in Pāli. I could make out some of it, but not much because he was chanting so quickly. It only took him about a minute and a half, and then he said

'Come on. Now you chant.' I said, 'Well, I don't know it by heart', so he said, 'All right, repeat it after me.' He rattled it off and I repeated it phrase for phrase. When I looked up again, all the other monks were standing up already. I was very disappointed.

Although in the Theravādin tradition the confession ceremony which has its roots in the rainy season gatherings has become a formality, this is not the only form of confession practised. For instance, even among Theravādins it does sometimes happen that a monk who feels something weighing on his mind goes and confesses it to his teacher. When you are living under the same roof as your teacher, the practice is that at the end of each day you go to him, bow down, and ask forgiveness for any offences of body, speech, or mind that you may have committed against him in the course of the day. For instance, you may not quite have liked something the teacher said to you, and an angry thought may have flashed across your mind. Well, you've got to confess it that night; you mustn't sleep on it. You've got to bring it out into the open and say 'This is what happened. I felt angry. I'm sorry, please forgive me.' If the practice is kept up in this way, a positive and open relationship between teacher and pupil is maintained.

In my own case, although I didn't have the opportunity to get to know most of my Tibetan teachers well enough to be able to make a real confession, I was sometimes able to open up to Dhardo Rimpoche, whom I got to know quite well.[27] Once or twice there was something that was making me feel uneasy, and I spoke to him about it. But there wasn't much opportunity for confession, and in any case I didn't think so much in those terms then as I do now. It was one of those things I had to find out for myself.

Ever since the time of the Buddha, confession has been considered important not only for monks, but also for lay people. Take the well-known story of Ajātaśatru, the king of Māgadha, who lived in the Buddha's time. Ajātaśatru had become king in a way all too common in those days. He had done it by murdering his father, King Bimbisāra, an old friend and disciple of the Buddha's. Although he had got the kingship he wanted, Ajātaśatru was uneasy in his mind. He couldn't forget what he had done; he could get no rest. One full moon night, after he had been tossing and turning for hours, he just couldn't stand it any longer. He got up to go and see the Buddha, who was staying with his disciples in the middle of the forest. Ajātaśatru went straight to the Buddha and confessed what he had done: evil had overcome him, and he had killed his own father for the sake of the throne. The Buddha heard and accepted

Ajātaśatru's confession, and then he gave a teaching. But although Ajāta-śatru heard the teaching and was receptive to it, the higher spiritual vision did not arise in him. The Buddha remarked that Ajātaśatru would have attained that vision but for the fact that he had committed that most serious and terrible of offences.

Mahāyāna Buddhism also has its tradition of confession. Indeed, throughout the Buddhist world, verses of confession are chanted as part of devotional practice. In the Mahāyāna tradition such verses – like the ones in the *Sūtra of Golden Light* – are particularly beautiful and elaborate. There are many texts that deal with the practice of confession in detail, and among them the *Sūtra of Golden Light* stands out for its great beauty and its comprehensive treatment of the subject.

We have already seen that the verses spoken by the golden drum, whilst focusing on the theme of confession, bring in other themes, and in fact take the form, more or less, of a sevenfold puja. A sevenfold puja is a form of worship in which one passes through a sequence of what might be called spiritual moods. First comes recognition of the Buddha, the Enlightened One, and the aspiration to commit oneself to the path of Enlightenment. Then comes confession of all those obstacles that stand between oneself as one is at present and the Enlightened being one aspires to become; then rejoicing in merit, in which one expresses delight at all the skilful actions performed by others. Then comes the request for a teaching; and lastly what is called 'transference of merit', in which one dedicates whatever fruits are borne by one's spiritual efforts to the good of all beings.

This is roughly the form taken by chapter 3 of the sūtra, although, the emphasis being on confession, there are three confession sections rather than the usual one, each with a slightly different flavour. Because each section brings out a different aspect of the spiritual significance of con-fession, we will look at each in some detail. To begin with, though, we will turn to the first utterances of the golden drum, which make clear the context in which confession should be made.

ASPIRATION: THE CONTEXT FOR CONFESSION

We could describe the first section of chapter 3 as a prayer for the progress of all sentient beings. To call it a prayer, however, is a very provisional description. The 'prayer' is just the sound of the drum, the golden light pouring forth from the drum, and more than that, it's the *effect* of the sound and the light – the beneficent effect of that sound and light on all sentient beings.

> By the excellent drum of golden light let the woes in the triple-thousand world be suppressed, the woes in the evil states, the woes in the world of Yāma and the woes of poverty here in the threefold world.[28]

The 'evil states' here are those of the beings occupying three of the six realms depicted by the Tibetan Wheel of Life: the realm of the animals, the realm of the hungry ghosts, and the realm of the hell-beings. Ultimately, of course, you have to get out of all six realms, but these three in particular are the evil states, the 'ill-farings'.

So as yet the aspiration isn't very high. There's just a prayer that these worldly woes may be suppressed. There isn't any reference to the attainment of higher spiritual states.

> And by this resounding of the sound of the drum may all troubles in the world be suppressed, may beings be without fear, free of fear just as great sages are without fear, fearless.[29]

Abhaya or fearlessness is mentioned very often in Buddhism. It is, for example, enumerated as an element in the Bodhisattva's practice of *dāna* or giving. Along with material things, culture, life and limb (if necessary), and the supreme gift, the gift of the Buddha's teaching, he is able to impart the gift of fearlessness. By his mere presence the Bodhisattva creates confidence and removes people's fear. Certainly freedom from fear is emphasized much more in Buddhism than in Christianity, where we may say fear is positively encouraged: 'The fear of the Lord is the beginning of wisdom.'

I can recall from my own experience one quite vivid instance illustrative of this difference between the two religions. It concerned the death of somebody I knew when I was living in Kalimpong – an elderly Englishwoman who had come out to Kalimpong and become a Buddhist. I came back from Calcutta one day and the first news I got on my return was that Miss Barclay had died, and that there was a dispute about the body. The local Catholic Christians were claiming it and wanting to give it Christian burial, but my students were resisting and saying no, she had become a Buddhist. So I hurried straight to her house and found several local Christians there, plus a number of my students, all Buddhists, and the police.

As I entered, the police inspector said to me 'Can you tell me what religion this lady followed?' I said 'Oh yes, she was a Buddhist.' My students said, 'There, we told you so, we told you so!' So the police officer said 'Ah, but can you prove it?' – and all the Catholics smiled. I said 'Yes.' The police inspector then said 'Well, can you produce the proof in the police station tomorrow morning?' 'Yes, certainly.'

We had an organization called the Young Men's Buddhist Association and Miss Barclay had become an associate member. She had signed the application form, and where it said 'Religion' she'd filled in 'Buddhist'. So, to cut a long story short, we claimed the body. We took it from the hospital mortuary back to the YMBA, and, as there was nowhere else, laid it out on the ping-pong table. The funeral had been announced for that afternoon and a lot of people came.

And here we get to the point of the story. Miss Barclay had known quite a few Christians in the area, including missionaries, and they all gathered in the sitting-room; and there were many of my students who had also known her. According to local custom, before someone was cremated you would go and have a last look at them. All my students, who were young Nepalese and Tibetans and Bhutanese, were keen to have a last look at Miss Barclay. She had been a good friend to them; she had often invited them for tea. So they were all going into the games room to take a look: 'Oh yes, she looks OK, quite peaceful ...' – that sort of thing.

But when I asked the Christian missionaries and ministers whether they would like to go in and have a look at Miss Barclay, they said, to a man, 'Oh no, thank you!' They clearly had a fear of death, or anything to do with it. Not one of them went in to have a look – they were simply afraid to – but all these quite ordinary Tibetan and Nepalese students went in without any hesitation. You couldn't quite say it was all in the day's work, but they were accustomed to it. It was what happened at home if their grandfather or their great-aunt died. Death was a natural thing, it was a part of life. There was nothing to be afraid of – you all had to die one day, everybody knew that. But these missionaries, even though they were preachers of religion, were obviously afraid.

Whether this was specifically to do with Christianity, or something more to do with modern life in general, it is difficult to say. But certainly there seems to be much more fear of this kind in the minds of people in the West. One shouldn't overstate this, of course; there is fear in everybody, otherwise there would be no need for prayers of this sort, or for Bodhisattvas to impart fearlessness. Indeed, the development of fearlessness is central to the practice of Buddhism, especially fearlessness in the face of death.

Very often we don't realize the extent to which we are under the influence of fear and worry and anxiety. Not very many people are completely free from fear, or even free from worry. To be fearless is quite an achievement; in fact, if you are fearless, you are practically Enlightened. By this I don't mean that Enlightenment confers the kind of fearlessness which is simply lack of imagination. I remember once hearing about wartime pilots, and apparently the best of them, the ace fliers, the ones who won decorations, were totally lacking in imagination. They weren't particularly fearless; they just didn't have enough imagination to realize that there was any danger. That isn't true fearlessness. If you are truly fearless, you see the situation clearly, you have no illusions about it, but you don't feel afraid. That is fearlessness as understood by Buddhism. After all, what is fear? You are usually afraid for yourself, or afraid of losing yourself. If you are fearless, therefore, you are practically free from egotism.

The basic fear is, obviously, fear of death, but there are many others. Perhaps surprisingly, a great number of people seem to be afraid of going mad. It seems as though they are already under quite a strain and just a bit more pressure will make them crack. It is noticeable that in the West there is more fear of insane people than you tend to find in India. Here, if a lunatic walked in and started acting the fool, so to speak, we wouldn't quite know how to take it, whereas Indian people wouldn't be embarrassed or put out at all, as long as he didn't do any actual harm. Perhaps this fear of lunacy indicates that in the West one identifies oneself more strongly with the rational part of oneself than people usually do in India, and one therefore tends to have difficulty finding a sense of fellow-feeling with those who have lost their reason.

There is also fear of humiliation. Bunyan's shepherd boy sings: 'He that is down needs fear no fall' – but all too often we *are* afraid of falling, afraid of not being able to live up to what people expect of us. We have a false idea of ourself which we try to live up to, and which other people expect us to live up to, and we feel insecure because we know that we are trying to live up to something false. We feel a sense of strain all the time, because we are afraid of disappointing people's expectations and feeling humiliated as a result.

If you have always thought of yourself as being very clever, and everybody else thinks you're very clever, you feel humiliated if you're made to look a fool because that isn't the image you have of yourself. But if you've got no illusions about yourself and don't try to live up to some unreal image, you're not vulnerable to humiliation in this way. If you've been a fool since the day you were born – and if everybody knows it and you know it too – you're not humiliated by being shown up as a fool. You're just being yourself.

If, as the sūtra prays, you become fearless, that is a great spiritual achievement, because it's only the Buddha, the Enlightened one, who is completely fearless. And as Buddhism has always attached great importance to the state of fearlessness, it should come as no surprise that the sound of the golden drum has the effect of removing fear.

A solitary retreat, when you spend time alone meditating and reflecting, is very likely to give rise to fear, because it deprives you of the activities and things through which you hide from your basic anxiety. Under more ordinary circumstances, if you start feeling anxious you go and talk to somebody or go to the cinema or do something else to distract yourself. But when you're on solitary retreat you can't do any of those things. There is no escape from anxiety, no escape from fear; you're brought right up against it. There is an element of this in everybody. It's as though it's there all the time, or much of the time, but we usually distract ourselves from it instead of facing it. When we're alone, though, it's a lot more difficult to run away.

If you are able to get away on solitary retreat, you may well find that at first you are keen to keep busy and fill in the day, because you are afraid of getting bored. But as the retreat progresses and you build up a higher level of positivity, you should be able to leave off doing so many things. You find you just don't need that kind of support. After a month or two you could conceivably end up doing nothing at all, and still pass the whole day quite positively – that is, being neither afraid nor empty nor bored nor anything else.

So if you get the chance to go on solitary retreat, or just to spend some time alone, you need to be careful not to use study and meditation to escape from feelings of anxiety. You do objectively need to keep yourself positively occupied, but we should be careful not to do things as defences against the anxiety which arises simply through being alone. It's fine to meditate all the time if it's a spontaneous and natural thing, but not if you are just meditating to keep anxiety at bay. Difficult as it may be, you need to allow yourself to feel afraid. You can't transform the feeling just like that, but if you make sure you are allowing yourself to feel it, it will pass sooner or later. You might find in the end that it is less trouble allowing yourself to feel the anxiety than spending all your time and energy keeping it at bay.

> Just as the great sages who know all in the cycle of existence are endowed with all the noble virtues, so may men be oceans of virtues endowed with the virtues of meditation and the seven members of enlightenment.[30]

The seven members – or factors – of Enlightenment are the seven *bodhyaṅgas*: recollection or awareness (*smṛti*), investigation of mental states (*dharma-vicaya*), energy or vigour (*vīrya*), rapture (*prīti*), tension release or bliss (*praśrabdhi*), concentration (*samādhi*), and tranquillity or equanimity (*upekṣā*).

Of course, the factors can't really be divided up quite so neatly. *Vīrya*, for example, although it is listed as a factor (it is also numbered as one of the *pāramitās* or perfections), is needed all along. Without some *vīrya*, some vigour, how can you investigate your mental states, for instance? But all the same, there is a kind of sequence in the factors. First of all you have mindfulness. Then with that mindfulness you examine all your mental states, to see whether they are skilful or unskilful. That is *dharma-vicaya*. Then, having investigated your mental states, you act upon the knowledge gained from the investigation, starting to weed out the unskilful mental states and cultivate the skilful ones. And for that you obviously need energy. Not only do you need energy for doing it, but once you have done it, you gain more energy, because the energy that was locked up in the unskilful mental states has been released. The release of energy leads to an experience of *prīti* or rapture – and so on.

The cycle of existence mentioned here is the *nidāna* chain, the Wheel of Life, and the suggestion is that the great sages have penetrated it through insight into all its aspects.[31] They know it thoroughly, have seen through it completely, and they are at the same time endowed with all the noble virtues.

> And by this resounding of the sound of the drum may all beings possess the voice of Brahma.[32]

Wishing that all beings may possess the voice of Brahma is in effect to wish that all beings may become Enlightened, because the Buddha is the one who possesses the voice of Brahma. The Brahma voice is made up of all possible sounds. Sometimes it's said that it is made up of the sixty-four sounds – there being sixty-four letters in the Sanskrit alphabet – which is to say that it expresses all possible combinations of words and sentences.

It says everything, but communicates to each person what they particularly need to hear. To say that the Buddha has the Brahma voice is therefore to say that when the Buddha speaks, everybody understands in his or her own way.

Take the audience of a talk about Buddhism. Everybody hears the same words, but they each take what they need. One person may say 'He said something that really impressed me – he said something about the Four Noble Truths.'[33] But someone else may say 'No, it was all about the life of the Buddha. I really liked that.' No doubt the speaker spoke about both those things, but for one listener it was the Four Noble Truths that registered, while for the other it was what was said about the life of the Buddha.

A talk, of course, has a certain length and includes various different topics, but the Brahma voice says everything at once, if you can imagine that. It's as though the lecturer had managed to speak about the Four Noble Truths and the life of the Buddha at the same time. The Brahma voice is the voice from which everybody picks out what he wants – or needs – to hear. In an ultimate sense we could say that the Buddha doesn't say anything at all, or that everything he says has the same meaning, and that what he says only seems to comprise different things because different people take it differently.

> May they touch the best enlightenment of Buddhahood. May they turn the pure Wheel of the Law. May they remain living for inconceivable aeons. May they preach the Law for the welfare of the world. May they destroy impurities, annihilate woes, suppress passion, likewise hatred and folly.[34]

This is all pretty straightforward; the essential meaning is again the wish that all living beings may gain Enlightenment. Turning the Wheel of the Law is a reference to the traditional image, the *dharmacakrapravartana*, the 'setting in motion of the Wheel of the Dharma'. According to some scholars there is some solar symbolism here, the Wheel of the Dharma being the sun-wheel, the sun with its rays.

> May those beings who dwell in an evil state, their limbs alight with blazing fire, hear the sound of the drum. May they take up the refrain: 'Homage be to the Buddha.'[35]

Here we are talking about what we would call hell, although the Buddhist hell differs from the Christian one in that it is not a permanent state. Even beings in hell may make spiritual progress in the long term. These lines express the wish that even beings in such a very unfavourable condition may hear the sound of the drum, in order that they may have some chance to escape from that state, and – eventually – become Enlightened.

> May all beings be mindful of their former births during hundreds of births, thousands of millions of births.[36]

First of all, it is worth questioning the point of remembering all one's previous births. Perhaps on the whole it is just as well that we *don't* remember our previous lives. It would probably be such a sordid and sorry tale. We might be terribly discouraged to see ourselves making the same mistakes over and over again. Looking back on the follies of this life is bad enough for some of us. If we peeked back into the previous life and it was no better, and the one before that even worse, and the ten or twelve before that absolutely catastrophic – well, we'd get depressed after the first few hundred. We might start thinking we had no hope. So we are better off, at this stage, only remembering this life – or bits of it. It does seem a merciful providence that wipes the slate clean every time we are reborn so that we can make a fresh start.

But when you have developed these higher spiritual faculties, then it's safe enough to look back and recollect your previous lives. Even if you look back on tens of thousands of wasted lives, it doesn't matter, because at least you're on your way now – you are in fact very near your goal. To say 'May all beings be mindful of their former births' is therefore to wish at the same time that all beings may attain a high level of spiritual development, because it is only then that it will be useful or even bearable to recollect all those previous lives.

> Continually mindful of the great sages, let them hear their word, for it is noble. And by this resounding of the noise of the drum may they always obtain a meeting with the Buddhas. May they avoid evil action. May they practise meritorious acts of good.[37]

Being continually mindful of the great sages means recollecting their lives and good qualities, or if they are alive, going to see them and listening to them. In speaking of 'their word' in the singular, the text seems to imply that all the great sages speak one word, that is, that all those who are really great sages give – at least in essence – the same teaching.

> For those men, Asuras, all beings who have desires and wishes, may I fulfil them all by this resounding of the noise of the drum.[38]

So here are all these beings who are full of desires and wishes. It's as though the sound of the drum fulfils their real wishes, what they are really after, perhaps even without knowing it. And here we touch upon a fundamental spiritual issue. Often we feel desires for all sorts of things we think we want, but even if we get what we thought we wanted, our desires remain unsatisfied. We experience this, of course, because we are so busy going after things we don't really want. Only too often when we have had it and enjoyed it – if it was enjoyable – we realize that we didn't really want it after all. We are not really satisfied; we have just been distracted or amused for a while, no more than that. When we think about it, we realize that we could easily have done without it – even have been better off without it.

But when you are in the grip of desire, it's hard to remember all this. When you think you want something, well, you think you want it. You can go through the same procedure time and time again, maybe hundreds of times, before you learn your lesson and accept that you're not going to get what you really want from that thing. It cannot give you real satisfaction – but it's difficult to give up hoping that it might be able to, and trying just once more. 'I'll give it another chance before trying nirvāṇa!' You have to really wallow in it before you know it's muck.

Even if somebody tells you that the object of your desire will be a disappointment, and on a rational level you can see that he is right, this still won't help if deep down you remain unconvinced. However rational and reasonable the arguments against doing it are, you may well feel compelled to do whatever it is anyway, just to see for yourself.

But, of course, there is really no need to try out everything personally. If somebody tells you that if you put your finger in the fire it will burn, you don't have to test it to see. You might put your finger near enough to get warm, and a bit nearer to get warmer, but that will be enough to convince you. It's a delusion to think that we have to experience personally everything that the Buddha has warned us does not lead in the direction of nirvāṇa. We just have to take the Buddha's word for it in at least certain areas, and not insist on a personal confirmation of the unsatisfactoriness of every vice.

It isn't even really necessary to experience something of every kind or category of vice. You can group them into one big group called 'worldly pleasures'; if you have had even a taste of one of them, that should be enough to disillusion you about them all. They all come under the same heading; they're all conditioned things, so they don't really differ in any essential respect from one another.

On the other hand, it could be quite dangerous to deprive yourself of all comforts on the basis of a purely rational understanding of the truth, before you have started to get any real satisfaction from practising Buddhism. If you did that, you could well feel so bored and frustrated, and find life so blank and meaningless, that you would be tempted to go to the opposite extreme. You must begin to enjoy being a Buddhist before you give up too much, otherwise you will associate being a Buddhist with a dull, dry, painful, difficult, joyless sort of existence.

This should not, of course, be used as a rationalization for not giving up anything at all. In fact, if you haven't got any enjoyment at all from the Dharma, it might be best to give up a few things and make things really uncomfortable for yourself. That might force the issue. Otherwise you could remain stuck indefinitely, just being mentally occupied with the Dharma, getting no real pleasure from it, and not being willing to give up even small things because you haven't yet started to enjoy the spiritual life. You could stay like that all your life. You might have to do something drastic, take a risk, make yourself really uncomfortable, get thoroughly bored and frustrated. Then you would have to get pleasure from the Dharma because you weren't getting it from anywhere else.

It is tempting to think that the golden light might be somehow reflected in the more refined worldly pleasures, but this is not so at all. It is true that in the case of aesthetic experiences at their very highest, like the music of Bach at its most sublime, you get distant reflections – or perhaps we should say echoes – of the golden light. But the golden light does not actually shine through even the most elevated aesthetic production; and it's not enough just to have a glimpse in the distance in an indirect, remote way. We have to make the experience our own, and this involves a regular, disciplined way of life directed to that end.

In modern times we have got into the habit of sampling experience with no corresponding commitment to what the experience is meant to represent. To take the example of music, we don't usually think of it very seriously. It doesn't involve us in any responsibility towards it; it's just available for us to use and enjoy. We go along to concerts because it's a pleasant sensation. But we could go along and experience them as a revelation which would make a real difference to our lives. It is the nature of the aesthetic experience that you are lifted out of yourself a bit – that's part of its value – and then dropped right back into yourself, virtually the same as you were before. Probably only a musician could listen to music with commitment. The rest of us are more like the so-called religious person who sits at home in the evening with a box of chocolates leafing through the life of Milarepa or the *Parinibbāna Sutta*. It's just an experience in a very superficial, untransforming sense.

We might have a taste of what Bach was trying to convey, but most of us can't become a musician like Bach. In the case of spiritual experience, however, it's different. Something is pointed out to us, or we experience something fleetingly, and then within the spiritual tradition we can make an effort, reproduce that experience within ourselves, and experience it fully. You might never become a Bach, but you can become a Buddha.

Of course, even if it doesn't result in lasting change, aesthetic experience can still be of benefit. If you are weaning yourself off, say, rather gross rock music, then to listen instead to the music of Bach is – at least in my view – very much a step in the right direction. Even if it doesn't reflect the golden light very clearly, it's a light of some kind. At least you are turning from something coarse and crude to something relatively refined, and that prepares the ground for the reception of the golden light.

So the sound of the drum is the giver of true satisfaction. Sometimes mediocre satisfaction blocks the path of true satisfaction; the good is the enemy of the best. We must learn to ask ourselves what we really want, because very often what we think we want is not really our heart's desire. We have got into a habit: we are used to it, we think we can't do without it, we think we enjoy it. But if we stop and think about our experience, we often have to admit that we don't really enjoy the things we usually do. We just don't know what to do instead. We fear that without our habitual activities we would be bored and dull, so we keep on doing them to stave off the boredom.

If you are unhappy, you can go out on the town, dull your perceptions, and pretend to be happy. Alternatively, you can stay where you are, knowing that you are unhappy but at least having some idea where to look for true happiness. Or, at the very least, knowing where you are *not* going to find it. It might sound strange, but in a way the unhappiness you feel is positive because it's simply the discomfort you feel when you are no longer trying to enjoy evanescent satisfactions.

You might perhaps feel, say on a Saturday night when everyone in the world seems to be going out to have a good time, that resisting the pull to join this social stream is somehow disintegrating. By losing touch with the 'social whirl' you feel you are losing touch with your own energy. This is because there is within you something that is in conflict with your more creative energies that responds to that pull. When you surrender to the attraction, all that has happened is that one part of you has triumphed over another with the help of outside forces. That certainly doesn't represent integration. You haven't resolved the conflict; you have just submerged it for the time being. You've temporarily ended the tension within you by yielding to the outside influence.

> For those beings who have taken birth in a fierce hell, their limbs alight with blazing fire, and, without deliverance and oppressed with grief, wander about, there will be quenching of their fires. Those beings whose woes are fierce and terrible in hells, among ghosts or in the world of men, by this resounding of the noise of the drum, may all their woes be suppressed.[39]

Here, if we come right down to earth, the quenching of the fires refers to our experience when we come upon something of a purely spiritual nature. It has the effect of making us realize that all our suffering is unnecessary; we have brought it upon ourselves through our own foolish involvement with certain things. When we realize this, our suffering just ceases.

In his dream Ruciraketu now not only hears a prayer that by virtue of the drum of golden light all beings may progress; he also actually sees the golden light helping them to progress. In this case the medium really is the message. The prayer of the drum, the prayer of the golden light, is self-fulfilling. As we have seen, the golden drum is the Absolute, the Buddha, as well as being the new Ruciraketu, and also the sūtra itself. So what Ruciraketu hears in this opening section is not just a pious wish that all sentient beings may progress. What he hears – and sees – is a sort of cosmic drama, a drama of the effect of the golden light of the transcendental on the darkness of the mundane.

He has in his dream a sort of spiritual vision. He sees that on the one hand there is the golden light, the light of truth, the light of reality; and on the other hand there is the darkness of confusion and bewilderment, the darkness of defilement and passion. And he sees that the darkness is struggling to overcome the light, and the light is struggling to overcome the darkness. He not only hears the prayer that 'the woes in the triple-thousand world may be suppressed' – he sees that in the case of at least some people woes *are* being suppressed. He not only hears the prayer that beings may be without fear; he sees some of them becoming free from fear. In the same way he sees people gaining Enlightenment, teaching the Dharma, destroying greed, hatred, and delusion. He sees people paying homage to the Buddha, worshipping the Buddha, recollecting the Buddha, meeting the Buddha, sees them performing skilful actions, sees the fires of hell being quenched, sees all woes being suppressed. In other words, Ruciraketu has a vision of the whole world being transformed. He sees darkness being overcome, and the golden light triumphant.

And he too feels the effect of the golden light. He too wants to be transformed. Not only that, he wants to co-operate with the golden light in its work of transforming the world and helping sentient beings to progress. And this is his response:

> May I be for those who are without deliverance, without rescue, without refuge, the deliverer, the refuge, the excellent protector.[40]

In other words, the *bodhicitta*, the will to Enlightenment, arises, and he takes the Bodhisattva Vow, the vow to attain supreme Enlightenment for the benefit of all sentient beings. The English word 'protector' can be confusing, because it is frequently used to translate two quite different Sanskrit words. When in the FWBO Sevenfold Puja, for example, the Buddhas are referred to as 'protectors', the word translated is *nātha*. On the other hand, the word generally used in connection with the protectors of the four quarters, the four great kings, whom we will come across later in the sūtra, is *pāla* – they are the dharmapālas. *Nātha* has rather a different significance from *pāla*. For instance, an orphan is called an *anātha* – someone without a protector. So *nātha* could even be translated as 'master'.

Ruciraketu's taking of the Bodhisattva Vow at this point reminds us that the sense of time in the sūtra is all askew. Ruciraketu is introduced to us as a Bodhisattva, which implies that he has already taken the Bodhisattva Vow, but here we find him, or rather the golden drum, taking the vow as though it hadn't been taken before. This shouldn't come as a surprise; after all, this is a dream, and dreams operate on a different time scale from ordinary life.

In fact, Ruciraketu in effect takes the Bodhisattva Vow again towards the end of the chapter:

> May all beings be such in virtue, appearance, fame, glory, with body adorned with the beautiful major marks and decorated with the eighty minor marks. And by this good act, may I ere long become a Buddha in the world; may I preach the Law for the welfare of the world; may I deliver beings oppressed by many woes; may I overcome Māra with his might and with his army; may I turn the Wheel of the excellent Law; may I remain for inconceivable aeons; may I satisfy beings with the water of nectar; may I fulfil the six unrivalled perfections just as they were fulfilled by previous Buddhas; may I smite the impurities; may I destroy woes; may I

extinguish passion, likewise hatred and folly. And may I be
continually mindful of former births for hundreds of births,
thousands of millions of births. May I constantly recollect the great
sages. May I listen to their speech, for it is noble. And by this good
act, may I always find a meeting with the Buddhas; may I utterly
avoid evil action; may I practise the good acts, mines of excellence.[41]

This paragraph starts off with an aspiration on behalf of all beings but
then it modulates into a sort of Bodhisattva Vow. There is an important
point to be made here. The bodhicitta, the will to Enlightenment – or
thought of Enlightenment, as it is sometimes (incorrectly) translated – is
transcendental. It is not a product of the mundane consciousness. One
cannot therefore really speak of 'my bodhicitta' or 'your bodhicitta'. It is
not an individual possession. In fact there is only one bodhicitta, just as
in reality there is only one Bodhisattva and only one Buddha. But the one
bodhicitta manifests through different individuals, through those that
make themselves receptive to it, like light refracting through a prism.

This is what has happened in Ruciraketu's case. He has made himself
receptive to the golden light, so that the golden light begins to work
through him. In short, he becomes a real Bodhisattva. And what a real
Bodhisattva does is practise the six perfections: generosity, ethics,
patience, energy, meditation, and wisdom. He works on himself, and he
does his best to help others. But unfortunately, what usually – indeed
always – happens next is that he comes up against obstacles within
himself, inner resistance. He becomes aware of many weaknesses and
faults, of much within him that is actually evil. He becomes aware of the
darkness within him. And this darkness resists the influence of the
bodhicitta, struggles against the golden light. What should the Bodhisattva do? What *can* he do? He can confess. He can confess his faults, the
evil that is within him. It is Ruciraketu's confession that takes the form
of the verses in the *Sūtra of Golden Light*.

Ruciraketu's experience is surely very much our own, even though our
experience may be on a lower level and a more restricted scale. We too,
perhaps, have seen the workings of the golden light in the world, or at
least our corner of it, and we too have wanted to make ourselves receptive
to that light, to allow it to work through us. So we too have breathed forth
our individual aspirations. We may not have taken the Bodhisattva Vow,
but we have at least resolved to work on ourselves and do our best to
help others in whatever way we can. But then we too encounter obstacles
within ourselves, inner resistance perhaps far stronger and more terrible

than anything Ruciraketu meets. So what can we do? Well, to begin with at least, we too can simply confess.

THE FIRST CONFESSION: THE VICTORY OF THE GOLDEN LIGHT

The word for confession in Sanskrit is *deśanā*, which means 'pointing out', 'indicating', 'explaining', 'expounding' – as in *Dharma deśanā*, which means the pointing out of the Dharma, the explaining of the Dharma. In the same way you get *pāpa deśanā*, the pointing out, the acknowledgement, of faults. *Pāpa* is often translated as 'sin', but I prefer to avoid the word because of its Christian connections. 'Faults', on the other hand, is rather weak. 'Evil' is probably the best translation. *Pāpa deśanā* is a pointing out, a confession, of the evil within us. But none of these expressions really does justice to one's actual spiritual experience at this stage. We need to go into the matter more deeply.

When you come into contact with the golden light, something of it enters into your system. It's a sort of spiritual food – the most concentrated and powerful kind of spiritual food imaginable. More than that, it's a sort of spiritual medicine. When it enters your system, it encounters all sorts of other things you have taken in: greed, hatred, delusion, wrong views.... There ensues a struggle between the golden light and the poison in your system, each trying to throw the other out. Sometimes, unfortunately, the unskilful states win, and succeed in expelling the golden light, which means an end to your spiritual life, at least for the time being. But happily this rarely happens. Once you have really taken in even a little of the golden light, it's very difficult to get rid of: in short, you're stuck with it.

So, does being stuck with the golden light mean that once you have come into contact with the spiritual path you can never fall back? Well, yes and no. It is only once you have entered the Stream that you are irreversibly bound for Enlightenment.[42] Up to that point, any spiritual experience or series of experiences you have is not irreversible, however long it may take to reverse the series.

However, it is probably true to say that once you have attained the level of reflexive consciousness that characterizes a human being, it is unlikely that you will lose it. From a Buddhist point of view, you have perhaps enjoyed reflexive consciousness for a very long time, through many births. What has developed over a long period takes a lot of undoing.

Even in the course of a single lifetime a human being can degenerate greatly through unskilful action – maybe through taking what is not given, or through persistent alcoholism, or even through murder. None the less, however degenerate, that person is still quite recognizably a human being, and reflexive consciousness is still quite clearly there, at least to some extent.

Once you have come into contact with the golden light, as long as your reflexive consciousness persists intact, you can't forget about your experience of that golden light, even though you haven't attained Stream Entry, even though you are not a Bodhisattva, and even though in theory you could fall right back to a very low state. In the long run you could, with a great deal of difficulty and as a result of a great deal of unskilful behaviour, shake off the golden light, but it is highly unlikely. None the less there is a sharp distinction between that state and the state of having achieved Stream Entry.

It is of course popularly understood that a human being might be reborn as an animal. Whether we can say that this really happens or not depends very much on what we mean by a human being. If we mean someone who has not only a human body but a fully and genuinely human consciousness, it is extremely unlikely that after he dies, he will be reborn as an animal. But if he has developed only a very rudimentary human consciousness, and even that has been degraded by unskilful actions, so that when he comes to die, his mental state is not much higher than an animal's, it seems not impossible that he should be reborn as an animal.

In Darjeeling years ago I happened to come across a man who kept pigs. He was a Nepalese Buddhist, but he was also a pig-keeper, and slaughtered pigs for market. He had his piggeries and slaughterhouse just below the place where I was staying, and every night I would hear the pigs screaming. When their throats were cut they emitted a dreadful, long-drawn-out scream which seemed to go on for minutes together. The pig-keeper spent all his time with those pigs, and he really did look like a pig. He had piggy features, a piggy expression – even a piggy build, with short legs and forearms almost like trotters. I got the impression that he was in close mental rapport with his pigs, and I would find it quite easy to believe that he had been reborn as a pig, especially as in the course of his life he had slaughtered hundreds and thousands of pigs.

So it depends what you mean by a human being. It seems highly unlikely, but it is plausible that in exceptional cases a person could be reborn as an animal, just as one can't help feeling that some animals have got such definitely human qualities that they could easily be reborn as human beings. The idea of humans being reborn as animals may seem to go against the grain of evolution. Having been cast up into the human state, having reached the stage of reflexive consciousness, how could one possibly fall back? But one of the characteristics of reflexive consciousness is that it can work against itself, destroy itself, commit suicide, as it were. For instance, when a man starts drinking to forget, he is deliberately trying to wipe out his truly human nature. It's as though reflexive consciousness has the power to turn round on itself and commit suicide. It's a two-edged weapon.

However, if you are fortunate enough to experience the golden light, then usually the golden light succeeds in throwing out, even throwing up, the poison. This makes it not just a spiritual food or a spiritual medicine, but a spiritual emetic. Once you have taken it, it compels you to vomit up all the evil in your system. It is in this vomiting up of mental and emotional poisons that the confession of evil really consists. It's much more than a verbal acknowledgement; it's an actual revulsion from evil. When we vomit physically, our stomach turns over and there's an upheaval; and it's much the same when we truly confess. There's a spiritual upheaval, and then up comes the poison and we spew it out. This way of putting things is graphic, I know – perhaps even offensive – but the truth of the matter is that confession can be a painful and unpleasant process, a process in which we may feel that we are spewing up not only the evil that is in us, but our blood and guts as well.

If we are in any doubt about what we should confess, the answer is simple: everything. We need to confess everything that is holding us back, everything that is preventing us from gaining Enlightenment. But this, of course, is by no means easy. There are some things that are very difficult, even impossible, to confess. This is because genuine confession is a powerful thing. Really to confess something is to give it up, not just verbally but in fact. If we are unwilling to confess something, it means that we are unable to give it up. And to the extent that we do not confess the evil within us, the evil we have done, we do not grow. We are hanging on to the past, to our old self, refusing to die.

Ruciraketu's confession is very comprehensive indeed. As far as we can tell, he doesn't leave anything out or hold anything back. There are three verses of confession in the sūtra, each with a slightly different emphasis. The first is simply a very full confession of all the evils Ruciraketu may have done. The second brings in the element of forgiveness, and the third adds the idea of evils committed under the influence of various 'oppressions'. Here is the first of the three sections:

And whatever evil, cruel act was done by me previously, I will confess it all before the Buddhas. Whatever evil I have done by not attending to my parents, by neglecting the Buddhas, by neglecting the good; whatever evil I have done by being drunk with the intoxication of authority or with the intoxication of high birth or by being drunk with the intoxication of tender age; whatever evil I have done, bad thought, bad word, by a mind dark with ignorance, under the influence of an evil friend or by a mind distracted by impurities, under the compulsion of sport or enjoyment, or through the influence of anxiety or anger, or through the fault of unsatisfied wealth; whatever evil I have done by my associations with ignoble people, by reason of envy and greed, or by the fault of guile or wretchedness; whatever evil I have done through failure to gain the mastery over my desires by reason of fear at the time of approaching troubles; whatever evil I have done through the influence of a flighty mind or through the influence of passion and anger or through being oppressed by hunger and thirst; whatever evil I have done for the sake of drink and food, for the sake of clothing, for a reason involving women, through the various afflictions of impurities; whatever evil of body, tongue and mind, bad action accumulated in threefold manner, I have done, together with similar things, I confess it all. Whatever disrespect I may have shown to Buddhas, doctrines, likewise to Śrāvakas, I confess it all. Whatever disrespect I may have shown towards Pratyekabuddhas or towards Bodhisattvas, I confess it all. If I have shown disrespect towards those who preach the Good Law or towards other meritorious beings, I confess it all. If I have unawares continually rejected the Good Law or shown disrespect towards my parents, I confess it all. Whatever evil I have done through stupidity or from folly or through being full of pride and arrogance, through passion, hatred or delusion, I confess it all.[43]

So this is Ruciraketu's first confession, and it gives a good idea of what is to be confessed. His first statement is:

... whatever evil, cruel act was done by me previously, I will confess it all before the Buddhas.

It is highly significant that the very first evil act that Ruciraketu confesses is cruelty. This is no doubt because cruelty is the behaviour which is most directly opposed to the Bodhisattva ideal. If you are cruel, you can't possibly be a Bodhisattva, because cruelty is the direct opposite of compassion. One of the words for cruelty is *nirdaya*, which means 'absence of compassion'. So if you want to be a Bodhisattva, the first thing you have to confess, the first thing you have to vomit up, is cruelty. Cruel acts are going to obstruct your path more than anything else.

This is why the Mahāyāna is particularly down on all unskilful actions that spring from hatred. Some Mahāyāna sūtras go so far as to say that in a sense it doesn't matter if you commit unskilful actions based on greed. At least that shows that you have some affinity for living beings, some inclination towards them. But hatred shows a different attitude altogether. A Bodhisattva cannot possibly entertain thoughts of hatred or cruelty. You can be a Bodhisattva if you've got a bit of greed left, but you can't be a Bodhisattva if you've got even a little bit of hatred left. It is no accident that cruel acts are the very first to be confessed here.

This is perhaps the reason some scriptures say that the Bodhisattva should not keep a cat. The cat is supposed to be cruel – that's the Indian idea – because it plays with and torments the mouse before killing it. So Indians regard the cat as a cruel, hard-hearted creature. The cat is said to be the only one of all those present at the time of the Buddha's parinirvāṇa who did not weep – apart from the Arhants, who were Enlightened. All the animals gathered there wept, but the cat just sat there, quite unmoved. So the cat has got rather a bad reputation in Indian myth and legend.

Cruelty is worse than hatred, and hatred is worse than anger. Anger is simply frustrated desire; it's the energy in the desire finding an obstacle and trying to burst through. Anger may be explosive, but it is often very short-lived, and you don't really wish the person who is obstructing you any harm. You just want to break through the obstruction; you don't want to hurt anybody. But when you hate, you have a fixed idea of some definite person or thing obstructing you, and you want to go all out to remove that person or that thing. In fact, if it is a person you feel hatred towards, you don't just want to remove them; you want to harm and injure them because you are so angry with them for having obstructed you. A species of hatred is enmity, which is the sort of vengeful hatred that pursues somebody and won't let him go, won't forgive him.

You can get angry with someone without ever being in any danger of hating them; you may even like them very much. But you can't hate somebody and at the same time be genuinely fond of them. You can certainly hate somebody and be in love with them – those are two sides of the same coin – but you can't hate a person you've got a genuine liking for. When you're angry with someone it isn't that you want to do them any harm – not intentionally anyway. You just explode because they are getting in your way. Anger can in a sense be quite positive in a way that hatred can never be. The danger is that if you regularly get angry with the same person for the same sort of reason, your anger will eventually consolidate into hatred.

Just as hatred develops out of anger, so enmity is to carry one's hatred beyond the possibility of forgiveness in pursuit of revenge. Cruelty goes a stage further. Cruelty is the inflicting of pain or suffering on someone beyond what is necessary to get them out of the way, and delighting in their suffering. And malice is the enjoyment of inflicting suffering on someone who has done you no harm at all. From the Mahāyāna point of view this is the most unskilful of all possible mental states.

This view is reflected in the general Mahāyāna approach to ethics. For example, when King Aśoka, the great Buddhist ruler of the Mauryan empire, exhorted his people to skilful actions, he always spoke in terms of being gentle, being patient, not giving way to anger. This was, for him, the basis of morality. He never said a word about, for example, sex. In our culture when we think of morality, the first thing that comes into our minds tends to be that we shouldn't do this, and we shouldn't do that. But in Buddhist cultures, if someone is said to be an immoral person, that means that he is rude, unfriendly, harsh in speech, inhospitable, and angry.

> Whatever evil I have done by not attending to my parents ... I
> confess it all.

After confessing any cruel acts committed, the next thing confessed – even before the confession of neglecting the Buddhas – is evil done 'by not attending to my parents'. If this sequence has any meaning at all, it suggests that not attending to one's parents is quite a serious matter. If you are on bad terms with your parents, it suggests, you can't make much spiritual progress. Your relationship with your parents goes so deep that if it isn't positive, there's a lot in you that isn't positive. This doesn't mean that you have to have a close relationship with your parents or see eye to eye with them. They may see things so differently from you that you may not be able to communicate with them at all. But at least your attitude should be one of goodwill. If it isn't, that is going to make things difficult for you.

If you feel that your parents are stifling you, if they are not allowing you to grow up, it is essential for you to leave home, literally or meta-phorically, and perhaps, on account of your attachment, you cannot but leave with some resentment. But if you really want to develop spiritually, sooner or later you must get over that. Even if your parents never understand what you have done and why, you must cultivate a positive attitude towards them. So long as you feel negative towards them and experience them as being restrictive and oppressive, that is going to get in your way. Our emotions are so bound up with our parents that if we hate them, we may well find it difficult to love anybody, or be capable of much devotion. Gurdjieff used to say 'A good man always loves his parents.'

I am not advocating the preservation of family life as a stuffy, claustrophobic affair. You need not feel dependent on the warmth of the cosy family group – far from it. From a Buddhist point of view you need to love your parents not just because you are their son or daughter, but because as an individual you are objectively grateful to them for what they have done for you in sponsoring your entry into the world. When Buddhism speaks in terms of a positive attitude towards one's parents, it means something more like *mettā* (loving-kindness) than love in the ordinary sense.[44]

This is true also of Hinduism at its best. A passage in the *Manusmriti* says that when a son reaches the age of sixteen, his father should no longer treat him as a son but just as a friend.[45] When you are sixteen, you are supposed to be grown up and independent, and you can start relating to your parents as an individual. Ideally your parents will accept you as such. Only then can there be a really positive mutual relationship between parents and children. When the children have grown up and become independent of their parents, and the parents have grown up enough to accept the change and relate to their children as individuals, there can be a very positive relationship. After all, we have known our parents all our lives, and that's a strong basis for a positive relationship.

If your parents have died, or you are not in contact with them, you can at least feel positively towards them, wishing them well wherever they are. If, by contrast, your parents are very much around, and find it difficult to let you go, you can find ways of handling that. If, for example, your mother worries about you excessively, you need not let that get in the way of developing positive feelings towards her. The first thing to recognize is that she is not just a worrying mother; she is a woman who is prone to anxiety. She doesn't just worry about you; she worries about all sorts of things. See her in that light, and you can feel more compassionate towards her.

After all, it is the function of mothers to worry. If our mothers hadn't worried about our material well-being when we were small, we wouldn't be alive now. Like the instinct of the hen to spread its wings over the eggs, it's a basic biological instinct with an obvious survival value for the species. So it is not surprising if your mother fusses and clucks around you – it is in her nature. If you manage to convince her that you have grown up and she doesn't need to worry any more about whether you are eating properly and keeping warm enough, then you can begin to relate to her as another human being. If not, you may just have to accept that she will want to keep fussing over you a bit.

The relationship with one's father may be more problematic, especially for young men, although it may also contain more possibilities. When one is very young, one's father often seems rather a threatening figure. But if a father has himself felt restricted by and dissatisfied with his way of life, he may be pleased that his son is not getting into the same rut. Even if he doesn't manage to say 'Well done, son. I'm glad you've made more of a success of things than I could,' he may well show that he is pleased with your success – not just your worldly success, but your success in human, even spiritual, terms.

> Whatever evil I have done ... by neglecting the Buddhas, by
> neglecting the good ... I confess it all.

This is simply the acknowledgement that one has not been worshipping and meditating on the Buddhas, not been listening to their teachings. Neglecting the good is neglecting to cultivate skilful mental states.

> Whatever evil I have done by being drunk with the intoxication of
> authority or with the intoxication of high birth or by being drunk
> with the intoxication of tender age ... I confess it all.

The word translated here as 'intoxication' is sometimes translated 'infatuation', and essentially it means pride in the sense of inflation. Take, for example, the intoxication of 'tender age' (or, better, 'youthfulness'). When you are in the full bloom of youth, you can get a bit carried away by the fact that you are young and vigorous, and this can lead you into all sorts of wild and reckless actions. 'Oh, I can get away with it. I'm young. I can stay out drinking all night. I can stand it.' You become rather over-confident, rather inflated, and you tend to look down on or get impatient with those who are elderly, or not as quick and strong as you are. This is the sort of thing meant by the intoxication of tender age.

The intoxication of authority is what we call being 'drunk with power', carried away by the exercise of your own influence. And if you are intoxicated by 'high birth', you feel terribly pleased with yourself on account of your breeding, your distinguished background, your old school, your university education, and so on. That intoxication isn't perhaps so common nowadays as it used to be. It has probably been replaced by something else – like celebrity.

You can also be intoxicated by wealth. This brings to mind the fable of the frog and the halfpenny. Once upon a time a frog was hopping along in a field when he found a halfpenny. Overjoyed at finding it, he hid it in his hole, and sat outside the hole puffing and swelling with importance because he was now the proud owner of a halfpenny. And as he sat there, an elephant happened to come by. The frog called out 'Don't you go stepping over my hole! Don't you know who I am? I'm the owner of a halfpenny!' But the elephant didn't even hear the frog. He just went on his way, and stepped over the frog's hole. The frog was so annoyed that he hopped along behind the elephant trying to kick him.

If your mind is intoxicated, this is how ridiculous and reckless you can become. You lose all sense of proportion. A lot of the foolish things we do arise from this sort of inflated idea of ourselves. Just as when you're drunk you feel you can do anything, even stupid, ridiculous, crazy things that you wouldn't normally think of doing, when you're drunk with youth or wealth or social position or power, you behave in a sense just as recklessly and foolishly. You think that because you are young or powerful or well-bred or famous you can get away with it. Intoxication leads to over-confidence; over-confidence leads to over-stretching yourself and making mistakes; and making mistakes leads to a disaster of one kind or another. Most of our unskilful actions are committed not out of deliberate wickedness but because we get so carried away that we start making mistakes – for which, sooner or later, we have to pay. This is what is being confessed here.

> Whatever evil I have done, bad thought, bad word, by an act badly done or by not perceiving a mishap; whatever evil I have done by the application of foolish reasoning, by a mind dark with ignorance, under the influence of an evil friend or by a mind distracted by impurities … I confess it all.

This confession encompasses the well-known classification of body, speech, and mind. 'Not perceiving a mishap' presumably means not perceiving the disastrous consequences that come from unskilful actions. For 'the application of foolish reasoning' we could substitute the modern term 'rationalization'. The evil done 'by a mind dark with ignorance' is clear enough.

But how about evil done 'under the influence of an evil friend'? What might that be? In the *Sigalovāda Sutta* an evil friend is described as one who says 'Come on, let's go and hear the singing, let's go and join the dancing, let's go and see the girls.'[46] In modern parlance it would be someone urging you to go and see a blue movie, perhaps.

And then there is evil done 'by a mind distracted by impurities'. This serves to remind us that very few people commit evil out of deliberate wickedness. It's more like foolishness, forgetfulness, unmindfulness. Dr Radhakrishnan said in a lecture on the Buddha that the Buddha thought of people as foolish rather than wicked, ignorant rather than rebellious. Christianity, of course, takes quite a different line.

> Whatever evil I have done ... under the compulsion of sport or enjoyment ... I confess it all.

By 'sport' is really meant play, playing around. Sometimes you're enjoying yourself so much that you start doing something really foolish or even reckless. You get a bit carried away. This sort of thing used to happen sometimes on the first retreats I led in England. In those days, people would either be so 'mindful' that they got stiff and self-conscious, or so spontaneous that they would run riot. My task as leader of the retreat was to keep trying to bring them back to the middle way. At one stage some of the women retreatants lost their mindfulness to such an extent that four or five of them were racing up and down the corridor shrieking aloud.

One of the great problems of the spiritual life is how to keep a sense of enjoyment and positivity while at the same time remaining mindful – but not so mindful that you feel as though you are walking around in a suit of armour. To follow the middle path of being mindful and aware, knowing exactly what you are doing, but at the same time being free and spontaneous and joyful, is the art of the spiritual life.

I remember once, in the very early days of the FWBO, going to visit one of our men's communities for some kind of celebration. When I got there, however, the atmosphere was far from celebratory – it was quite stiff and joyless, and I wondered what on earth was the matter. I took a walk in the garden and noticed that some tomato plants needed to be staked up with bamboo canes, so I asked a couple of men if they would mind doing that. They said 'Yes, all right' in a rather dull sort of way, and I left them to it. When I came back ten minutes later, I found them having a 'sword-fight' with two lengths of bamboo – and they looked so happy and joyful, happier than I'd ever seen them before. At the same time, they were clearly allowing themselves to express their aggressiveness. When I reflected on this later, I concluded that they had been being over-mindful, and had not been allowing their more playful sides to emerge.

You learn to draw the line between joy and intoxication when you are able to realize that you are losing your mindfulness. On the other hand, if you become stiff and self-conscious, that's not real mindfulness either. Your awareness has become 'alienated'. Most people tend to begin practising Buddhism by being 'over-mindful' (or rather, falsely mindful), because they usually start off by being completely unmindful. It's as though you have to go to the other extreme for a while and learn to be mindful, and then – not exactly forget about mindfulness, but let go and loosen up a bit. Of course, if you're not careful, you go to extremes again, and need to introduce more mindfulness and awareness. You just have to see which extreme you're tending towards at the moment, and correct the imbalance. The aim is to reach the middle ground where you've got lots of spontaneous, happy energy, but you're mindful at the same time.

Although mindfulness is certainly a key factor in the development of individuality, so is spontaneity. Even 'animal' spontaneity can be turned into a more truly human or even spiritual spontaneity. It's as if there's a certain energy in spontaneity which is refined and made more aware as you become more mindful. Clearly some people need to check their exuberance and high spirits, but others need to get their energies flowing and express themselves more freely. It may be that they need to forget all about mindfulness for a while and let their hair down.

It isn't, of course, that you have spontaneity and mindfulness going on side by side; they are completely blended. It's like the deep absorption of creative activity. When you are painting a picture, for instance, your energy is freely flowing, but at the same time you are aware. You know just what you are doing, but you are not stiff – everything is flowing freely. This is the kind of state I'm talking about, but raised to a much higher pitch of intensity. Sometimes it happens in an emergency. When you've got to do something quickly, all your energy is mobilized, but at the same time you are very aware and alert – you know exactly what you are doing. In a dangerous situation you can act quickly and spontaneously, but very effectively, with full awareness of the total situation.

Whatever evil I have done by my associations with ignoble people, by reason of envy and greed, or by the fault of guile or wretchedness; whatever evil I have done through failure to gain the mastery over my desires by reason of fear at the time of approaching troubles ... I confess it all.

The first part of this confession is easy to understand; the second may not be quite so obvious. It seems to be drawing attention to the fact that sometimes one is 'unmanned', as the old-fashioned expression has it, by fear at the thought of approaching troubles, and one just loses control over oneself, including control over one's desires.

This frequently happens in wartime. People living under dangerous conditions become a bit reckless. It's as though life isn't as valuable as it used to be; 'Eat, drink, and be merry, for tomorrow you may well be dead.' According to some authorities people's behaviour in wartime has a biological significance. With a lot of people getting killed, nature is interested in replacing them as soon as possible, hence the letting go of conventional moral restraints. It's as if there's an instinctive linking of death with reproduction. Chasing pleasure before battle certainly isn't the result of fearlessness in the face of death. If anything, it's the opposite. In a sense you know that you're going to die, but in another sense you're refusing to face up to it; you're grabbing at life and pleasure almost compulsively right up to the last minute to screen that fact from yourself.

The idea of asking oneself what one would do if one had three months to live may be a cliché, but one's response can be quite revealing. How would you spend the time? Would you go on the booze? Would you go away on solitary retreat? Would you read all those books you've never had time to read? What would you feel like doing? What would be the first thought that came into your head, once you'd got over the initial shock? There is probably something you would regret not being able to do before you die.

> Whatever evil I have done through the influence of a flighty mind or through the influence of passion and anger or through being oppressed by hunger and thirst; whatever evil I have done for the sake of drink and food, for the sake of clothing, for a reason involving women, through the various afflictions of impurities; whatever evil of body, tongue and mind, bad action accumulated in threefold manner, I have done, together with similar things, I confess it all.

'The influence of a flighty mind' and 'the influence of passion and anger' emphasize once again that one is very unlikely to do evil out of deliberate wickedness. One might think that evil done 'through being oppressed by hunger and thirst' – presumably stealing – need not be confessed because one must get one's food and drink somehow, but perhaps the implication is that one should have worked or begged for food rather than stealing it. The related confession – of evil done 'for the sake of drink and food and clothing' – might be evil committed by way of wrong livelihood. And we can each fill in for ourselves the details of evils done 'for a reason involving women' and 'through the various inflictions of impurities'.

> Whatever disrespect I may have shown to Buddhas, doctrines, likewise to Śrāvakas, I confess it all. Whatever disrespect I may have shown towards Pratyekabuddhas or towards Bodhisattvas, I confess it all. If I have shown disrespect towards those who preach the Good Law or towards other meritorious beings, I confess it all.

In a way this is a confession of disrespect to the Three Jewels: Buddha, Dharma, and Sangha – the Sangha (spiritual community) being represented by the śrāvakas, the 'hearers'.[47] Showing disrespect to the Buddhas includes not practising their teachings – as well, of course, as being actually disrespectful in their presence if they happen to be alive in your time. Disrespect to doctrines would mean not listening to the teachings or not considering them carefully. And in the Indian context to which the sūtra refers, disrespect to śrāvakas would mean – if you were a householder – things like not providing for the needs of the Buddha's monk disciples, addressing them contemptuously, or telling them to be off when they came on their almsround.

> If I have unawares continually rejected the Good Law or shown disrespect towards my parents, I confess it all.

This confession is significant not just because we come back to parents again, but because of this notion of rejecting the Good Law continually. It amounts to a confession of culpable ignorance. You've got the opportunity of hearing and knowing about the Dharma, but you deliberately ignore that opportunity. In a way, therefore, you are – unawares – continually rejecting it.

> Whatever evil I have done through stupidity or from folly or through being full of pride and arrogance, through passion, hatred or delusion, I confess it all.

This is the end of the confession. The last three faults confessed are of course *lobha*, *dveṣa*, and *moha*, the three roots of all unskilful thoughts, words, and deeds.[48]

The noticeable thing about the confession as a whole is that it doesn't list any concrete examples. It seems more concerned with laying down general principles, presumably because individual actions need to be evaluated differently according to circumstances. The general principles given aren't so very abstract, however – they are near enough to actual experience for us to be able to translate them into personally relevant examples under these various headings.

When one is making a confession it is generally best to stick to facts and confess quite specific things – nothing too rarefied or unreal. There is no need to confess the fact that you haven't contemplated nirvāṇa every day for the last month; that can probably be taken for granted. It would be more useful to confess all the small, mean, sordid things you've done or not done, like getting out of taking your turn with the washing up, that sort of thing. It can be very salutary to experience a kind of disillusionment with yourself, to see that you are not quite the decent person you thought you were. You've got all sorts of mean, nasty little streaks in you. You see that clearly and then confess it, own up to it, bring it out into the open. It is not enough to speak in a pseudo-Jungian way of 'recognizing the shadow side'. You have to feel thoroughly ashamed of it and really want to get rid of it. It is not a rather romantic 'shadow'; it's an unpleasant, smelly stain.

However, as we have seen throughout this passage of the sūtra, it is important to remember that for almost all of us, the evil we do is not done out of deliberate wickedness. We do evil through ignorance, or through making a mistake, or under the influence of some basically unskilful mental state. We don't actually set out to do evil.

On the other hand I have very occasionally met people who have said 'Yes, it's wicked, and I know it's wicked, but I'm going to do it anyway. It's what I want to do.' It's almost as though they are possessed by some demon. They are so caught up in an extreme negative emotion, whether it be hatred or jealousy or the desire for revenge, that they really don't care whether they do evil or not. Such people are comparatively rare, and even more so are those who determine to do evil quite gratuitously.

There is a distinction to be drawn between people who act wickedly in full knowledge that they are doing so and people who do evil things believing that they are in the right. The man who places a bomb in a railway carriage knowing that people are going to be killed or injured by it may genuinely believe that he is not doing evil. He may say that he is fighting for a good cause, fighting for justice. If people have to be killed for the sake of the cause, that's too bad; he regrets it, but it can't be helped. Such a person will not admit that he is doing evil.

We can see a similar if less extreme mental confusion at work in the case of people who eat meat. Many of them wouldn't dream of killing a pig, but they don't hesitate to go out and buy pork chops, even though they know somewhere in their minds that there is a connection between the slaughterhouse and their lunch. Or perhaps a lack of imagination is at work, and they really can't make the connection.

In short, I don't believe that we all have the potential for the worst kind of evil in the same way that we all have the potential for Buddhahood. It is difficult to predict what someone will do or not do under certain conditions, but my feeling is that there are some people who would refuse to do certain things under whatever circumstances.

THE SECOND CONFESSION: FROM GUILT TO OPENNESS

May the Buddhas watch over me with minds attentive. May they forgive my sin with minds given over to compassion. On account of the evil done by me previously even in hundreds of aeons, I have a troubled mind oppressed with wretchedness, trouble and fear. With an unhappy mind I continually fear evil acts. Wherever I go there is no enjoyment for me anywhere. All the Buddhas are compassionate. They remove the fears of all beings. May they forgive my sin and may they deliver me from fear. May the Tathāgatas take away for me the defilement of impurities and acts. And may the Buddhas bathe me with the surging waters of compassion. I confess all the evil previously done by me and I confess all my present evil. For the future, I undertake to refrain from all acts evilly done. I do not conceal whatever evil I may have done. The threefold bodily act and the fourfold with the voice, as well as the act in three ways with the mind, all this I confess. What I have done with my body, what I have done with my voice, and what I have thought with my mind, the tenfold act I have done, I confess it all. May I avoid the ten evil acts. May I practise the ten good acts. I will remain in the tenth stage. I will become an excellent Buddha. Whatever evil act I have done bringing an undesired fruit I will confess it all in the presence of the Buddhas.[49]

This may come as a surprise, or even a shock, but the essence of confession is that you confess without any feeling of guilt. In fact, so long as you are experiencing guilt – irrational, neurotic guilt – no genuine confession is possible. You may experience intense regret, you may feel deeply ashamed of what you have done, and angry with yourself for doing it, but if it is real confession, you will not feel guilty.

It isn't easy to say what guilt is; it is perhaps significant that the etymology of the word, which is Anglo Saxon, is unknown. But this complex phenomenon, so pervasive in Western culture, can be analysed into at least three factors.

First, there's the consciousness of having done wrong, or at least of having done something which somebody else did not want you to do. You may not think it wrong yourself, but the fact that somebody else didn't want you to do it gives you the feeling that you have done something wrong.

Then there is fear of being punished when you are found out, and if you haven't done anything wrong yet, there is the fear of punishment if you were to do it and get caught. The fear of being found out leads to all sorts of complications: secrecy, concealment, deceit, falsehood, hypocrisy, evasiveness, withdrawal, and blocked communication. There is also the acute discomfort and frustration of not being able to do freely what you want to do, to say nothing of the resentment you feel.

But the essential nature of guilt still remains unfathomed. The third factor is perhaps the most telling one of all. The person who does not want you to do something may be someone you love and who loves you, someone to whom you are strongly, possessively, even violently attached, someone on whom you are emotionally dependent, someone without whose love you feel you cannot live. If you do what they don't want you to do, they will not only punish you; in anger they will withdraw their love from you. In other words, they will virtually condemn you to death, the most terrible of all punishments.

So guilt is the painful consciousness of having done, or even having wanted to do, something which will forfeit us the love of someone on whom we are emotionally dependent. Guilt arises for most of us very early in life, when, of course, the person whose love we are afraid of losing is our mother. All of us have suffered from this to some extent, and some continue to suffer from it in adult life.

As well as feeling guilty in relation to one person, we can feel guilty in relation to the group to which we naturally belong. We tend to seek the approval of the group – our family, our work-place, our society – and we find it difficult to live with its expressed or implied disapproval. Many people will go to almost any lengths to be reconciled to the group. They will say anything required of them, even confessing to crimes they have not committed: this is evident particularly in the political lives of totalitarian states. Sometimes these wretched, unfortunate people even believe their own false confessions. After all, the group must be right. The sort of 'confession' which is made in fear of the disapproval of the group is very different from the kind of confession whose spiritual significance we are considering.

Christianity and the other theistic religions, however, trade heavily on this sense of irrational guilt. According to these religious systems God is a person, a person in whose favour we all need to stay. The religious person loves God, or at least he tries to – and he has been told that God loves him. But there are all sorts of things that God doesn't want him to do, things which in fact make God angry, but which he, the believer, wants to do – or has even done already. So he feels guilty. He feels that because he has offended God, God doesn't love him any more, or even hates him. He may then start hating God, and feel guiltier than ever.

But the true individual confesses not because he can't live without the approval of the group, or of his mother, or of God, but because he wants to develop as an individual. He or she can never feel guilty, because he or she is not emotionally dependent on anybody. And in the *Sūtra of Golden Light* it is Ruciraketu who represents the true individual – or at least one who is trying to be a true individual. A true individual is one who has developed reflexive consciousness, one who is not only aware, but aware that he is aware. He is emotionally positive – full of friendliness, joy, compassion, and equanimity – and has a profound and heartfelt faith in the transcendental. Moreover, his energies are not blocked, but free and flowing and unified. He is therefore completely spontaneous, and at the same time completely responsible, aware of the consequences of his actions both for himself and for others, and acting in accordance with that awareness. Above all, perhaps, the individual is not a member of the group. He thinks, feels, and acts for himself, and is in no way emotionally dependent on the group's approval. He confesses because he wants to get rid of everything that stands between him and the realization of his ideal, not because he wants to be received back into the favour of the group.

This is clearly not the basis of confession in, for example, the Roman Catholic church, which encourages people to confess their sins against God's law out of a sense of guilt and fear of punishment. It is drummed into Catholics that if they die with a mortal sin unconfessed and unabsolved, they will go straight to hell forever. And because confession is made to a priest, who represents the group to which they belong (i.e. the church), Catholic believers have incurred, in transgressing God's laws, not only the wrath of God but also the disapproval of the group as represented by the priest. Some people are even more afraid of the priest than they are of God – which puts the priest firmly in control over the believer. This kind of confession may have some element of psychological value – at least it's a bit of a safety valve – but from the Buddhist point of view it has no spiritual significance at all.

In Bombay many years ago I knew an Indian Catholic priest, a middle-aged man who was a great scholar and knew many languages. When I got to know him he was beginning to rebel against the church to which he belonged, the 'Roman racket', as he used to call it. I once happened to meet him on Christmas Day, and noticed that he was looking very upset. I knew him well enough to ask what the matter was, and he told me that he had spent the whole of Christmas Eve hearing people's confessions. 'I feel absolutely sick,' he said. It wasn't that anyone had had anything very terrible – or even very interesting – to confess. It was just the usual catalogue of petty dishonesties and slight impurities. What had sickened him was the atmosphere of fear and guilt with which he had been in contact. He was sickened by people's desperate need to escape punishment and creep back into God's favour, their readiness to grovel and their relief at being let off with a few Paternosters and Ave Marias.

Now you'll never find genuine confession, confession as understood by Buddhism, sickening. On the contrary, you will find it inspiring – because genuine confession is made without any feeling of guilt. Yes, we naturally fear the karmic consequences of our unskilful actions. But those consequences arise naturally as a result of what we have done; they are not meted out by anybody as a kind of punishment. The law of karma is simply a description of the way things happen. Actions have consequences. If you have committed an unskilful action, you will have to suffer the consequences of that action. The law of karma is not administered by the Buddhas. It isn't their business.

So the Buddha, unlike the Christian God, does not sit in judgement over people, does not give out punishments and rewards. Because of the way we have been brought up, we may well approach the Buddha with a fearful, guilty mind, thinking of him as a punitive father figure, but this is completely to misunderstand the nature of Buddhahood. If you fear the Buddhas, you don't really see them as Buddhas at all. The compassion of the Buddha is utterly unwavering. There is no question of asking for forgiveness, still less of grovelling for mercy. The Buddha isn't a sort of

God, a father figure who might get angry with you or punish you. You can approach him without any apprehension at all.

This may well be difficult for us to take on board. If we don't think of the Buddha as an ordinary, rather nice human being, we are likely to think of him as God, with all God's attributes – including a tendency to get angry and send people to hell when he is offended. But the Buddha is quite a different kind of character. If we feel guilty, we may not be able to help somehow feeling that the Buddha's attitude towards us has changed, however slightly. Even if we know that he doesn't get angry, we may imagine that he has at least become a bit reserved or a bit distant. It is difficult to realize that whatever we have done, the Buddha's feelings for us do not change one iota. If we happened to meet him, he might speak quite sternly to us, but his attitude to us would essentially be unchanged.

This is very much the flavour of the opening lines of this second verse of confession in the *Sūtra of Golden Light*. Ruciraketu asks the Buddhas to 'watch over me with minds attentive', but this is not to be understood as a call for the Buddhas to pay attention. The Buddhas are there all the time, as it were – their minds are always attentive. What Ruciraketu is really saying is 'May I remember the Buddhas with an attentive mind' – reminding himself to be aware of the fact that the Buddhas are watching over him. Similarly, although he asks the Buddhas to 'forgive my sin', this is simply a reminder of the unchanging compassion of the Buddhas.

It isn't the case, on the other hand, that in forgiving us the Buddhas are somehow able to take away the effects of karma. The fact that we confess our evil deeds does not mean that we are going to escape their consequences. Even the Buddha himself had to suffer certain things in his last life as a result of the actions of previous lives. So when in the Vajrasattva mantra one asks for one's karma to be purified, that doesn't literally mean that karma is destroyed. It's more that by virtue of the practice you reach a level on which, although you're experiencing the results of karma, it doesn't really affect you – it doesn't matter any more.

One mustn't think of karma in too mechanical a way. According to some Buddhist sūtras, the consequences you reap relate directly to the evil action you have committed – 'an eye for an eye, a tooth for a tooth' – but one cannot really think of karma as though it were an exercise in bookkeeping. I don't think we can literally take it that if you punch somebody on the nose in this life, somebody will punch you on the nose in your next life. In fact, there are some minor karmas which lose their force and never bear fruit at all if they don't have the opportunity to do so within a certain length of time – although you do inevitably reap the consequences of all major karmas.

So, to sum up, when you ask the Buddhas to forgive your faults, you're not asking them to wipe out the consequences of your foolish actions. You know that that would be quite impossible, even for the Buddhas. When you say 'May the Buddhas forgive my sin' you're not begging them to change their minds and stop being angry with you. You are just trying to realize – for your own benefit – that the attitude of the Buddhas hasn't changed towards you, and will never change, whatever you do.

> On account of the evil done by me previously even in hundreds of aeons, I have a troubled mind oppressed with wretchedness, trouble and fear.

While there is no place for irrational guilt, it is equally important that one should not feel comfortable with one's unskilful actions. The sūtra's words here capture how one feels when one has committed unskilful actions that one knows to be unskilful. (Leave aside hundreds of aeons, it could have been last week.) If you have committed an unskilful action you *should* feel guilty – that is, you should feel troubled and even wretched. If someone commits a highly unskilful action, like striking another person, and when taken to task for it, they turn round and say 'What right have you got to try and make me feel guilty,' this is quite a serious confusion of thought. No one can impose upon you, as a Buddhist, the painful consciousness of having done wrong. But when you do experience such a painful realization, with or without the help of others, then this is a very positive and appropriate thing.

> With an unhappy mind I continually fear evil acts.

This is how you feel if you have really taken on board that actions have consequences – perhaps because you have already started to experience the consequences. Sometimes we fail to confess not through lack of trust but because we don't realize sufficiently strongly that what we have done is unskilful. Very often we have got into such a strong habit of committing certain unskilful actions that our conscience has become rather blunted. The solution is simply – although this is easier said than done – to develop more mindfulness. Say, for instance, you were rather greedy at supper time. Is that something to be confessed? It depends how strongly you feel it. If you think to yourself 'I was a real pig. Anyone who saw me would have formed a bad impression of what Buddhists are like' – well, confess it.

We need to develop more and more sensitivity of this kind. It is a matter for concern that some people seem unable to recognize unskilful or even highly unskilful actions. There are quite a few people who aren't particularly bothered about telling a lie, even when it's not a white lie. And some people aren't particularly bothered about not keeping their promises.

Wherever I go there is no enjoyment for me anywhere.

If your sensibilities are sufficiently acute, this is how you are going to feel. You are conscious of having performed unskilful actions, and perhaps you have already begun to reap the consequences. You know that due to your past bad habits you are in danger of performing even more unskilful actions, and reaping further unpleasant consequences, and this is very much on your mind. You know that there isn't any true enjoyment for you, because there is nowhere to run to escape the consequences of karma. All you can do is confess and make a fresh start.

Hence the next lines of the text:

All the Buddhas are compassionate. They remove the fears of all beings. May they forgive my sin and may they deliver me from fear.

What is important is not to escape the consequences of your unskilful actions – indeed, that's impossible – but to get rid of your feelings of guilt, fear, and worry. You can do that by confessing. Even though you will go on experiencing the consequences of your previous unskilful actions, it doesn't matter any more. You say 'All right, never mind. I'm just paying off old debts; I'm not accumulating any new ones. I am going forward now.'

May the Tathāgatas take away for me the defilement of impurities and acts.

This is to be understood in much the same way as the idea of the Bodhisattva 'placing' people in the tenth *bhūmi*, the highest stage of transcendental development before becoming a Buddha. Literally speaking it is totally unfeasible; it is to be understood as a rhetorical expression of the Bodhisattva's heroic ambition. In a sense the Buddhas are 'taking away our defilements' all the time, but we have to realize that ourselves.

May the Buddhas bathe me with the surging water of compassion. I confess all the evil previously done by me and I confess all my present evil. For the future, I undertake to refrain from all acts evilly done.

This is very important. It is not just a question of confessing what you have done. You have to make a firm resolution to turn over a new leaf, not to commit those unskilful actions any more. This is, of course, roughly what goes on when we make New Year resolutions. The turning of the year is a good time to confess and leave behind the foolish things you have done. You can take the opportunity, perhaps, to write down in black and white all the things you regret having done. You probably haven't done wicked things – most people haven't got the guts for that – but you could write down all the foolish, mean, silly things you did, or were betrayed into doing, or happened to do without thinking. Never mind how many sheets of paper you have to use. Write them all down, burn them, and say 'May I never do these things again in the coming year. May I stay free from all these things.' You are sure to feel much lighter after doing that. The value of confession as a spiritual practice is that you bring something to light, you objectify it, and to that extent you get rid of it, at least for the time being. If you do it sincerely, you feel cleansed, and lighter than you did before.

Good though the practice of making resolutions is, for a really effective practice of confession we are going to need to make our confessions known to someone else. No, not to an authority figure in a little wooden box. Confession is most effectively made to other individuals, others who are treading the spiritual path as we are. It can of course be made to those who are individuals *par excellence* – the Buddhas and Bodhisattvas. In the sūtra Ruciraketu confesses in the *presence* of all the Buddhas. But the reason Ruciraketu can confess to the Buddhas is that he can see and hear them. In our own practice we may recite the Sevenfold Puja and 'confess', as it were, to the Buddha, but we rarely, if ever, have a vivid sense of the Buddha's actual presence. This is not, therefore, confession in the full sense. Full confession means confessing specific offences – including those committed in thought – to others of whose presence we are conscious, and who are conscious of us, others who will hear our confession and accept it.

Furthermore, we need to make our confessions to people on the same spiritual path as ourselves – our spiritual friends or teachers. But why should this be so? Why can't we confess to someone we meet on the bus, or at least to our ordinary friends? There are, broadly speaking, two main reasons. First, we need to confess to people with whom we can be really open; and second, our confession needs to be heard by people who understand its significance for us.

The first of these reasons is highlighted by one of the most important sentences of this passage of the sūtra:

I do not conceal whatever evil I may have done.

We often conceal things not just from other people, but even from ourselves. We don't like to admit that we have done something wrong, that we have made a mistake. It's a form of humiliation to feel that we have not lived up to our image of ourself. Someone once said that when you sit down to write your autobiography, the first thing you become aware of is what you are going to leave out. Almost inevitably you don't tell the whole story. 'Oh no, I'm not going to say that. I'll say everything else, but not that.' To be happy for others to see you exactly as you are, warts and all, is very difficult. Usually there is some little nook or cranny of your character or your life or your past that you don't want anybody to know about. You don't even think about it yourself very much; you hide it even from yourself. Nietzsche said 'Memory says I did such and such, pride says I couldn't possibly have done it, and pride wins.' Ideally, of course, it should be possible to lead such a life that you can be open with everybody – one's life should ideally be an open book – but most people have at least a few pages, not to say the odd chapter or two, which they would prefer other people not to look at.

It's a strain relating to others with only a part of yourself, keeping back another part that they are never allowed to see. If you never relate to them as a complete, whole person, they don't know who you are, or at least they don't know the whole of you. This doesn't mean that if you have committed a crime you should tell it to everybody – that might be unwise – but certainly there should be a few people with whom you can be completely frank. Assuming you share with them a common spiritual ideal, they will be for you the spiritual community in the full sense. If you don't have friends whom you can trust totally, you are in quite a difficult position.

What prevents many of us from confessing and from being more open generally is the feeling that if other people knew us as we were, then they would no longer accept us. 'If people knew what I was really like, they wouldn't want to have any more to do with me.' But within the context of the spiritual community you are still accepted, even though people may strongly disapprove of what you have done. You may find it difficult to make that distinction – and it may be difficult for your friends in practice – but in principle they will try to retain the same mettā for you even though they may be very grieved at what you have done. To be open, you have got to have this kind of confidence in other people's genuine, basic goodwill towards you, which you are convinced will remain unchanged under all circumstances. Even if they tell you off, it will be with basic good will.

Of course, trust – the confidence that people will deal with you from a basis of love rather than from a basis of power – cannot be forced, even in the spiritual community. True confession cannot be the kind of mechanical procedure which goes under the name of confession in so many parts of the Buddhist world. You need to be in close, trustful communication with the person to whom you confess. And you can only trust people if you feel they are not going to hurt you, not going to take advantage of your openness. In a way you need to feel that their attitude towards you is basically like that of the Buddha. Whatever you have done, they are going to forgive you. Their basic attitude towards you is not going to change; they will have the same mettā for you even after you have confessed, when they know the worst about you.

The kind of openness developed in a spiritual friendship is of a higher order than that present in ordinary friendship, although openness and freedom of communication on the more ordinary human level does prepare the way for more distinctively spiritual communication. It would be rather surprising if someone went straight from not trusting anybody on the ordinary human level to trusting them in terms of spiritual friendship. You don't usually make that sort of leap unless you have had some quite exceptional, dramatic spiritual experience.

Confession is simply a specific aspect of one's general openness towards people one really trusts. In that sense it is nothing special; it's just a continuation of something one is doing all the time. That doesn't mean that confession is a casual matter. One needs to take the cultivation of openness with people very seriously, and that means taking confession seriously too. In the same spirit of openness, there may be occasions on which you need to point out the faults of your spiritual friend, or they to point out yours. Here, however, one must proceed with great caution. You can't attempt to point out another person's faults unless you are reasonably confident that they trust you, at least to some extent, depending on the seriousness of the matter that you are pointing out.

If you find yourself hesitant about revealing your actions to someone you genuinely believe to be more developed in a spiritual sense than yourself, it is likely to be because you know they will regard your action as unskilful. If you take the plunge, though, you will find that the more evolved the other person is, the more possible it is, in a sense, for you, assuming that you are relatively unevolved, to be open with them.

It takes a long time to become confident enough in another person to be able to confess to them. It also takes a lot of effort. It doesn't happen automatically, even if you spend a lot of time with them; you have to make a definite effort. It comes as quite a relief when you can be genuinely open with somebody, knowing that you don't have to keep up any pretences because you will be accepted for what you are. Your every single action won't be condoned, but *you* will be accepted. It is best to have nothing to confess, nothing to hide, but if we had to wait until we had reached that blameless state before we could be open, most of us would have to wait a very long time. It is the test of real openness, the test of true friendship, that you can be open even though there are unskilful things you would rather not have done. In fact, if you confess, your friend knows that you trust him, and may well become more open with you. If you can't be open with him, and he can't be open with you, it's not much of a friendship.

But why do we approach confession so cautiously? Why can't we just be open with everybody? The main problem is fear of what people will think. This is odd in a way. After all, they don't have it within their power to do you any harm or damage. Unless you have committed some crime which could land you in prison, why shouldn't everybody know what you've been up to? What does it matter if everybody in the whole city knows that you got drunk the weekend before last? So what?

We may also hold back because of an attitude left over from childhood. As children, when we are just starting to feel more independent, we delight in keeping things from our parents. We think gleefully 'If they knew, they'd have a fit!' Somehow we feel very clever, as though we have scored over them. That may be fair enough when we are small, but we need to grow out of that sort of attitude. If we feel towards the whole world as a child feels towards its parents, we haven't really grown up yet.

We tend to be very dependent on what people think of us. We want their approval, or at least we want to avoid their disapproval. Ironically enough, the things we can't bring ourselves to be open about are often the things that most people aren't really bothered about anyway. You may sometimes have the experience of trying to tell somebody something about yourself that you think is really awful. You find it excruciatingly difficult to bring it up, but then you notice that they aren't taking much notice of what you are saying because it is so insignificant to them. It simply hasn't registered. You may have imagined that you were going to stop them in their tracks, you may have been waiting for them to gasp in horror, but they just say 'Oh yes' and start talking about something else. They're not overwhelmed, shocked, or horrified at all. In other words, you have been attaching far too much importance to whatever it was that you did.

I had a friend many years ago who used to say to me 'If you really knew what I was like, you wouldn't want to have anything to do with me.' This went on for about two years. In the end, when he finally brought himself to confess what it was – it wasn't something he'd done, only something he'd been thinking – I burst out laughing. For two years he'd been convinced that if I knew what he was thinking, I'd never want to speak to him again. It was ridiculous. But this is so often the way we build things up in our minds.

The converse of this is the point we came across earlier: that we need to take our unskilful behaviour sufficiently seriously. And this brings us to the second reason for making our confessions to friends who are on the same spiritual path. Suppose you make your confession to an ordinary friend, a friend who does not share your spiritual ideals. Suppose, for instance, you confess that you got a bit drunk last weekend, or that you haven't meditated for a whole week. An ordinary friend won't be able to understand what those things mean to you, and therefore won't understand your distress. They may even say, with the best of intentions, that you are upsetting yourself unnecessarily. In this case there will be no real communication, and therefore no real confession. You will not have been able to vomit up the evil and get rid of it.

You need to confess to friends who understand what unskilful behaviour is, not just pals who pat you on the back and say 'That's just the sort of thing everybody does.' Friends of that kind tend to let you off rather lightly, so that your 'confession' doesn't amount to very much. You may not be proud of what you have done, but you may not be very much ashamed of it either. However, even that sort of openness is better than none at all. At least you have got the attitude of opening out, provided you're not just covertly boasting about some rather interesting aspect of your murky past.

If you go to a psychiatrist, or get talking to someone you meet when you're travelling, and end up admitting to certain intimate things – perhaps *because* you are talking to a stranger – that is perhaps a step in the right direction. At least you have said it out loud, and you may be able to go on to make a genuine confession. But it is important to be clear about the difference between admitting to something and truly confessing it. If you confess within the spiritual community, it is quite a different experience. Your spiritual friends will know what you are talking about, and they will be sympathetic with your distress, and genuinely concerned. At the same time they won't be really worried, because there is real communication, and therefore genuine confession, and also therefore real steps being taken to reject the evil that is in you.

When you really aren't sure whether or not you have been unskilful, the solution is easy – consult your spiritual friends. Say 'Look, what do you think? Have I been unskilful? Give me your opinion.' This is one of the things that spiritual friends are for.

If it feels like a challenge to confess, that's a good thing, because it shows that you are really confessing, not just treating confession as a formality, as it has become in so many parts of the Buddhist world. But if it is too much of a challenge to approach someone and tell them you have something to confess, you could do what I suggested earlier – write your confession down and ceremonially burn it in the context of a puja. That would be half way between confessing to the Buddha and confessing to a person. You need not even show the piece of paper to anybody: the fact that you have written it down means that you have owned up to what you have done, brought it out into the open as an objective reality. After all, someone might get hold of that piece of paper. You have taken the risk of letting it out.

The ideal time to confess is as soon as you have acted unskilfully, as soon as you are painfully aware of having made an ethical blunder – or as soon as you can get hold of your spiritual friends. The longer you hold back from confessing, the longer you are at a standstill in your spiritual life.

Confession, however, is not something you do once and for all. Moral defeats, unfortunately, are always being suffered, at least in the mind. Until Enlightenment has been attained, there is always some kind of evil or another within us to be got rid of. According to the Mahāyāna tradition, therefore, confession is a part of life. We need to be confessing all the time. Confession, in short, is crucial to the spiritual life.

THE THIRD CONFESSION: THE OPPRESSIONS OF EXISTENCE

We have seen that in his second confession Ruciraketu confesses to committing the ten unskilful acts – three of body, four of speech, and three of mind. The third and last confession adds a new element: the confession of evil heaped up through various oppressions.

In the oppression of existence or through foolish thought, whatever severe evil I have done, in the presence of the Buddha, I confess all this evil. And I confess that evil which has been heaped up by me in the oppression of birth, by the various oppressions of bodily activity, in the oppression of existence, in the oppression of the world, in the oppression of the fleeting mind, in the oppression of impurities caused by the foolish and stupid, and in the oppression of the arrival of evil friends, in the oppression of fear, in the oppression of passion, in the oppression of hatred and by the oppressions of folly and darkness, in the oppression of the instant, in the oppression of time, by the oppressions of gaining merits, standing before and in the presence of the Buddha, I confess all this evil.[50]

The word translated as 'oppression' is the Sanskrit *saṃkaṭa*, for which the dictionary gives the following definitions: 'brought together, contracted, closed, narrow, strait, crowded together, dense, impervious, impassable, crowded with, full of; a strait, difficulty, critical condition, danger to or from'. That gives one quite a good idea of what *saṃkaṭa* means, and makes it clear that this term 'oppression', though not bad, is not a fully adequate translation by any means.

The *saṃkaṭas* are those factors by which one is surrounded, which crowd in upon one, which oppress one, which squeeze and limit one. This suggests that there are all sorts of unskilful acts that one performs, as it were, under duress. Our unskilful acts are not those of a free untrammelled will. And if only conditions had been a bit more favourable, we might not have done them at all. There are so many factors in existence which oppress us, making it more likely that we will do something unskilful, and more difficult for us to act skilfully. Circumstances are so often against us. Our surroundings tend almost to compel us to do what is unskilful. Not that that is really any excuse, ultimately, because it is due to our weakness that we feel the oppression *as* oppression. But once again we come back to the point that people are not deliberately wicked; it's more that they are weak and give in to pressure.

The list of oppressions is a long one: existence, birth, bodily activity, the world, the fleeting mind, impurities caused by the foolish, the arrival of evil friends, fear, passion, hatred, folly and darkness, the instant, time, gaining merits. The sūtra confesses evil committed under the oppression of all these things. So clearly they are not factors that we occasionally encounter and have to resist; they are things that surround us and almost crush us all the time. It's not as though they are just there but don't bother us; they are all around us, hemming us in, breaking in upon us, weighing upon us, and restricting our movements. They are a constant chronic danger, and if we are not conscious of the fact it is because we go along with them to such an extent that there is nothing in us to be oppressed.

The list begins with 'the oppression of existence'. This implies that conditioned existence itself – just being a human being – is pressurizing us to perform unskilful actions. All you have to do is go out for a little walk and you see all sorts of things that cannot but give rise to unskilful thoughts, even unskilful activities, on your part. To be more specific, city life, we could say, is an oppression. In the city, we have to put so much energy into keeping the world at bay – keeping the world from encroaching upon what we have gained already in the way of mindfulness and positivity – that we don't have much left over with which to make real progress. Still, we have to admit that this only happens because something within us has an affinity with these oppressions of the world.

The sense in which 'foolish thought' might become an oppression is fairly obvious. Thoughts are running through our minds involuntarily all the time. We don't deliberately set out to think an unskilful thought; it just pops into our head. We didn't ask it to come, we didn't want it to be there; it just came. This is our experience. We call it 'our' thought, but sometimes it seems as though it is coming from outside, invading us. When we sit to meditate, we try to concentrate our minds, keep them clear and pure, and all these unskilful foolish thoughts keep rushing in and undoing all our best efforts. This is how we feel. And yet we cannot escape the fact that these thoughts are our own; they belong to us.

Then, 'the oppression of birth'. According to some psychologists, birth itself is a traumatic experience. There you are in the womb before birth: warm, relatively quiet, quite comfortable. Then suddenly you are violently squeezed through a narrow aperture, and come out at the other end into a terrible bright light to be seized, slapped, and plunged into water. This must surely be a very traumatic experience. You are slapped to make you breathe, rubbed with a rough towel, then dressed, all tied up. And then you start feeling hungry. This might well be described as the oppression of birth.

But next, in what way might bodily activity be an oppression, or even 'various oppressions'? Well, think about it. You wake up in the morning, you've got to get up and dress yourself, go to the lavatory, brush your teeth, and then you've got to eat. All these are bodily activities which are needed to keep you going. Sometimes there seem to be so many of them that you forget what you are living *for*. As you get older, physical existence becomes more and more of a burden. In the end you can hardly walk, or even get up from a chair without help. You can't get on to a bus without a helping hand. Maybe you can't dress yourself or go to the toilet without help. This is when this oppression really strikes home – although when you are young, you sometimes get a foretaste of it when you are ill. You can't think of very much at all beyond your physical state, your aches and pains, your medicine, and so on.

As for 'the oppression of the world', this could be taken in a narrower sense than the oppression of existence, to mean the whole of social life. Indeed, whatever the specific oppression may be, it is all-pervasive. Take, for instance, 'the arrival of evil friends'. It is not that we occasionally meet an evil friend, someone who is going to try to induce us to perform unskilful actions; we are surrounded by them. Go for a ride on a bus; there they all are. Go to watch a football match; there they all are. We are surrounded by people who are in a sense 'evil friends', in that their influence on us is not a positive, skilful one.

The oppressions of fear, passion, hatred, folly, and darkness we have already touched on in the previous confession sections. But this section continues to add new elements. For example, there's 'the oppression of the instant', having to act or make a decision when one may be off guard. And then 'the oppression of time', or as we would say 'pressure of time', is what so often seems to keep us from skilful action. Certainly under the conditions of modern life we often feel that we don't have enough time to do things properly, or think about what the skilful way to act would be. We act hastily, and the chances are that we act unskilfully.

Even gaining merits, according to the sūtra, is an oppression – odd as it may sound. What the sūtra is of course pointing to is the danger of getting too attached to our merit. If we think of the spiritual life in terms of acquiring merits too much then it becomes quite oppressive so far as our real spiritual life is concerned. The text doesn't explicitly say so, but I take it that the merits referred to here are of the lower kind, the kind which guarantee you a place in a higher heavenly world after death. I don't see how merits which are dedicated to Enlightenment could be an oppression. Oppression, after all, only arises when you are trying to do something skilful and external factors are getting in the way. Life itself can get in the way, time can get in the way, but merits that are dedicated to Enlightenment surely can't get in the way.

This list draws attention to the fact that there are all sorts of unskilful factors in existence which are always pressing in on us, and from which it is very difficult for us to escape, because we are experiencing them all the time. They never let up. It's as though there is some force at work in the world almost compelling us to do unskilful things against our better judgement and our own wishes. If we are surrounded by these things, sooner or later they are going to have some definite effect. It is not that they give rise to unskilfulness in some mysterious, indirect way. If we are constantly surrounded by evil friends, sooner or later they will have some influence on us. The list is of course selective; all unskilful or unhelpful factors are of this nature.

This is not to suggest that the individual is absolved from responsibility for his behaviour. In confessing the evil you have committed, you accept responsibility for it. It may be understandable when you fail to stand up to the oppressions, but it is your responsibility to stand up to them. If something is not your fault, why should you confess it? There would be no point. The fact that you confess means that you accept responsibility, even though you were strongly tempted. To make a technical distinction, one could say that these oppressions are the occasion of unskilful actions, but not their cause. You are their cause, and therefore the responsibility is yours. Perhaps you are very strongly tempted, but you still have the capacity to resist.

As you become integrated, you don't exactly feel less oppressed, but you feel less pulled around by the oppressions. If you are unintegrated, you are split and divided. When part of you wants to meditate, another part of you doesn't, so if there is any external pressure not to meditate, that can work on you quite easily through the part of you that doesn't want to do it anyway. If you are split, the part of you that is in sympathy with the oppression is vulnerable to its influence.

If you've got a sort of 'traitor within' that is in cahoots with the 'enemy without', you are in a difficult position. In addition to being under pressure from the oppression, you are divided within yourself so that one part of you is putting pressure on another. It is much easier to deal with external pressures when there is no inner conflict. If, for instance, as you go around the city you see advertisements featuring models in scanty attire, but there is nothing within you which is susceptible to that, they can bring as much pressure to bear on you as they like – nothing much will happen. On the other hand, if there is already a traitor lurking within, so to speak, the combined forces of the traitor and the adverts are likely to overwhelm you. If you are divided within yourself you are more likely to succumb to external pressure, but if you are more integrated, you can withstand a corresponding degree of pressure from the environment.

It is a good thing to be aware that there are all sorts of factors in the world that almost oblige us to behave unskilfully. We don't get much co-operation from the world; pressure is brought to bear on us all the time to act in the usual – that is, the unskilful – way. We live in the midst of an oppressive situation and we may feel that we have to block out a lot of things just to survive the day. This is why it is so good to get away on retreat from time to time, to experience the lightness and happiness of feeling that the pressure is off – at least for the time being.

It's a moot point as to whether being aware of oppressions *as* oppressions is really much help. If there's a terrific noise outside while you are trying to meditate, you can certainly become aware of what is happening, but that won't help you to meditate if the noise is still there and you are still being bothered by it.

One could say that it is through having to deal with the oppressions that one becomes strong, but I think there is a point beyond which that doesn't work any more. If you lift weights in the gym, that can certainly strengthen you, but if you are elderly and weak, they may put so much strain on your heart that you drop down dead. It's much the same psychologically. Having to put up with a certain amount is strengthening, but there's a limit to what you can sustain.

From this it follows that you must *know* how much you are able to bear. And if a situation is insupportable, you just have to withdraw from it, if at all possible. For instance, you might be living with someone with a terrible temper. You might be able to handle that for a while, but suppose another person with the same kind of temperament came to live with you as well. You might have to admit that you just couldn't bear to live with two people of that sort – they would just depress you, which wouldn't help you or anybody else. It is better to get out than to go under. We shouldn't be ashamed to admit that our resources are limited. Yes, we need to be strong, but we have to weigh up our own strength and decide what we can reasonably expect from ourselves. Usually we can manage more than we think we can, but we also have to be realistic and not destroy ourselves through false ideas about what we ought to be able to put up with. This is not to say, I should add, that we should necessarily accept our limitations and weaknesses. Sometimes there are certain parts of oneself that shouldn't be indulged or protected.

To sum up, oppression involves some external factor – whether social or psychological – that exerts pressure on us to be unskilful. We need not start feeling sorry for ourselves, but we should recognize quite realistically that by the very fact of living in the world we are up against it. All too often the world, far from co-operating with us in our efforts to be more skilful, almost pushes us in the other direction.

THE EFFECTS OF CONFESSION: PURIFICATION AND REJOICING

The effects of confession should by now be quite clear. When we have truly confessed, we feel cleansed and purified. We feel that we are back on the path, that we can go forward once more. The state in which we find ourselves is beautifully exemplified by the Vajrasattva visualization practice. This is a Vajrayāna practice, but in spirit it is very close to the verses of confession that Ruciraketu hears in his dream.

In the practice you visualize Vajrasattva seated directly above your head on a white lotus throne. He is pure white in colour, like the colour of freshly fallen snow on which the morning sun is shining. He is in the prime of youth, with long flowing black hair, and his expression is smiling and compassionate. In one hand he holds a vajra or dorje, balancing it against his chest, and in the other he holds a bell, resting on his knee.[51] In his heart you see a deep blue syllable *hūṁ*, and around it, like a garland, the one hundred letters of the mantra of Vajrasattva, also white in colour. The garland of letters revolves in a clockwise direction around the deep blue *hūṁ*, and as they revolve you see drops of pure white nectar oozing from them. This nectar falls down on to the crown of your head in a great stream, through the median nerve and down through all the nerve centres in your system, washing away all evil, washing your whole being absolutely clean. You become pure, transparent, shining, like a crystal vase. And having washed away all the impurities, the nectar accumulates within you, so that little by little you become like a crystal vase full to the brim with pure white curds.

When you have reached that state, you see that the whole sky is filled with pure white lotus flowers edge to edge. Upon each lotus flower is seated a pure white Vajrasattva, and beneath each Vajrasattva is a sentient being, being purified just as you are. You see that you are a pure being in a pure world, a pure being among pure beings. Then you feel that you really have confessed and been forgiven.

Once we have confessed to the Buddhas, it is only natural that we should feel intensely grateful to them for hearing and accepting our confession, and that we should therefore sing their praises as Ruciraketu does in the *Sūtra of Golden Light*.

I worship the Buddhas, who are like oceans of virtues, mountains gleaming with the colour of gold like Sumeru. I go for refuge to those Buddhas and with my head I bow down to all those Buddhas. Each one is gold-coloured, shining like pure gold. He has fine eyes, pure and faultless like beryl. He is a mine blazing with glory, splendour and fame. He is a Buddha-sun removing the obscurity of darkness with his rays of compassion. He is very flawless, very brilliant, with very gleaming limbs. He is a fully enlightened sun. His limbs are as prominent as pure gold. He refreshes as it were the blazing fire of those whose minds are consumed by the fire of impurities with the sage's meshes of moonbeams. His sense-organs are beautiful with the thirty-two excellent major marks, his members greatly gleaming with the very brilliant minor marks. With meshes of beams full of glory, merits, and splendour, he stands amid the darkness like the sun in the three worlds. Your members resembling silver, crystal or copper, with the various pure, magnificent colours of beryl, with meshes of rays manifoldly and variously adorned, coppery red like the dawn, you shine, great sage, like the sun. For one who has fallen into the river of the cycle of existence, in the midst of the flood of disaster, afflicted with anxiety, in the water of death, in the billow of old age, dry up completely with the meshes of rays of the Buddha-sun the ocean of woe, whose current is extremely harsh and cruel.[52]

The whole passage, like so many in other Mahāyāna sūtras, gives an impression of inexhaustibility, abundance, and richness, and this is really the whole point of it. It is emphasizing that the Buddha has got far more than just two or three rather monumental and abstract virtues. He is a veritable treasure chest of virtues and merits.

Here the imagery itself – the sun, the mountains, moonbeams, beryl, silver, copper, crystal, dawn, water – is all universal; there's nothing specifically Indian about it. But perhaps the disordered extravagance of it, the lushness, is rather Indian. There isn't much form to all these epithets and comparisons, no arrangement or symmetry. They are heaped on top of one another pell-mell. It may all seem a bit excessive, even alien to us. We may prefer a more 'Zen-like' approach – just one twig of blossom carefully set in a simple vase – but the Indians like to heap up hundreds of flowers all over the place, with no particular arrangement at all. If the Zen-like approach expresses a *real* intensity of stillness and concentration then this may be what we need. But a quiet tasteful restraint – a palette of pastels – is not really a virtue in itself, at least in a devotional context. Better to let ourselves go a bit, be a little less careful even, if by 'careful' we mean being buttoned up and timid.

Of course, the Western tradition is not entirely lacking in this type of prodigality of expression. Thomas Traherne rather lets go of the reins in this way in his *Centuries of Religious Meditations*. So does Shelley in his 'Ode to a Skylark', in which some of the images – for example, comparing the skylark to a high-born maiden in a palace-tower, or a glow-worm – are plainly a little absurd; but I used to teach this poem to students in India, and they loved all these comparisons. English critics usually agree that some of the similes could have been cut to make the poem more compact and unified, but the Indians certainly wouldn't think like that. For them, it could go on as long as it liked.

One could say that this is the difference between the gothic and the neoclassical style. The basic distinction is between a 'heaping-up' style and an 'eliminating' style, and it is exemplified in the Western cultural tradition as well as in Eastern Buddhism. Compare, for example, a Quaker meeting house, so plain and bare and unadorned, and a post-Reformation rococo Catholic church, all odds and ends of tinsel and velvet and lace and plaster and paint, with an effect either effervescent or tawdry. The difference between the Theravāda and the Vajrayāna approach is similar; and they both have their merits. English people tend to shy away from exuberance and profusion, but perhaps that's something we need to overcome.

Of course, it can go too much the other way. Some Tibetan temples get so full of things that they become quite oppressive. So many people have given them so many things – none of which can be thrown away or even given away – that every nook and cranny has an image or a thangka in it, plus umpteen sets of water bowls and umpteen lamps. The temples sometimes look really crowded, especially as things are often put in glass-fronted cases against the wall. It all tends to look a bit museum-like and dusty and moth-eaten. Everything has to be kept because some pious soul has donated it, but sometimes you really wish that you could throw away a few things. I have sometimes thought that Tibetan Buddhism itself is like that – a bit museum-like. There's too much of it, too many odds and ends in it.

So a middle path is probably needed. Every now and then it's good to go in for a bout of lavish and exuberant munificence, but you can't live with that all the time. And sometimes you feel like being very austere and simple, but you can't live with *that* all the time either. For day-to-day practice, a middle way is probably best. Have your shrine rich, but not cloying, austere but not dull. Festival days are the occasions for real lavishness – spare no expense on decorations and lamps and candles, and really splash out on the flowers.

> I worship the Buddha, whose members shine like gold, whose members gleam with the colour of gold, a mine of knowledge, chief in all three worlds, beautiful, whose members are adorned with very brilliant marks. Just as the water in the ocean is immeasurable, just as the earth is endless with its particles of dust, just as Meru is endless with its stones, just as the sky has an endless limit, so indeed are the Buddha's virtues endless. Even all beings cannot know them. If one should weigh and ponder them for numerous aeons, one could not know the last virtues. The earth with its rocks, mountains and oceans, it is perhaps in aeons possible to count and know, and the water in the ocean may perhaps be measured to a hair-point: it is not possible to know the end of the Buddha's virtues.[53]

The Buddha is the one who has reached or realized the Unconditioned. And just as the Unconditioned is not really accessible to thought and cannot be fully expressed, so it is with the Buddha. The Buddha's virtues are immeasurable, inexpressible. There are two ways of trying to get this across. You can either just make the statement 'The Buddha's virtues cannot be expressed,' or you can exhaust your powers of expression trying to describe them, which is what this paragraph in effect does. The second method probably gives a better impression of the inexhaustibility of the Buddha's virtues than the bare logical statement.

In many spiritual traditions there are said to be two main avenues of approach to reality: the negative way and the affirmative way. The negative way consists in denying of the Unconditioned everything that is conditioned. You say of the Unconditioned 'It isn't this, it isn't that. It is nothing to do with space, and nothing to do with time. There is no beginning and no end. It is neither light nor darkness, neither good nor evil, neither existence nor non-existence. It's beyond all that.' But the affirmative way consists in saying that the Unconditioned is light – not any ordinary light, but the absolute light, the brightest light, the purest light, the greatest light. Or it says that the Unconditioned is beautiful, but not any ordinary beauty, not any worldly beauty. It is far more beautiful than even the most beautiful thing that we see and experience. It is beauty itself, beauty *sans pareil*.

Both of these, of course, are just ways of seeing things. Strictly speaking we can't think of reality at all, but for practical purposes we have to think about it. And basically there are only these two ways in which we *can* think about it: either by negating with regard to the Unconditioned everything that is conditioned, or by thinking of the Unconditioned in terms of the conditioned at its very height, at its very best, beyond what we ever actually experience within the conditioned.

Well, there is a third way, actually. There is also the approach through paradox, through the forcible juxtaposition of contradictory terms, as when you speak of 'dazzling darkness'. Such contradictions give at least some people some hint of what reality is like. The Buddhist Perfection of Wisdom texts operate through conceptual paradoxes in this way, as well as using the negative approach.

But clearly the *Sūtra of Golden Light* favours the affirmative approach, using images and pictures and lavish descriptions. It contains just one very short chapter on śūnyatā, and that is a sort of clumsy version of the Perfection of Wisdom teaching.

The natural consequence of confession is twofold: to rejoice in merits, both one's own and other people's; and to dedicate one's merit to Enlightenment. We get the first hint of this after the second confession:

> Those who in this Jambudvīpa and in other world-spheres do a good
> act I congratulate on it all. And whatever merit has been gained by
> me by body, voice or mind, through that merit-root may I touch
> excellent enlightenment.[54]

Rejoicing in the merits of others gives one strength and inspiration. It also counteracts any tendency to envy and greed because it encourages disinterestedness. You are just as glad if somebody else does a good action as if you had done it yourself. If you manage to cultivate a positive attitude of appreciation, you may feel that in a way you *have* done it yourself.

For some people rejoicing in the merits of others is not easy. When we think about other people's good qualities, we may even feel quite uncomfortable. The reason for this is that we feel inferior; and we feel inferior because we don't have those good qualities ourselves. This is what riles us. We look at it all in a jaundiced, prejudiced way. Instead of thinking 'Jane is a very kind person,' we start thinking 'She's much kinder than me. She probably thinks she's better than me. And what's worse, when other people look at us, *they* probably think she's better than me.' The more we think about it, the more inferior we feel. We may imagine that

Jane thinks herself superior to us when the thought has never entered her head. She may even be quite oblivious to our existence. If somebody else's virtue makes them superior to us in a way that makes us feel put down, we are likely to underestimate or depreciate their good qualities, just to keep ourselves, as we see it, on a level with them.

If we have some merits of our own to rejoice in, we may find it easier to rejoice in the merits of others because we feel more on a level with them, but in fact that's just a concession to our weakness. We should be able to rejoice in the merits of others regardless of whether or not we have any merits at all. In fact, the fewer merits we have, the more reason there is to rejoice in the merits of others. If you haven't got any merits of your own, thank goodness somebody has! If there are merits around in the world they should be a natural cause for rejoicing.

The sort of merit the text has in mind is probably the merit that people produce, so to speak, without reference to you personally. But of course even our response to good actions done expressly for our benefit is not necessarily straightforward. Some people rather resist the idea of others doing good to them because they feel it puts them under an obligation. You might be reluctant to borrow a lawn-mower from the people next door, say, because that would mean that you would be under an obligation to lend them something in return. But in trying to avoid being under any obligation you might in the end virtually cut off the relationship altogether. If you have contact with people at all, you simply can't help becoming involved in a network of mutual obligations.

Perhaps when we are unwilling or reluctant to rejoice in other people's merits, we are being a bit too self-conscious. We may need to forget about ourselves and where we stand, and just rejoice in somebody's merits in a quite impersonal way. When the sun is shining, you don't feel jealous of the sun because it has the light and you don't have it. You simply enjoy the sunshine. In the same way, just rejoice that somebody is producing some merits and making the world a brighter and better place. No matter who it is, whether it is you or somebody else, at least those merits are being produced.

After rejoicing in the merits of others, Ruciraketu goes on to dedicate whatever merit he has gained himself to Enlightenment. This dedication is bound up with the 'three aims'. According to some texts there are three possible aims in life. You can wish for well-being in this present life, you can wish for a happy rebirth in some future existence, or you can think in terms of gaining Enlightenment; and you can dedicate your merit to any one of these. To put it simplistically, you can say 'By virtue of this meritorious act may I be happy and healthy and strong in this life,' or you can say 'By virtue of this good action may I have a happy heavenly rebirth after I die,' or you can say 'By virtue of this good action may I gain Enlightenment for the sake of all.' The Bodhisattva, of course, does the third, and this is the one that is meant here.

We clearly need to guard against self-consciousness of an unhelpful kind in matters of this sort. Yes, you have an ultimate ideal, and you sincerely wish that whatever good you are doing may not be frittered away but may contribute to the attainment of that ultimate ideal. Clearly, however, you shouldn't do that in a self-conscious way, any more than you should do anything else self-consciously. You don't tell people that you're off to meditate because you want to gain Enlightenment. You just say 'I think I'll go and meditate.' But in your own mind you are aware that this is the direction in which you are moving, and the goal for the sake of which you are mobilizing all your energies and resources, including the resources represented by your merits. You just wish that if you do have any merits, they may redound to ultimate Enlightenment.

Does it, then, really make any difference what you dedicate your merit to? If you dedicate it to a happy present life, or to a future life, does that make any concrete difference? The traditional Buddhist view is that it does, because your motivation is always the decisive factor. The Chinese Buddhists distinguish between 'pure' merit and 'impure' merit – colloquially they are called 'white merits' and 'red merits', white being the colour of the spirit and red the colour of the earth. The merit of the first and second aims is impure because it is tainted with self-interest, whereas the merit dedicated to the third aim is free of any such taint.

Pure merit tends to be deeper and more powerful than impure merit, inasmuch as it's not that you earn merit as if it were a sort of commodity or income which you can decide to invest either for your own benefit or for the benefit of all. You could say that the returns on an investment of merit for the sake of all are infinitely greater than a personal investment, but it is not quite like that either. Depending on whether you put them into worldly or spiritual things, the merits themselves change, because it's not just merit, it's *you*. Your merits are you.

The idea of a Bodhisattva's dedication of merit is above all to help him eliminate any trace of selfishness. He lets go of the idea of working for himself or benefiting himself in this or a future life. He just wants to dedicate whatever resources he has to Enlightenment for the sake of all. In this way he gets rid of all traces of self-seeking.

Usually when we do good we have in the back of our mind somewhere the idea that it will be of some benefit to us personally, in a narrow and individualistic sense. The Bodhisattva tries to counteract that natural – and, it should be said, perfectly healthy – tendency by saying 'Whatever merits I produce, may they not go to my personal advantage in this or a future life. May they help me to gain Enlightenment for the benefit of all, so that I may be of use to everybody.' This helps him to overcome the individualistic attitude represented by the other two dedications, which is of course quite incompatible with the Mahāyāna and the Bodhisattva ideal. It guards against our natural tendency to look after number one even in what we like to think of as our spiritual life.

The two strands, rejoicing in the merits of others and dedicating one's own merits to Enlightenment, are brought together after the third confession section:

> Whatever beings here in Jambudvīpa and whatever also in other world-spheres perform various, profound merits, I congratulate them all on this merit. By this my congratulation on their merits and by the merit obtained by me through body, voice or mind, may there be fruitful success for my resolve. May I touch supreme, flawless enlightenment.[55]

This comes just after a long passage of general good wishes. Enjoying spiritual happiness and well-being ourselves, it is only natural that we should rejoice in the spiritual happiness and well-being of others, as Ruciraketu does here. You often have this at the conclusion of a puja or even the conclusion of a Mahāyāna sūtra. It's just an expression of good will towards all living beings – that you wish for all of them all good things, both material and spiritual.

> Everywhere in the spheres of all beings may all the woes in the world be extinguished. May those beings whose senses are defective, whose limbs are deficient, all now become complete in senses. May those who in the ten directions are diseased, powerless, whose body is injured, and who are without salvation, all be delivered quickly from their disease, and may they obtain health, strength, and senses. May those beings who are in danger of being threatened or killed by kings, thieves, or scoundrels, who are troubled by hundreds of different fears, may all those beings who are oppressed by the advent of troubles be delivered from those hundreds of extreme, very dreadful fears. May those who are beaten, bound and tortured

by bonds, and situated in various troubles, distracted by numerous thousands of labours, who have become afflicted by various fears and cruel anxiety, may they all be delivered from their bonds; may the beaten be delivered from the beaters; may the condemned be united with life; and may all those who have come upon troubles become free from fear. May those beings who are oppressed by hunger and thirst obtain a variety of food and drink. And may the blind see various forms, the deaf hear delightful sounds, the naked obtain various garments, poor beings obtain treasures. And may all beings be blessed with abundant wealth, corn, and various jewels. May the experience of woe harm no one and may all beings be endowed with good fortune. May they have beautiful, gracious, auspicious forms and continually have a heap of numerous blessings. As soon as they think of them, may there be for them food and drink as they desire, great abundance, and merits, lutes, drums, and pleasant-sounding cymbals, springs, pools, ponds, and tanks. As soon as they think of them, may there be for them lotus-ponds of blue and golden lotuses, food and drink, likewise clothing, wealth, gold, ornament of gems and pearls, gold, beryl, and various jewels. May there be no sounds of woe anywhere in the world. May there be not one being of opposing mien, and may they all be of noble aspect, creating light for one another.

Whatever success there may be in the world of men, may it arise for them at their thought. As soon as they think of them, may all their desires be fulfilled through their merit and its fruit. May they rain down three times from the trees perfume, garlands, unguents, incense, powder, various flowers. May the beings accept them and be joyful. May they do honour, inconceivable, to all the Tathāgatas in the ten directions, to those completely enlightened, to the Śrāvakas, to the pure, flawless, firm Law. May beings avoid the low states of existence. May they avoid the eight evil instants. May they obtain the supreme, chief instant. May they always obtain a meeting with Buddhas. May they always be high-born and have their treasuries replete with abundant wealth and corn. For numerous aeons may they be thoroughly adorned with beauty, complexion, fame and glory. May all women constantly become men, strong, heroic, intelligent, and learned. May they constantly proceed to enlightenment and be active in the six perfections. May they see the Buddhas in the ten directions, comfortably seated under excellent jewelled trees, sitting together on seats of precious beryl. May they hear them expounding the Law. The evil acts obtained by me, what I obtained previously in the oppressions of existences, whatever the evil acts bringing undesired fruits – may they all without remainder be destroyed. May all beings who dwell in the bondage of existence, bound with firm fetters by the fetters of the cycle of existence, be delivered from their bondage by the hands of wisdom. May they be delivered from their woes. May they become Buddhas.[56]

The 'eight evil instants' represent eight spiritually inauspicious conditions under which one may be reborn: not being born with a human body, not being born male, not being born when there is a Buddha around or at a time when the teaching is known, being born in a border country among barbarians – and so on. It's a standard list – Gampopa gives it, for example, in the *Jewel Ornament of Liberation*. Of course, auspicious rebirth is dependent on merit, so what you're really wishing for is the merit to cause you to be reborn at a favourable time.

The phrase which jumps out at us here is 'May all women constantly become men.' You find this prayer or aspiration in many Buddhist texts. In a way it's wishing the person who happens to be a woman a better chance in the next life. This basically means accepting that the female psycho-physical constitution is generally less conducive to Enlightenment than the male psycho-physical constitution. Many women will consider this to be an outrageous put-down, but it is really just like a man praying to be reborn at a time when there is a Buddha around. He isn't putting himself down in any way; he is just aspiring for more favourable conditions.

If a woman makes a strong effort to gain Enlightenment, the Buddhist view is that she will probably be reborn as a man anyway, because she will in this life have transformed herself into someone with mental and spiritual qualities which tend to be more often found in men, even though she still has a woman's body. A woman who seriously takes up the spiritual life is in effect – psycho-spiritually – a man.

This aspiration doesn't mean, therefore, that a woman can't make any spiritual progress. She doesn't have to pray to be reborn as a man in order to make a start. If she is very determined, she can certainly make a great deal of spiritual progress in this life. It is simply that as a woman she's got more of a handicap – though heaven knows men are handicapped heavily enough themselves! It isn't easy for *anybody* to practise the spiritual life.

This is a tricky area for some people. I know from my own experience that quite a few women resent any suggestion that they are in any way 'inferior'. I certainly don't want to exaggerate any disability, but where there is any kind of obstacle, you don't make it any easier for yourself to grow spiritually if you insist on denying it, and resent any reminder that it is there. The only way you can make progress is to recognize it and deal with it, or at least take it into account. Otherwise it is going to get in the way.

So if a woman, *as a woman*, is at some disadvantage, it is much better to acknowledge it and say, 'Well yes, it is a disadvantage, but never mind. I'm going to take it into account and I'm going to make progress none the less.' If you deny it, you are only blocking the path of your own development. And it's just the same in the case of men, if there is any specific disability in their case. The important thing is that development is possible, Enlightenment is possible.

Women are quite often concerned about what they see as discrimination against women in Buddhism, and they sometimes home in on Buddhist scriptures which seem to suggest that women are being put down. But there is one text that makes the whole matter quite clear. It comes in the passage of the Pāli Canon where Mahāpājapati comes to the Buddha seeking ordination. At first the Buddha refuses her request. The Buddha's attendant Ānanda, clearly wondering whether Mahāpajāpati has been refused ordination because of a lack of spiritual capacity in women, asks the Buddha directly 'Are women capable of the highest spiritual attainment?' And the Buddha says 'Yes.'

This, so far as Buddhist tradition is concerned, settled the matter once and for all. No one has ever suggested that the Buddha might not have said it; his words here are absolutely categorical, and all other texts have to be interpreted in their light. This is the basic Buddhist principle – and it is underlined by other Pāli Canon texts in which the Buddha emphasized women's capacity to gain Enlightenment.

One might further say that although Buddhism has recognized that women have certain disadvantages, it is only Buddhism, among all the major religions of the world, that has stated categorically that women are capable of the highest spiritual attainment. The question isn't even asked in Christianity. Women can be 'saved'; you can have female saints; but if you start talking in terms of a female 'saviour' – or even of a woman priest in some circles – you run into difficulties. But in Buddhism it has always been said that women are capable of, and have achieved, whatever spiritual attainments men have achieved. There are examples in Buddhist history of women who, whether young or old, have attained Enlightenment, so we know it is possible. The Buddha himself had very accomplished female disciples, so did Milarepa, the Enlightened Tibetan ascetic, and so did Padmasambhava, the great guru of Tibet. In Buddhism women have been able to occupy any spiritual position that men have been able to occupy. There have been not only bhikkhus but bhikkhunīs, not only male gurus but female gurus. There is nothing in Buddhism to prevent a woman from exercising any spiritual function whatever, and this is the only religion of which one can say that.

So Buddhism has this double attitude. It is very realistic, and at the same time very idealistic. It does say that there are certain disadvantages for women, but on the other hand it says that women can gain Enlightenment, and that whatever spiritual path or function is open to men is also open to women. One has to take both of these together. Buddhism is essentially seeing things as they really are, at every possible level. In the long run it is surely encouraging for women to recognize whatever difficulties there are but to feel confident at the same time that, if they really want to, they can transcend all difficulties whatsoever.

According to the Buddhist tradition, the main difficulty as far as a woman is concerned is her biological constitution. She is built to produce children, and usually isn't happy unless she is doing that, or having something to do with that process. Of course, there are many women who say in all sincerity that they have no biological urge to have children. And certainly today women are free in an unprecedented way *not* to have children. It is, however, probably true to say that the majority of women would not feel truly fulfilled if they had not had at least one or two children. But once that urge or desire has been fulfilled, they can commit themselves to the spiritual life, if that is what they want to do.

One could say that a woman who has had her children but who is still young and vigorous would be well placed to follow the spiritual path. When a woman has passed child-bearing age, when her children are grown up, she is completely free to go ahead with the spiritual life. In a way, the only path open to her then is a spiritual path, or at least a path of individual development and responsibility. What else is she going to do with her life? This is the question that confronts her. One might even say that women may perhaps have a handicap when it comes to following the spiritual path in the earlier part of life, but that this is not the case later in life. The only difficulty, it would seem, is the purely practical one of bringing it to the attention of such women that they have a great opportunity, of pointing out to them that they have reached an extremely favourable time in their lives.

Many women feel that their whole life is over by the time their children have left home. In a sense, they are right. Their life as women in the narrower sense *is* over; but their life as aspiring individuals is just beginning.[57] A woman in such a position can think 'Biology isn't going to bother me any more. That has had its necessary fulfilment. Now I can devote my life to being an individual. I'm going to grow beyond the boundaries of the family, even the boundaries of the extended family.'

But, of course, there is really no need to wait until your children have left home. You can have any number of children, whether as a mother or as a father, and still commit yourself to spiritual development. And there are plenty of people with no responsibilities at all, with no children, who drift in and out of involvement with the spiritual life and never think of really committing themselves. So the question that still has to be asked is whether there is something inherent in women as women which makes them less inclined to the spiritual life than men.

I have tentatively reached the conclusion that the spiritual life is more difficult for women because they are less able than men to envisage something beyond, something purely transcendental, and are therefore less able to orient themselves in that direction. They can think in terms of psychological – even psycho-spiritual – development, but they seem to find it more difficult to think in terms of spiritual development in the direction of a specifically transcendental goal. This seems to be true even of women who are relatively free, who have had their family life and brought up their children. They may not be able to commit themselves to the spiritual life because their female conditioning is still very strong and limits their horizons, so that they are unable to see beyond a worldly career.

Of course, both men and women tend at first to think of Buddhism in terms of personal development; that's the current tendency in the West anyway. And many people stay involved with it in that way, with no more than a vague appreciation of anything beyond merely psychological and social development. This sort of misapprehension, as a way into the spiritual life, is all right up to a point. But it seems difficult for women to get a more purely transcendental dimension into view. They may be very devoted to Buddhism, or to a particular Buddhist group, but devotion should not be mistaken for commitment. One may be devoted to the group, or to certain people in it, but not committed in the sense of seeing a transcendental factor above and beyond the mundane and psychological, and making that one's personal aim.

Most women don't commit crimes as some men do, they don't become psychopaths as some men do, but they are also not as likely to be geniuses as some men are. They are not as good or as bad; men's range is much wider. Women tend to be more stable, in a way more integrated, than men, but that integration tends to be on a lower level. It is true to say of both men and women that some people are integrated on a relatively low level, while others are less integrated but have elements in their total unintegrated being which are higher than any of those in the person who is integrated on a lower level. Gifted and richly endowed people can be quite unintegrated, which means that if and when they do integrate themselves, there is a rich synthesis, and they become much more highly evolved than others who are more stable but less exceptional. There are many people who are quite integrated on their own level, while others who are capable of much higher experiences, or much deeper insights, are relatively unintegrated. In a way, the greater the range of your experience and the further it goes, the more difficult it is for you to become an integrated person, because you have more to integrate.

Integration takes place around a central, focal point, so to become integrated you have to decide what your centre – your ultimate aim – is and gradually get everything going towards that. It is important for richly endowed people to have an ultimate goal or ideal to work towards; otherwise they have no means of integration. The ordinary person will survive without such a goal just because they are integrated on their own level, but the more gifted person really needs a centre in relation to which he can integrate himself. Otherwise he goes to pieces – goes from one extreme to the other, or disintegrates into some sort of madness. This is where the transcendental factor, the sense of something beyond mundane existence, comes in, and in this respect, as I have said, women seem generally to be at something of a disadvantage.

Women seem to derive a great deal of their sense of self-worth from a sense that they are valued by somebody else, especially by a man, rather than from their own estimation of themselves. But if they are to evolve as individuals, they have to develop that self-respect, to value themselves and not wait for men to value them. Many women see this quite clearly and work on it, but it isn't at all easy for them.

One way women can work towards individuality is by developing more independence and initiative. This is not to say that men are always full of independence and initiative, but I think this is something that women in particular need to concentrate on cultivating. From a purely social and cultural point of view, both men and women need to be more independent of one another. The stereotype of the helpless male who can't even sew a button on a shirt is the other side of the picture. There are certain things that men tend to rely on women for, instead of doing them for themselves. By and large, social and cultural practices and interests may encourage women to be dependent, but women need not accept the limitations that society places upon their independence. Women are not the weak, dependent creatures that society very often makes them out to be.

This is where women's communities – communities in which women committed to the spiritual path live and practise together – are so useful. They remove completely the illusion that a woman is a poor, weak creature, a sort of clinging vine that needs to be propped up by some strong man. Through living in communities, many women have discovered with delight that they can do everything themselves. They are quite independent; they can look after themselves in every respect. This doesn't mean that they start disliking or hating men. In fact, they tend to get on with them better than before, because they relate to them from a position of independence, with no element of clinging, and they don't have to play any games to get their own way. If they want something, they insist on having it, openly and straightforwardly.

Some women derive a great deal of inspiration from female archetypal figures – *ḍākinīs*, for instance.[58] This is quite positive, but one shouldn't start to think of ḍākinīs as a glorification, a 'pseudo-spiritualization', of femaleness, and a justification for remaining female in a non-spiritual or even anti-spiritual sense. The archetypes can be misused in that way, just as the Tantra generally can be misused as a justification for almost anything. Female Bodhisattvas can also be misunderstood. Essentially a Bodhisattva is no more female than male, no more male than female. Having a female Bodhisattva doesn't mean putting a halo round the head of ordinary, untransformed femininity.

This raises the question of what 'transformed femininity' might be. I am using 'femininity' to represent the softer spiritual qualities – tenderness, gentleness, and compassion. 'Feminine' qualities, like 'masculine' qualities, are capable of being exercised on a higher level, in a refined and purified form. For instance, just as masculine competitiveness can be refined and sublimated into a healthy rivalry, feminine nurturing qualities can be refined and sublimated into something like compassion, care for life in a broader sense. But transformed femininity is not at all the same thing as transformed femaleness. Femaleness – in the sense of the earth mother, reproductive, sense-oriented quality – cannot be transformed; it has to be abandoned.

Both men and women need to rise above sexual polarity. But it is important to make a distinction between rising above it – incorporating both poles within oneself – and falling below it because one is inadequate to take the role of either a man or a woman. This is probably more noticeable in men than in women. You find men who are 'intermediate' in a way – but in a very weak way. It's as though they haven't been able to be men. Perhaps they find the role of being a man in the modern world so daunting and demanding that they just don't feel equal to it, so they sink back into being childish. It is a great mistake to confuse this with a genuine synthesis, psychological and spiritual, of the sexual polar opposites. A weak male is not a man who has succeeded in developing his feminine side. He is a man who has not been able to be a man. He needs to work on becoming a man, then he can think of developing his feminine side if he likes.

Perhaps there are some men who are born as 'weak males', who can't really change much in this lifetime, but they shouldn't be taken as a norm for healthy men, much less still regarded as people who have risen above sexual polarization. This isn't to say of course that one is less of a man just because one is gentle. One could be strong and even aggressive when necessary and still have very gentle characteristics. What I'm thinking of is the man who cannot be anything but gentle. He is not able to be strong, dynamic, aggressive, even when the situation requires it.

The man who is unable to be a man and the woman who is unable to be a woman have a superficial resemblance to some sort of androgyne, but it is not the real thing. The next level up is the real male and the real female, and then, at a higher level, the more integrated individual who is still biologically male or female (it is not a question of physical hermaphroditism) but who, in the case of the biological male, has developed and integrated his feminine side and, in the case of the biological female, has developed and integrated her masculine side. They remain differentiated biologically, but they are integrated as individuals, so there is no extreme psychological polarization, and they get along much better and more happily because they are more individual.

It is important to distinguish these three levels; very often the first is mistaken for the third. Sometimes you find people trying to damp down a man's natural masculinity – restrain it, discourage it – under the impression that they are thereby making him more 'integrated', but that's nonsense. In the same way, some try to encourage a woman to give up her more womanly qualities, make herself something neutral and sexless, under the impression that she is thereby becoming more of an individual. But it is possible to be a real individual and at the same time a real man or a real woman. You don't develop by impoverishing yourself. You integrate the 'old' rather than discarding it. So if you are a woman, be a woman; if you are a man, be a man. Accept it, develop it, make the most of it, but gradually rise above it and incorporate it into something more completely human, more truly individual.

And if you are a woman, part of accepting that you are a woman is that in some ways you are going to have to make more effort, at least at the beginning of the spiritual life. To plunge into the spiritual life you need zest and enthusiasm, drive and thrust, and – in short – a man seems to have that more readily than a woman. In this context we should perhaps bring to mind the Buddhist background of karma and rebirth. You are not reborn as a man or a woman by accident, but because you already have an affinity for that particular bodily form. You have been embodied in the first place because you had an inclination towards embodied existence. You wanted to be reborn; you wanted to experience the physical world through the physical senses; otherwise you would have been reborn in a *devaloka*, a heavenly world where there is no distinction of gender.[59] This is the traditional teaching. And the first great choice that confronts 'you' is whether you are to be reborn as a man or as a woman. You aren't suddenly landed with a male or female form without having done, so to speak, anything to deserve it.

So if one were a sort of neutral consciousness hovering in the bardo state, what inclinations would cause one to want or even choose (supposing it was a free choice) to be embodied as a woman or as a man? It seems to me that if you had the choice, and you wanted to lead an adventurous life, you would probably choose to be embodied as a man. And what stops a woman leading an outward-going, adventurous life would seem to be something to do with her biological nature.

All this is not to say that if you are a man you are yourself superior to women. It is just that you tend to have a natural advantage which you may or may not make use of. And if you are a woman, this is not to say you are yourself inferior to men; you simply have a natural disadvantage, from a purely spiritual point of view, which you may or may not choose to try and overcome. This, I'm sure, is why in many Mahāyāna sūtras one encounters the aspiration that all women may become men – in other words, may this particular individual assume in her next existence a

psycho-physical constitution more suited to the attainment of Enlightenment. You are wishing well towards that being. In the same way, you
might wish that they should be reborn at a time when there are Buddhas
and the Dharma is being taught. Women need not feel put down or
discouraged; on the contrary, they can feel encouraged to overcome all
obstacles and attain true individuality.[60]

The phrase 'May there be not one being of opposing mien, and may
they all be of noble aspect, creating light for one another,' is one I haven't
come across in any other text. It suggests a sort of creative communication
which helps both parties to move forward, each shedding light on the
path for the other. It's very much in the spirit of the whole paragraph,
which again is rather lavish. The text might just as well have said 'May
all living beings win happiness both mundane and transcendental,' and
left it at that, but the Mahāyāna likes to enumerate things very concretely
and vividly – which is no doubt much better, at least for the majority of
people.

The chapter ends with some final good wishes:

> Whoever worships and praises the Buddhas continually, with mind
> believing, pure, spotless, by means of this Confession, which is
> praised as a cause of ripening, and abandons the evil states for sixty
> aeons, and whoever, men, women, brahmins, warriors, with these
> celebrated verses, will praise the sage, standing with hands in the
> gesture of reverence, recollecting births in all existences, he will have
> his body adorned with all members and with all senses, endowed
> with various merits, with virtues, and he will be continually
> worshipped by kings among men. Such will he be in each place of
> birth.
>
> Not under one Buddha have they performed good, nor even under
> two, nor four, nor five, nor ten, but they in whose ear this Confession
> will have sounded have performed good under thousands of
> Buddhas.
>
> So ends the third chapter, the Chapter on Confession, in the
> excellent Suvarṇabhāsa, king of Sūtras.[61]

So in order to meet with this sūtra you must already have accumulated
quite a few merits. You must have come into contact with a number of
Buddhas – in different lives, because you only get one Buddha at a time.
According to tradition the earth could not bear the weight of more than
one Buddha at a time.

Again the sūtra is typical of the Mahāyāna in going in for lavish praise and rejoicing on a grand scale. Mahāyāna sūtras always try to give you an impression of vastness and infinity, multiplicity and abundance. They try to widen your perspective. Perhaps it is only in this way that the compiler of the sūtra could express what he really felt; he couldn't do it in a more sober fashion. It must have been very inspiring for the people who took it perfectly literally.

The general impression given by the whole chapter is one of joy and exuberance. It goes with a real swing. Even though there is so much said about faults and evil, the overall impression is very positive. There is nothing morbid about it, no atmosphere of sin and guilt. It is not abstract or abstruse; it states the spiritually obvious in an understandable, straightforward way. It is non-conceptual, direct, and immediate in its appeal. You just have to allow yourself to be carried along by it.

This joy comes across in a number of the Mahāyāna sūtras. Everybody is so overjoyed that a Buddha has appeared, that there is the Dharma to be followed, a sangha to make offerings to, stupas to worship. Everybody is overwhelmed with joy, and they think how lucky they are, and how wonderful it all is. It is very pure, colourful, innocent, and child-like, although there is no suggestion of immaturity. This is the traditional atmosphere and spirit of the Mahāyāna. For the average Mahāyāna worshipper, religion has always meant something colourful and joyful, exuberant and happy; and being involved with religion means being generous, outgoing, hospitable, kind, affectionate, welcoming, open, clear, and joyful.

And this is the ultimate spiritual significance of confession: to clear away all darkness and evil so that we can experience the freedom and joy of a pure heart and mind. When we have not only seen the golden light at work in the world and been touched by it ourselves, but purified ourselves of the evil within us, the path to ultimate perfection lies clear before us.

Part Two

TRANSFORMING WORLD

3

The Protectors of the Dharma

So far we have been concerned with the development of the individual, with the transformation by the golden light of the individual self. Now we can begin to make the transition from transformation of self to transformation of world. So – first things first – what is the 'world'? I mean the question not in an abstract or philosophical sense but quite literally. These days we are very used to seeing the world, and the universe, in a particular way. We are so used to 'knowing' about the world in a scientific sense that it is easy to forget that only a few centuries ago the world people 'knew', the pre-Copernican world, was a fundamentally different one. It may still be hard for us to imagine that there could be any other way of seeing the universe than the 'right' way, the scientific way.

But the ancient Indian Buddhists saw the universe quite differently. And to see it as they did, we will have to use our imagination. To begin with, imagine space, nothing but space, infinite space, stretching in all directions. Then, as you continue to look, seeing more and more deeply, you will see that diffused throughout that infinity of space is air, air of a deep blue colour. Within that blue air you gradually discern two currents of air, two 'blue winds', blowing in opposite directions. And these winds take the form of two crossed vajras, each of which is millions of miles in length.

Now imagine that resting on those two vast crossed vajras you can see a great mass of waters, forming a flat disc. And on these waters, towards the edges of the disc, you see four continents or islands, each with two subcontinents. All these continents and subcontinents have bases of solid gold. The eastern continent is called Videha. It is white in colour and shaped like the crescent moon. The southern continent is called Jambud-vīpa; it is blue in colour and shaped like the shoulder-blade of a sheep. The western continent, Godānīya, is round, like the sun, and red in colour. And the northern continent, Uttarakuru, is square, and green in colour.

Then, right at the centre of the waters, there towers a great mountain, Mount Meru. It stands eighty thousand miles above the waters, and extends eighty thousand miles below them. It has four faces, rather like a pyramid, and each face is made of a precious substance. The eastern face is of silver, the southern face of lapis lazuli, the western face of ruby, and the northern face of gold. Surrounding Mount Meru is an ocean 80,000 miles wide and 80,000 miles deep. Surrounding the ocean is a ring of golden mountains, 40,000 miles high and 40,000 miles wide. Then surrounding that is an ocean of the same dimensions. Altogether there are seven circular oceans and seven rings of golden mountains, their dimensions gradually diminishing as one moves outwards, although of course the diameter of the circles they form progressively increases, so that the last ring of golden mountains is only 625 miles high and 625 miles wide. Outside this are the waters on which float the four continents and the eight subcontinents. The entire system is enclosed by a great iron wall, the purpose of which is to shut in the light of the sun and the moon and the stars. This wall is said to be 312½ miles (or *yojanas*) in height, and more than 3½ million miles or *yojanas* in circumference. Outside that great iron wall there is only darkness until another universe is reached.

According to ancient Buddhist tradition there are thousands and millions of such universes throughout space, each with its own Mount Meru, continents, mountains, and oceans – and its own sentient beings and Buddhas. This cosmology would seem to be almost entirely an Indian Buddhist production. The only element which might be Tibetan – apart from a little colouring here and there – might be the blue winds and the two crossed vajras. The details are to be found in traditional texts like the *Mahāvyutpatti* – a sort of Sanskrit dictionary compiled to help translators of texts from Sanskrit into Tibetan – and the *Abhidharma-kośa*.

The Indian view of the universe presents, of course, a very different picture of the universe from the modern Western one. However, it has its own validity. I once met a young Tibetan lama who had been studying Western academic subjects and I asked him which he thought was true: the traditional Indo-Tibetan picture of the universe or the modern Western one. He was a very young lama – in fact he was the reincarnation of a very famous Gelugpa lama – but although he was so young, the reply he gave was not only cautious but in my view quite correct. He said 'The two pictures are useful for different purposes.'

I wouldn't like to comment on the usefulness of the modern Western picture, but there is no doubt about the usefulness of the traditional Buddhist picture, at least so far as its own definite spiritual purposes are concerned. For one thing, it provides the concrete symbolism on which is based a good deal of meditational and devotional practice, especially in the Vajrayāna. One of the most important of all Vajrayāna practices is what is known as the offering of the mandala. Mandala literally means 'circle', and in this context it means the whole circle of conditioned existence as represented in the Buddhist picture of the universe. The practice is quite complex. In the course of your devotions you build up a three-dimensional model of the universe, complete with Mount Meru, the four continents, and so on. (You do this in your imagination, using heaps of rice on a metal tray to symbolize the different elements of the world picture.) This model universe you offer up to the Buddha, or more usually to the guru – especially after receiving teaching or initiation – together with suitable prayers and meditations.

This offering up of the whole universe is a very natural response. After all, you have received the Dharma, something that is infinitely precious, something that is going to transform your whole life – so what are you going to give? It is not a question of giving *in return*; you give because you feel like giving, because you feel so grateful. You want to give everything that you possess, including your own life, your own self. Indeed, you feel that if you were master of the whole universe, you would give that. So this is what you do. It is only by making such an offering that you can express what you feel. For you at that moment the mandala *is* the universe, the universe *is* the mandala.

The traditional Buddhist view of the universe also provides the cosmological background to the Buddha's teaching, and is present, explicitly or implicitly, in the Buddhist scriptures, especially perhaps in the Mahāyāna sūtras. In chapter 6 of the *Sūtra of Golden Light*, for example, the Buddha speaks of the 'whole triple-thousand, great-thousand world-sphere, in which there are a hundred million moons, suns, great oceans, [and] Sumerus....'

We have seen something of the 'landscape' of the universe – its mountains, oceans, and islands – but we have not yet been introduced to the beings who inhabit this universe, some of whom will be playing a key role in this chapter of the sūtra. We ourselves inhabit Jambudvīpa, the southern continent. Jambudvīpa is the smallest of the continents, only seven thousand miles in diameter, and according to ancient tradition its inhabitants are rich and prosperous, and perform both skilful and unskilful deeds.

To meet some of the other inhabitants of this universe we need to take a closer look at Mount Meru. The mountain is divided horizontally into eight tiers, four below the waters and four above. The four tiers below the waters contain the hells, which are occupied by various classes of tormented beings, suffering the results of their unskilful actions. And the four tiers above the water are inhabited by various classes of demigods: the yakṣas (sublime spirits), the nāgas (the serpents or dragons), and so on.

Then above Mount Meru are the various heavens of the gods, which begin, according to some accounts, 80,000 miles above the summit of the mountain. First of all there is the heaven known as the 'Heaven of the Thirty-three' – that is to say the thirty-three gods, the thirty-three Vedic deities. Their king is Indra, who occupies a wonderful palace in the midst of this heaven. Next come the Suyima gods, and next above them is the heaven of the contented gods, the Tuṣita Heaven. Then there's the heaven of the gods that take delight in their own creations, and then a heaven of gods who take delight in others' creations. So altogether, including the heaven of the four great kings, there are six heavens.

According to Buddhist teaching the whole of conditioned existence is divided into three great planes or levels: the plane of sensuous desire; the plane of pure form – archetypal form, if you like; and the formless plane. All the heavens mentioned so far fall, like the human realm, within the plane of sensuous desire.

All six heavens of this plane are inhabited by both gods and goddesses, and therefore in each of these heavens there's the possibility of sexual gratification. The higher one ascends, however, the more refined in form that gratification becomes, just as the heavens themselves become progressively more refined the higher one goes. In Indra's heaven, as among human beings, sexual gratification is achieved through copulation, among the Suyima gods simply by holding hands, among the contented gods by means of a smile, among the gods who delight in their own creations by prolonged gazing, and among the gods who delight in the creations of others, by a mere glance – nothing more.

Above the heavens of sensuous desire with their gods and goddesses are the heavens of the world of pure form. These are inhabited by sixteen or eighteen (accounts vary) classes of Brahma gods. In the first three heavens live gods in the company of Brahma, gods in Brahma's retinue, and great Brahma gods. Then in the next three heavens we have the gods of lesser light, the gods of limitless light, and the gods of sonant light (that is, light which is also sound, sound which is also light). Above them are a further three heavens, in which live the gods of lesser purity, the gods of limitless purity, and the gods of radiant purity. And then there are still a further seven (or nine) heavens inhabited by more classes of Brahma gods. The last five of these heavens are collectively known as pure abodes, and here are born all those who on earth have broken all five lower fetters, and attained the path of no return – that is, the path of no further rebirth in the world of human beings, or indeed any realm below the pure abodes.

All the heavens of the plane of pure form are inhabited only by masculine divinities – angels, if you like – and they appear there spontaneously, without any need for the whole business of sexual reproduction. Above the heavens of pure form with their angels are four heavens of the formless plane, inhabited by gods without form.

One can draw correspondences between all these various heavens and the dhyāna states experienced in meditation. Each of the groups of heavens of the Brahma gods corresponds to one of the first four dhyānas, and the heavens of the formless plane correspond to the four formless dhyānas.

To complete our survey of the population of the ancient Buddhist universe, we must come down quite a long way, back to the level of the Heaven of the Thirty-three. In the air at this level is the circle of the eight goddesses: the goddesses of sensuousness, garlands, song, dance, flowers, incense, lamps, and perfumes. These goddesses occupy positions in the eight principal directions of space. They are young and beautiful, and of different colours – white, yellow, red, green, and so on. They all hold in their hands articles corresponding to their natures and their names. Then, immediately outside these goddesses, also suspended in the air in fixed positions, are the seven precious things – the precious wheel, the precious gem, the precious queen, the precious minister, the precious elephant, the precious horse, and the precious steward – plus the vase of treasure. And then in the inmost circle, immediately around Mount Meru, are the sun, with its chariot drawn by ten horses, the moon, with its chariot drawn by seven horses, the precious umbrella of sovereignty, and the banner of victory. And in the centre of it all, in the palace of Indra, is heaped up the entire treasure of gods and men. It's as though in Indra's palace you can find everything that gods and men could possibly desire. In one of the Gospels it is said 'Where your treasure is, there will your heart be also.' So treasure represents what you desire. And Indra's palace is the place where all your desires are fulfilled – at least your desires up to that level, for there are many heavens and realms above the Heaven of the Thirty-three.

There is just one group of beings in this extraordinary universe that we have not yet met. If we look again at Mount Meru, we will see that there are four figures standing on or near the summit, or perhaps each on a subsidiary peak half way up the mountain, in each of the four directions. These are the four great kings, the four protectors of the world.

First of all there's Dhṛtarāṣṭra. His name means 'Upholder of the Land', he is white in colour, and he is the protector of the eastern quarter. He is king of the gandharvas (heavenly musicians) and of the piśācas (vampires). Then there is Virūḍhaka, whose name means 'Growth'. He is yellow in colour, and protects the southern quarter, and he is king of the pretas or hungry ghosts and of the kumbhandas. Thirdly there is Virūpākṣa, 'He of the Bulging Eyes': the protector of the western quarter, he is red in colour, and rules over the nāgas, the serpents or dragons, as well as the puṭanas or fever-spirits. Finally there is Vaiśravaṇa, whose name means 'Greatly Learned'. He is green in colour, he is the protector of the northern quarter, and he rules over the yakṣas or sublime spirits and the rākṣasas, the flesh-eating demons.

All four kings are powerfully built, of defiant mien, and armour-clad. They are often represented in Buddhist art, especially in frescoes inside the vestibules of temples (two on either side of the entrance to the main hall) or in the form of free-standing, often quite gigantic images. And, of course, they appear in the *Sūtra of Golden Light*.

As we have seen, the Buddha is teaching the sūtra surrounded by Bodhisattvas and many other beings. At the beginning of chapter 6 of the sūtra we discover that among these beings are the four great kings. They have apparently been present in the assembly all along, but they have made no contribution to the proceedings until this point. They now rise to their feet, salute the Buddha, and begin to speak. The kings speak a number of times, as does the Buddha – this is the longest chapter of the sūtra – but we can get a general sense of their significance by focusing on their opening speech. In this speech, the four kings make two statements and four promises. Firstly, they extol the merits of the *Sūtra of Golden Light*. Secondly, they declare that the sūtra nourishes them in – as we shall see – quite a curious and significant fashion. Then they make their four promises: to exercise their sovereignty over the different classes of demi-gods according to the Dharma, to protect the whole of Jambudvīpa, to protect the monks who proclaim the sūtra, and to protect the kings who patronize the monks who proclaim the sūtra.

On the subject of the first statement there is just one point I would bring out here. This is that the various grounds upon which the four great kings extol the sūtra are of two main kinds: spiritual and worldly. For instance, they extol the sūtra because it has been taken care of by multitudes of Bodhisattvas and bestows supreme blessings upon all beings: but they also extol it because it repels foreign armies and removes hunger and illness. In effect they are saying it transforms life or self and it transforms the world.

Now for the second statement of the four great kings – that the *Sūtra of Golden Light* nourishes them. What they say is this:

> When, dear Lord, this excellent Suvarṇabhāsa, king of Sūtras, is being expounded in detail in the assembly, by merely hearing this Law and by the nectar juice of the Law, the divine bodies of us four great kings together with our armies and retinues will wax with great might. In our body there will be produced prowess, strength and energy. Brilliance, glory and splendour will enter our body.[62]

How is it that the mere hearing of the sūtra should have this effect on the bodies of the four great kings? What are we meant to understand by 'hearing the sūtra'? In order to understand this, we will need to understand more deeply who the four great kings are and what they really represent. There are principally four points to be made.

First, the four great kings occupy the lowest of the heavens of the plane of sensuous desire. They are definitely heavenly beings, but of a very low order, in fact of the lowest order. At the same time they are in touch with the beings that inhabit the earth – not only human beings, but also the various kinds of non-human beings. From the point of view of the world this has decided advantages. The kings occupy an intermediate position, a kind of borderland between the more crude and the more refined, the more chaotic and the more harmonious levels of the plane of sensuous desire. Because they are in direct contact with the earth they are in a position to intervene in its affairs, but because they belong to the heavens, their intervention is sure to be of a positive nature.

The four kings are known as the *lokapālas*, the guardians of the world. In traditional Hīnayāna Buddhism *hiri* and *ottappa* – shame and blame, as they are usually translated – are called the two lokapālas, because without them there can be no moral order. This would seem to imply that there is no great difference between the lokapālas and the dharmapālas of the Vajrayāna tradition – 'dharma' here having a strong ethical connotation. The Vajrayāna, however – as might be expected – gives a somewhat different slant to things in that it sometimes portrays dharmapālas as very fierce, wrathful beings who are in essence Enlightened Bodhisattvas. This makes them quite different from the four kings – the lokapālas – who are not Bodhisattvas but definitely mundane beings, albeit of a very high order.

The second significant aspect of the four great kings is that they are leaders of different hordes of non-human beings. These non-human beings are of many different kinds, of all sorts of shapes and sizes and even colours. Some are very beautiful, or at least capable of assuming beautiful shapes, but most are horribly misshapen and ugly. For example, the nāgas, the serpents or dragons, are associated with water and with treasure, and they can make themselves large or small, visible or invisible. They often have a good understanding of the teaching, but they don't practise it. The yakṣas are rather terrible, and often of enormous size. The gandharvas, the perfume eaters, are so called because they live on perfumes just as human beings live on solid food. They are musicians in the palace of Indra, in the Heaven of the Thirty-three, and are said to be very uxorious.

The asuras are fierce, war-like spirits, sometimes compared with the giants of Greek mythology, and they are constantly fighting the gods of the Heaven of the Thirty-three. The male asuras are extremely ugly, but the females are very beautiful. The garuḍas are enormous, golden-winged creatures like eagles, who feed upon nāgas. And then there are the kiṁnaras. The name kiṁnara means 'What? Is it a man?' and they are so called because they resemble men to some extent, so that when you see one you might not be sure whether it is a man or not. According to some authorities they have horns on their heads; according to others they have men's heads and bird's bodies. Like the gandharvas, they are musicians in the palace of Indra – the males sing, the females dance.

There are very many other kinds of non-human beings: vampires, nightmares, ghosts, ghouls, bogles, fever-spirits, and so on. Between them they represent the whole mass of gross, chaotic, turbulent energies that swirl about on this earth plane of ours – energies that can only too easily assume negative and destructive forms. And each of the four great kings rules over a particular group of these non-human beings. In other words, they keep the gross, turbulent, chaotic energies of the earth plane under control. They are not able to transform them, but at least they can prevent them getting too much out of hand.

It is only the four great kings who are in a position to render this kind of service. The gods of the higher heavens couldn't do it. Their energies are so refined that they have no point of contact with nāgas, yakṣas, rākṣasas, and so on – perhaps they are not even aware of their existence. So the four great kings perform a very useful service. They belong to the heavens, but they are in touch with the earth, and they are therefore able to keep the powerful natural energies of the earth under control, and prevent them from having a disruptive effect on the human world.

The third point to be made about the four great kings is that they are protectors of the world, protectors of the four quarters. But what are they protectors against? The kings themselves make this clear in their first speech. Addressing the Buddha, they say 'We will rout the hordes of Bhūtas, who are pitiless, whose minds are without compassion, who take their glory from others.' Bhūtas are evil spirits. They are the forces that are hostile to humanity, inimical to spiritual development, the energies that refuse to accept the control of the four great kings. All the kings can do about them is keep them at bay, keep them out.

It is because they are protectors or guardians in this way that the kings stand on either side of the entrance to the temple, neither inside nor outside, but on the threshold. After all, a temple is not just a building. A temple is an enclosed, sacred space, where sacred, symbolic actions are performed. It is therefore a space that only integrated energies can be allowed to enter. The central position in the temple is occupied by the Buddha or an equivalent figure such as Padmasambhava or Avalokiteśvara, and other positions are occupied by Arhants, Bodhi-sattvas, spiritual teachers, gods and goddesses, all harmoniously grouped around the central figure. Even the nāgas and yakṣas and other non-human beings may have a place. It depends on just one thing: whether they truly worship the Buddha, whether they go for Refuge, whether they place themselves at the service of the Dharma.

One might well ask, of course, how non-human beings like pretas and yakṣas can possibly place themselves at the service of the Dharma. The answer to this lies in what we make of this kind of symbolism. Let's take an example from rather nearer home: the figure of the Greek god Hermes. Who or what is Hermes? We might say that in Greek mythology he is the messenger of the gods, and that might seem like a satisfactory answer, but it is not really an answer at all. If you read up about Hermes it becomes clear that he was a deeply complex figure with all sorts of aspects, some of them apparently quite contradictory. In order to gain even a little idea of who or what Hermes is or was, you have to comb through the available material very carefully. You have to examine all the hundreds of references to Hermes in the *Iliad* and the *Odyssey*, and gradually build up your picture of him. It's simply not enough to say 'Hermes was the messenger of the gods' and leave it at that. That could even be quite misleading, in that it might give people the idea that they know all about him.

It's like that with all the mythological figures mentioned in the *Sūtra of Golden Light*. It is not enough just to say 'The pretas are hungry ghosts – so how can hungry ghosts be put at the service of the Dharma?' You have to study the pretas – who are they? what are they? – and try to get some understanding of what they are really like. Then perhaps you can begin to see how they can be put at the service of the Dharma.

Let's apply this to the case of the nāgas – the dragons or serpents. What might they represent? The protector of the western quarter of the world – that is, *our* quarter – is Virūpākṣa. And Virūpākṣa is the leader of, among other classes of non-human beings, the dragons. But what exactly are these dragons? We mustn't confuse them with our own British dragons, the kind of dragon that was killed by St George. The Buddhist dragon is quite a different kind of creature. According to Buddhist tradition dragons are highly intelligent. They often have a very good understanding of the Dharma, but – and here's the rub – they don't practise it. In particular, they don't observe the precepts. This is perhaps why in Indian Buddhist art dragons are usually represented in serpent form, with big heads, long thin bodies, and no arms or legs. They have no limbs because they don't do anything. They think and understand, but they never practise – they never act upon what they know – so they don't need limbs.

I once read a book written by a Chinese Buddhist monk who in passing made the statement that dragons are not so common nowadays as they used to be. I must say, however, that I don't agree with him. I think that if anything dragons are more common than they used to be, at least in some parts of the world. In the West dragons are very common indeed. Here there are lots of people who understand the Dharma very well, who know all about śūnyatā and Zen, all about the One Mind and the Abhidharma, all about the esoteric Tantric teachings, but who never even think of practising the Dharma. Such dragons – for dragons can take human form – are very common in some Buddhist circles.

In some ways the intellectual dragons of the West are the worst dragons the world has yet seen, because they hardly recognize the authority even of Virūpākṣa. It's as though even that degree of organization has broken down. The nāgas have broken away from Virūpākṣa, and perhaps all the other beings and creatures have broken away from their respective guardian kings too. There's a degree of confusion, a degree of chaos, that has perhaps never existed before. Perhaps the most immediately danger- ous dragon at large today is represented by the scientific community, in so far as its research and development programmes – that is, the direction of its search for knowledge – are unaffected by ethical considerations. For many members of this enormously influential community, it's as though they have sold themselves to the devil for the sake of professional success, material security, and prestige.

As Buddhists, what we need to do is invoke the help of Virūpākṣa, the protector of the western quarter, to bring our dragons under control. We have to bring our own one-sided intellectual activity under control – by being receptive to the golden light and practising the Dharma. In this way we will bring the nāgas within the portals of the temple.

The temple is also a mandala, a harmonious arrangement of psycho- logical, spiritual, and transcendental energies around a common central principle: the principle of Enlightenment. So by bringing the nāgas within the portals of the temple, we are also building the mandala. And the four great kings are also guardians of the four gates of the mandala. They prevent the entry of any hostile force, any unintegrated energy – that is to say, any energy that is not prepared to align itself, on its own level and in its own way, with the principle of Enlightenment. The four great kings are the guardians of the threshold, a function of great impor- tance. On the one hand they have to keep out the hostile unintegrated forces – otherwise the harmony of the mandala would be disrupted. On the other hand, they have to admit the energies which are integrated and ready to be admitted – otherwise the potential richness of the mandala would be impoverished.

Within the Buddhist tradition there are also other beings who guard the gates of the mandala. These are the four *gaurīs*, the 'fair ones'. They are said to stop people leaving the mandala by means of hooks. From a Western point of view this might sound rather violent, but in Buddhism these hooks are associated with fascination. A 'fascinating woman' can be said to 'hook' men not by violence but just by exerting her charm; and a Bodhisattva does the same. The Bodhisattva draws us to Enlightenment with beauty, revealing Enlightenment as the truly beautiful. The gaurī represents that kind of fascination. For your own good you have to be kept within the mandala, but by the very nature of the situation you can't be kept there by force. So the gaurīs would seem to represent the more fascinating aspect of the lokapālas, the aspect that makes you want to stay within the mandala rather than leaving it as you might otherwise be tempted to do.

If, say, the mandala is decorated with flowers and looks very beautiful, even though you may not be spiritually drawn to what the mandala represents, at least you like it in there. It's attractive, it's beautiful – and that helps you to stay. That is the gaurīs at work with their hooks. The spiritual community is also a mandala. Here too the four great kings have a function. Disruptive energies must be kept out, otherwise the spiritual community will be destroyed, but positive, integrated energies must be welcomed, otherwise the spiritual community will not grow.

The fourth and last point to bear in mind about the four great kings is that they are immensely powerful. This characteristic is brought out well in paintings and images, in which the kings are usually depicted as men a little past the middle of life, and powerfully built, often with enormous bulging muscles. In some ways they resemble the Heracles of Greek mythology, but unlike Heracles they are clad in armour. They represent enormously powerful, positive energies, energies which are not very spiritual or refined but at the same time not quite earthly. Such energies are sometimes described as crude, and crude they certainly are in comparison with the more refined energies of the higher planes. But crude energy is not to be despised – it has an essential part to play in the world. The energy represented by the four great kings is not only enormously powerful, but also extremely free and active. It is not blocked or repressed, but always available to keep turbulent earthly energies under control and repel anti-spiritual forces.

It should now be a little more clear who the four great kings really are, and what they really represent. They represent the forces of balance and harmony in the cosmos, especially in the all-important borderland between the human world and the heavenly world, or, if you like, between the psychological and the spiritual. They represent, indeed, the possibility of transition from the one to the other.

We should also now be in a better position to understand the kings' statement that the *Sūtra of Golden Light* nourishes them. Clearly, this statement is not to be understood in an exclusively literal sense. What nourishes them is the golden light, the light of the transcendental. And they *need* that nourishment. We can understand from this that the positive energies of the cosmos, the energies that make for balance and harmony, however powerful they are, will sooner or later pass over into the opposite and become negative if they are not nourished by the transcendental.

This has important implications. On the level of the individual human life it means that there is no such thing as purely *psychological* positivity in the sense of a positivity whose support comes only from a psychological source. There is no such thing, even, as purely *spiritual* positivity. What, after all, is the criterion of what is positive and what is not, what is skilful and what is not? From a Buddhist point of view, the skilful is something that provides a base for the development of a connection with the transcendental. And what in practice provides a base for the development of the transcendental is the positive. So without that reference to the transcendental, how are you going to determine what is genuinely positive? You have no means of ascertaining the difference between the positive and the merely pleasant, between what is genuinely positive and what simply gives personal satisfaction. You just can't be sure that what seems to you to be positive really is positive without that reference to the transcendental.

There is another consideration to take into account here. Suppose you experience a positive mental state in the ordinary psychological sense; if you have at least a concept of the transcendental, and you know that the positive can provide a basis for the transcendental, you then have an incentive to sustain that experience of the positive. One could go so far as to say that without a reference to the transcendental you have no fundamental reason to develop or sustain positivity.

This means in practice that you need to have a personal connection with someone who has had experience of the transcendental. If you can only refer to it as a memory or an ancient tradition, it loses its sustaining power. This is what happened in the Buddha's day in the case of the brahmins. Their ancestors had been knowers of Brahma, had attained to Brahma, but by the Buddha's time the brahmins could refer to no such experience, so they could not sustain the spiritual tradition.

We can look at this in terms of the symbolism of the Tibetan Wheel of Life, in particular that of the realm of the gods. The gods appear to have a very positive experience of life, but unless they have some awareness of the transcendental, their positivity cannot function as a basis for the realization of the transcendental. According to tradition the gods are simply reaping the reward of previous skilful actions. What sustains their positivity is karma. When their positive karma runs out, so to speak, they will fall from their positive state unless from within it they can envisage the transcendental. But if they do have this vision, then it will provide a basis not just for the realization of the transcendental but also for the extension of their positive experience.

If we accept all this, it follows that we cannot be truly human without going for Refuge. We are human by accident, as it were, or just for a short time; we can't sustain our human state without some reference to the transcendental factor. Our reason for creating the fresh positive karma which will sustain a positive state is ultimately a transcendental reason.

Even after a transcendental experience has ceased to be a living thing and is only a memory, the memory continues to exert some influence for a time. But eventually, if there hasn't been a fresh impulse from or experience of the transcendental, all the positive volitions that have depended on that transcendental factor become weaker and weaker. A society can run on the memory of a vision for a while, but not for long. For instance, over the past hundred years or more many people have ceased to believe in Christianity but have continued to live according to Christian ethics because there was still some momentum left in those ethics. In recent times, though, the momentum has slowed down and many people see no reason for continuing to follow Christian ethics.

It is not just that the only true, lasting positivity is that which has its ultimate sanction in the transcendental. Nourished by the transcendental, positivity will be more positive even on its own level than it could possibly have been without it. As the four great kings say, 'In our body there will be produced prowess, strength and energy. Brilliance, glory and splendour will enter our body.' Here 'body' does not mean body as distinct from mind, but the whole personality, the whole being. In other words, nourished by the golden light, the kings will be greater and more kingly than ever, and they will exercise their distinctive functions more effectively than ever. Similarly, one who goes for Refuge will not only develop spiritually but will also become more of a human being. Distinctively human qualities are nourished by the spiritual, nourished by the transcendental. It is almost possible to say that you can't be a human being unless you go for Refuge. Ultimately it is only the Enlightened human being who is the true human being.

On the level of collective human life, there can be no healthy culture or civilization without some basis in transcendental values, however deeply hidden those values may be. A purely secular culture is really a contradiction in terms – though this certainly does not mean that we in the West are flung back into the arms of orthodox Christianity. There are other alternatives.

Having declared that they are nourished by the Dharma, the four great kings make their four vows. The first, their promise to exercise their sovereignty over the different classes of demigods according to the Dharma, means that their rule will not be an expression of arbitrary, egoistic will, but will express spiritual power – not their own power but that of the Dharma. They will simply be the channels through which this power is transmitted, through which it reaches the hordes of non-human beings. And in becoming such channels they will be all the more truly themselves.

The kings' second promise is to protect the whole of Jambudvīpa, which is the known material world, the human world. The four great kings promise to keep out all hostile forces that threaten to disrupt the fabric of a positive, healthy, human society – that is, a society in which it is possible for the individual to develop. At present the services of the four great kings are very badly needed – in fact, their strength is being strained to the utmost, especially in our western quarter, where hostile forces are trying to break in at a number of points.

Their third promise is to protect the monks who read or recite the sūtra and explain its meaning, and to give them their encouragement. Objectively this means that the grosser energies of the cosmos will co-operate with the monks in their work of proclaiming the sūtra. Subjectively it means that the monks themselves will integrate their own grosser psychophysical energies so that they can use them for this purpose. After all, one needs a lot of energy to proclaim the Dharma – not only spiritual energy, but sheer physical stamina. This too the four great kings promise to give.

Fourthly, they promise to protect kings who patronize the monks who proclaim the sūtra. Here 'kings' means governments – social, economic, and political systems that are organized to assist spiritual development. Such 'kings' perform in their respective systems the same function that the four great kings perform in the cosmos at large, and it's only natural, therefore, that the four great kings should protect them. They represent the same spirit on different levels of operation. I will go into this more in the last chapter, which is concerned with the upholders of the moral order.

These four vows, together with the four great kings' commitment to protecting the sūtra, mean that, just as the hordes of non-human beings submit themselves to the four great kings, similarly the kings submit themselves to the golden light. In other words, the earthly energies submit to the heavenly energies, and the heavenly energies submit to the transcendental energies. Thus is the profound principle of spiritual hierarchy introduced. The four great kings, indeed, can even be said to symbolize this principle. They exercise sovereignty over what is below them, while at the same time willingly accepting the sovereignty of what is above them. The kings therefore also represent the principle of world transformation. The world can only be truly transformed if it submits to the golden light, if it is receptive to the golden light – that is, if it organizes itself in such a way as to assist the manifestation of the golden light in the life of the individual.

Having come so far, it is worth exploring in what sense the four great kings can be said to exist. The question hangs, of course, on what one might mean by 'exist'. I have to say that when I was studying this section of the sūtra I had the sense that the kings were gathered around me, not so much as separate entities, but more like four clouds joined together. I certainly didn't have the impression that my experience of them was purely subjective. I felt that they did exist in some objective sense, though obviously I can offer no proof of that.

It is perhaps not too far-fetched to think of the four great kings as representing forces of balance and harmony in the cosmos, and as such having a real influence on the world. It does seem to be the case that there is a principle of balance at work in nature, even in the human body. When it becomes ill, the healthy organism has a natural tendency to compensate and heal itself. If an imbalance in the environment is brought about, perhaps by a man-made disaster, there also nature seems to have a tendency to put itself right. Perhaps the four great kings represent that tendency writ large in nature as a whole. They are not separate from nature; they are a part of it, although they do have distinct personalities. They are not standing outside nature and interfering with it like a mechanic tinkering with a car.

There are no obvious counterparts to the four great kings in Western mythology, although King Arthur perhaps comes close. If we disregard the specifically Christian aspects of his mythology, he can still be seen as a king fighting with the forces of evil, like the four great kings. Of course, King Arthur is defeated in the end, which the four great kings never are, apparently, so perhaps he doesn't quite do. Another parallel might possibly be drawn with St George, who is at least a legendary figure, in that he doesn't seem to have had a historical existence at all, except in the same kind of remote sense as King Arthur. And then there's the archangel Michael, who is traditionally depicted as fighting with devils.

The only way to invoke the power of the four great kings is to think about them or concentrate on them. My own experience of their presence no doubt happened because I was concentrating intensely on them. They may have mantras – and the Vajrayāna has pujas that include the making of offerings to them – but such practices would only help to invoke them to the degree that one was concentrated and absorbed in the thought of them. The explicit practices would only help one to become concentrated on that basis.

This means that you would have to be *interested* in the four great kings. If you thought of them as no more than a bit of outmoded Tibetan mythology, you certainly wouldn't be able to invoke them. You have to have some feeling for them, just as for any other mythological figure. If you absorbed yourself in material dealing with Hermes you would have a sort of experience of Hermes. It's the same with any archetypal figure, because they all correspond to something in the human psyche. You can contact them through that aspect of the psyche which corresponds to them, but first you have to activate it.

It is not only the four great kings who come forward and promise to protect the sūtra. In subsequent chapters, other deities come forward and make similar promises. In particular, three goddesses promise to protect the sūtra: Sarasvatī, the goddess of learning, Śrī, the goddess of wealth, and Dṛḍhā, the earth goddess. The promises of the four great kings represent the general principle of the transformation of the world through submission to the golden light, whilst the promises of the three goddesses represent the working out of that principle in different spheres of human life and activity. What those spheres are, and how that principle works out in them, we shall see in the course of the next three chapters.

If we submit to the golden light, we will be able to transform our own life, our own self, and also co-operate in the transformation of the world. And if we do that, in our own small sphere we too shall be one of the protectors of the Dharma.

4

BUDDHISM AND CULTURE

THE WORLD IS TRANSFORMED when it becomes wholly receptive to the golden light. And by 'the world' in this context I mean the sum total of unenlightened human activities. Agriculture, commerce, the arts, the sciences, medicine, law, government, administration, diplomacy, transport, communication, advertising, entertainment, sport ... together all these things make up the world. And they become receptive to the golden light by placing themselves at the service of the spiritual development of the individual. This may of course mean that they have to recognize that they cannot be of any service whatsoever to the individual in his or her spiritual development. In that case they must just quietly abolish themselves – that is the best service they can render.

When all the different activities that make up the world have placed themselves at the service of the spiritual development of the individual, the world will be transformed by the golden light. It will be a world 'fit for individuals to live in', a world that will help individuals to grow.

Of course, to say that all the activities that make up the world should place themselves at the service of the spiritual development of the individual is only a manner of speaking. After all, those activities don't carry on of their own accord; they are carried on by people. It is therefore people who must place themselves at the service of the spiritual development of the individual. Only then will the world be transformed. And the vast majority of people have, of course, no intention of doing anything of the sort. They are going to carry on with their particular activities with no reference whatsoever to the golden light and the spiritual development of the individual.

But this does not mean that nothing can be done. The difficulty can be overcome; the world can still be transformed. It can be transformed through teams of spiritually committed individuals taking up different human activities and orienting them in the direction of the golden light in such a way that they conduce to the spiritual development both of those who carry out the activities and those who come into contact with them.

Through becoming involved with as many of these activities as possible, people committed to spiritual development can bring into existence a world within a world. A transformed world within the untransformed world can be brought into being – and gradually expanded.

In exploring the role of the four great kings, we have encountered the general principle of world transformation. We have seen that the world can be transformed only if it becomes receptive to the golden light. From now onwards we shall be concerned with the transformation of specific aspects of the world: culture, the environment, economics, and even politics. The first three of these are represented in the sūtra by three goddesses – Sarasvatī, Śrī, and Dṛḍhā – each of whom come forward and promise to protect the sūtra, thereby placing the department of human activity that they represent at the service of the development of the individual.

The first of these great goddesses to step forward is Sarasvatī. At the beginning of chapter 7 she comes forward, salutes the Buddha, and makes a number of promises relating to the monk who preaches the *Sūtra of Golden Light*. We'll come to what these promises are, but first, who is Sarasvatī?

This is a question we wouldn't have any trouble answering if we happened to be in India, especially if we happened to be there during the five or six weeks after the end of the rainy season. In many parts of India this particular period is known as the 'pujas', and it's so called because at this time a whole series of Hindu religious festivals and celebrations in honour of various Hindu gods and goddesses is held. It's a very festive season: everybody is happy and cheerful, and more friendly than usual. The sky is blue, the sun shines, a gentle breeze blows – it's the most enjoyable season of the whole year. People often take a holiday from work because they just don't feel like working. They buy new clothes, they go to see their friends and relations, they exchange presents, and of course they go, usually in the evening, to worship the various gods and goddesses. In some parts of India, for instance in Bengal, special images are made just for the puja season and installed in temporary shrines in places accessible to the public. In India people go to the puja rather as in England they go to football matches or bingo, and they go in their tens or even hundreds of thousands. On the occasions of very special festivities, some of which come around only every ten or twelve years, they even go in their millions.

And one of the most popular of the gods and goddesses worshipped in the puja season is Sarasvatī. The images made of her are usually of clay, and life-size, sometimes even a little larger than life, and beautifully painted and decorated. The goddess is depicted as a beautiful young woman with long flowing tresses, wearing a brocade Benares sari, usually red with a golden border. She is seated on a white *haṁsa*. Usually *haṁsa* is translated as 'swan' but actually it's a goose. Indian cultural associations with geese are quite different from Western ones; in India the goose is a beautiful, elegant bird that conjures up all sorts of religious associations. So Sarasvatī is seated on a white goose, and she holds a veena – an Indian musical instrument something like a lute – in her lap.

In India different deities are particularly worshipped by different classes of people. Businessmen, merchants, traders, and shopkeepers worship Ganesha, the elephant-headed god who removes obstacles, and Lakshmī, the goddess of wealth. Those who go in for physical training – athletes, musclemen, and weightlifters – worship Hanuman, the monkey god, the great devotee of Rama, who is renowned for his physical strength, energy, and enterprise. Women and girls, on the other hand, are particularly fond of Krishna, not so much because he preached the *Bhagavad Gītā* as because he dances at night in the forest with the gopīs – the cow-girls, or, more poetically, the milkmaids.

Sarasvatī is worshipped in particular by the students. On the eve of her festival her altar is piled high with exercise books and textbooks, pens and pencils, even india rubbers. In making these offerings the students are invoking Sarasvatī's blessing, and asking for her help in passing the forthcoming examinations, which follow rather too quickly for comfort on the pujas. Sarasvatī is the object of the students' devotion because she is goddess of learning, of education – in a word, of culture.

The name Sarasvatī does not give us any clue as to her actual function. It means 'abounding in water', sometimes translated even as 'watery'.

This is because it is the name, as one might guess, of a river, a river in north-western India. So how did a river come to be transformed into a goddess of learning and culture? As is usually the case in India, this is a very long story. It goes back several thousand years, to the time when the Aryans invaded India. No one really knows where they came from, but they entered India from the north-west, with their horses and chariots, and gradually subdued the original inhabitants of the land. And with these invaders came not only their warriors and rulers, but also their priests, the famous brahmins.

By this time the brahmins had developed an elaborate system of ritual and sacrifices. There were sacrifices for every conceivable purpose, every conceivable occasion, and these sacrifices were often performed on the banks of a river. In those days there were no temples. Everything was done in the open air. Being smooth and sandy, with a flat surface for the construction of the altar, a river bank was the ideal place for a sacrifice, and it provided plenty of water for the ritual ablutions to which the brahmins attached great importance. Moreover, on the banks of the river, perhaps far from human habitation, there was seclusion, there was peace and quiet. The banks of the Sarasvatī were particularly favoured for the celebration of these Vedic sacrifices, so much so that an association grew up between this river and the whole sacrificial system.

A great deal of brahminical culture was based on the sacrificial system, or grew out of it. For example, in the course of the sacrifices, the famous Vedic hymns were recited. These were often of great poetic beauty. There were hymns to the sun and the moon, hymns to the dawn and the winds. There were hymns to the thunder-god Indra, to the heavenly twins and the heavenly horses, and so on. These hymns, which are often very glorious in their language and conception, represent the beginnings of Indian literature. Some may have been composed even before the Aryans entered India. Their language is very archaic, so much so that even by the time they arrived in India it had become quite difficult to understand. This prompted the brahmins to develop a whole science of etymology called *nirukti*, along with grammar, phonetics, and prosody. The hymns were often chanted to special tunes, so here we have the beginnings of a certain kind of music. Moreover, the altars used in connection with the brahminical sacrifices were very elaborate. They had to be constructed in a certain way, of a certain size and shape – in one case like an eagle with outstretched wings – and even of a certain number of bricks. These exact specifications led, so it is said, to the development of arithmetic and geometry.

So it is safe to say that a great deal of Indian culture – even high Indian culture – was associated with the sacrificial system, and in particular with the banks of the Sarasvatī. By this time the river had 'become' a goddess in her own right. Like all ancient peoples the ancient Indians identified natural features such as rivers, mountains, and lakes, the sun and the moon, and the earth itself as deities. They saw them, even experienced them, as gods and goddesses. And quite early in Indian cultural history there appears a river goddess called Sarasvatī who is particularly associated with culture.

But the process of development did not stop there. In the Vedas there are several hymns to an ancient and rather shadowy goddess called Vāc. Vāc means 'speech' – not ordinary speech, but speech in the sense of powerful, significant, even creative speech – and incidentally, the fact that the ancient Indians made a goddess out of speech and addressed hymns to her shows that they realized the great importance of human communication. Anyway, in the course of centuries Sarasvatī gradually assumed the attributes of Vāc, so that in a manner of speaking Vāc became absorbed in the goddess Sarasvatī.

It is important to note that Vāc represented speech, the *spoken* word. As yet there was no such thing as writing in India, at least not for religious purposes. Writing was something profane, fit only for keeping records of accounts and so on. Thus the culture of which Sarasvatī became a personification was an orally transmitted culture, with teachings handed down from teacher to pupil by word of mouth. In such a culture memory is of tremendous importance. If someone's memory fails, knowledge that is of lasting value to the community may be lost. Sarasvatī therefore also became associated with good memory. We can draw a parallel here with the nine muses of ancient Greek mythology. The muses are the personification of various arts and sciences, the companions – some accounts say the daughters – of Apollo, the god of poetry, music, and prophecy. And the mother of the muses is Mnemosyne, whose name means 'memory'. Memory, in other words, is the mother of all the arts and sciences; in all pre-literate societies there is no culture without memory.

Of course in India the oral traditions were eventually written down, and when this happened, Sarasvatī became not just a goddess of the spoken word, but also a goddess of literature and scholarship. She also began to be regarded as the wife of the god Brahma. Brahma is one of the *trimūrti*, the three principal embodiments of the divine, in Puranic Hinduism: Brahma the Creator, Vishnu the Preserver, and Shiva the Destroyer.

This then is the Sarasvatī who is still worshipped in India today, more than a thousand years after all these developments took place. She is the goddess of education and culture, the embodiment of communication, the personification of memory, the patroness of literature, both sacred and profane, and the wife of the god Brahma, the Creator. It is therefore quite interesting that her appearance in chapter 6 of the sūtra is the first time she appears in Indian literature.

The question is, what is she doing there? She is clearly a Hindu goddess. What is a Hindu goddess doing in a Mahāyāna Buddhist sūtra? How does she come to be there? In chapter 3 we found a brahmin appearing in Ruciraketu's dream. Now here we have a Hindu goddess playing an even more important part in the sūtra. What does this mean?

The first thing to remember is that Hinduism is not a universal religion like Buddhism or Christianity or Islam, but an ethnic one like Judaism or Shinto. It is the sum total of the beliefs and practices of the Indian people over a period of three thousand years. Whilst there are some aspects of Hinduism that are concerned with the spiritual development of the individual, on the whole, like other ethnic religions, Hinduism is much more concerned with the preservation of the group. Sarasvatī therefore represents the cultural heritage of the social group – that is, she represents Indian culture.

But what is 'culture'? It's quite an interesting word. In English its primary meaning is tillage, rearing, production, as in agriculture, horticulture, floriculture, and so on. It then has its applied or derived meanings – as in physical culture, mental culture – so that in the end the word comes to mean something like 'development'. We have the cultured person or cultivated person – that is to say, the person who is developed in an all-round manner: physically, mentally, emotionally, and morally.

The Sanskrit equivalent of the English word 'culture' conveys much the same meaning, but with an interesting difference of emphasis. It is *saṃskṛti*, which means 'the perfected' and is contrasted with *prakṛti*, 'the natural'. *Saṃskṛti*, in other words, is the product of human art, while *prakṛti* is the product of nature. We find this difference reflected in the sphere of language. The ancient Indian classical language Sanskrit is the perfected form of language – language which has been regularized, polished, refined – whilst the language Prakrit is the natural form of language, the vernacular. Sanskrit is spoken by educated, cultured people, whilst Prakrit is spoken by the uneducated, by the masses. We can see this difference at work in certain classical Indian dramas. The leading characters speak Sanskrit, whilst the other characters, including servants and women, speak Prakrit.

Students of the history of Buddhism may wonder how it was that Buddhist scriptures came to be written down in the polished, cultured Sanskrit rather than the vernacular Prakrit. After all, didn't the Buddha expressly forbid the monks to teach the Dharma in Sanskrit, asking them instead to teach it in the everyday language of ordinary people? Well, the Buddha did say something like that, but the word he used was not *saṁskṛt* but *chandas*. This was what is known as 'Vedic Sanskrit', the language in which the Vedas were composed. It was originally the language spoken by the Aryans, but by the time of the Buddha it was a 'dead' language, as Latin, for example, is today. The Buddha did not want his words to be translated into what was for most people a dead language; he preferred that the Dharma should be available to people in their own language, whatever that was.

Once a religious tradition is embodied in a particular form of language, it tends to remain embodied in that form, due to religious conservatism – religion is always conservative, it would seem. Meanwhile, the ordinary spoken language goes on changing, so that eventually a difference develops between the language of sacred texts, whether oral or written down, and the ordinary, everyday language. And this is what happened in the case of Vedic Sanskrit. The Vedas existed in that particular archaic form of the language that couldn't be changed due to the sacredness of the Vedas, but language went on changing. That was how Sanskrit and Prakrit developed, the two being basically the same language – one in a more refined, the other in a less refined, form.

By the time the Mahāyāna sūtras came to be written down, Sanskrit – not Vedic Sanskrit but classical Sanskrit – had become a sort of lingua franca that was much more widely understood than Vedic Sanskrit had been in the Buddha's time. The Mahāyāna sūtras were written down in Sanskrit simply because it was the language that was most widely understood. There was no departure from principle; the idea throughout was to make the Buddha's teaching accessible to as many people as possible.

The fact that the Buddhist scriptures were translated into Sanskrit didn't mean that they were accessible only to 'educated' people. As I have said, in dramas the more upper class characters spoke Sanskrit whilst the servants spoke Prakrit, but they could all understand one another. It's a bit like the difference between standard English and broad Cockney, except that Prakrit was also a literary medium – the Jains, for instance, used Prakrit quite extensively.

All this is perhaps a little beside the point but it does put us in a better position to understand the significance of Sarasvatī's appearance in the *Sūtra of Golden Light*. As we have seen, she represents the culture of the group – specifically Indian culture – but she also represents what that culture itself represents, what *saṁskṛti* represents. She represents human nature in its more developed state, human activities in their more polished and refined forms. We could even say that she represents the cultivated person, the cultivated mind.

I introduced Sarasvatī's appearance in the *Sūtra of Golden Light* by saying that she promises to protect the sūtra, but this is not, strictly speaking, quite correct. What she actually promises to protect is the monk who preaches the sūtra, who communicates the golden light of the Dharma. And the Dharma – what we call 'Buddhism' – is not an ethnic religion but a universal one, a spiritual teaching addressed to the individual, or the person who is trying to become an individual. The golden light is the light of the transcendental, the light of Truth, the light of Reality, the light of the Buddha.

For this golden light to be communicated, a language, a medium of communication, is needed, not only literally but metaphorically. And that medium of communication has to fulfil two requirements. First of all, obviously enough, it has to be common to both parties. The monk who is preaching the sūtra and those to whom he is preaching it have to speak the same language. And secondly, that language has to be sufficiently refined, sufficiently transparent, to communicate at least something of the splendour of the golden light.

The preacher of the Dharma in the *Sūtra of Golden Light* is trying to communicate the golden light to the people of India, and he therefore has to speak the language of Indian culture. Only the language of culture is sufficiently refined to act as the medium of communication for the golden light, and only the language of Indian culture is familiar enough to be intelligible. So this is what the appearance of the great goddess Sarasvatī represents. She stands for the coming together of universal and ethnic religion, the coming together of Buddhism and Indian culture. More specifically, she stands for the coming together of the spiritual ideals of the Mahāyāna and the rich and vital culture of the Indian Gupta period, the period that also produced some of the most distinguished Buddhist art.

Furthermore, in promising to protect the monk who teaches the Dharma, she shows how ethnic culture places itself at the service of universal religion. Although we encounter it here in unusually dramatic form, this is by no means a unique situation. Universal religion, in fact, always speaks the language of ethnic culture, at least to begin with. To begin with, in a sense, there is no other language for it to speak. The Buddha himself spoke the cultural language, or rather languages, of his day. At that time there seem to have been two languages: the language of the Brahmanas and the language of the Śramaṇas; the Vedic language and the non-Vedic or even anti-Vedic language; perhaps even an Aryan language and a non-Aryan language.

As we saw in the last chapter, the *Sūtra of Golden Light* speaks the language of Indian cosmology and mythology. It speaks of rings of golden mountains and circular oceans, gods and goddesses, and various classes of non-human beings. But, of course, Buddhism did not stay confined to India, and as it spread throughout Asia it came into contact with other ethnic cultures, especially with those of Central Asia, China, Japan, and Tibet, and these cultures also placed themselves at the service of the Dharma. Buddhism gradually learned to express itself in terms of Chinese culture, Japanese culture, and so on.

Now the Dharma has come to the West. Individuals of Western origin are coming into contact with the golden light, and even wanting to communicate it to other Westerners. And to do this they have to express themselves in terms of Western culture. Buddhism has to learn the language of Western culture. This raises a number of interesting questions. Can Buddhism be separated from Eastern culture? Is an acquaintance with Eastern culture essential for the understanding of Buddhism, or can Western culture place itself at the service of Buddhism? What *is* Western culture? Can the Dharma be taught without the medium of culture altogether? Before we can answer all these questions, we need to take a more detailed look at chapter 6 of the sūtra.

By virtue of its miscellaneous character – miscellaneous even for such a transcendental rag-bag as the *Sūtra of Golden Light* – the sixth chapter is representative of the kind of material that a late Mahāyāna sūtra often includes, even though it is quite a short chapter, no longer than four pages in the English translation. It opens with Sarasvatī saluting the Buddha, and then making various promises. She promises to bestow upon the monk who preaches the Dharma five gifts or blessings.

First of all, Sarasvatī promises to bestow eloquence 'for the sake of adorning the speech of the monk who preaches the Law'. The monk is likely to be a follower of the Mahāyāna, an aspirant to the Bodhisattva ideal, and he is naturally going to want to share the Buddha's teaching with as many people as possible. And this is going to mean that he must be able to put it across effectively. He needs the power of communication, he needs eloquence, and this is what Sarasvatī gives him. This eloquence is not a matter of textbook rhetoric, not a matter of the tricks of the trade of the professional after-dinner speaker. It is finding easy, natural expression for the genuine feelings of the heart in appropriate thoughts, words, and images.

Secondly, Sarasvatī promises to bestow a good memory. This is clearly necessary for a preacher of the Dharma. There are references in the sūtra to its being written down, but memorizing it is still considered to be important, even today in some parts of the Buddhist world. I remember one of my own Tibetan teachers telling me how many pages of scripture he had to memorize each day when he was a novice monk of seven years old. The method of preaching the Dharma in ancient India was rather like a sort of public seminar. The custom was for the monk to recite a few lines of the sūtra or other text, and then give his own detailed explanation, perhaps with illustrative stories. In this manner he would make his way through the whole sūtra from beginning to end. He might be reciting it and discoursing on it every day for several hours, and in the case of the longer sūtras this might go on for several months. Clearly a good memory was needed, and this is what Sarasvatī promises to bestow.

Thirdly, she promises to arrange the substance of the monk's speech so that it is well spoken. The content of Mahāyāna sūtras is frequently not only very difficult, but also very disorganized. It is all mixed up and disconnected, even confused. If he is not careful, the monk may get lost, as it were, in the impenetrable jungle of the sūtra, may not perceive its real message. This is certainly the case with the *Sūtra of Golden Light*. It may not be one of the most difficult of the Mahāyāna sūtras as regards content, but it is certainly one of the least well arranged, at least in conventional literary terms. So here too Sarasvatī lends a hand, helping the monk to expound the sūtra in orderly, systematic fashion.

To be able to expound the sūtra in this fashion, the monk must obviously have an understanding of it, and this is Sarasvatī's fourth gift: great illumination and knowledge. It is not enough for the monk to be able to recite the words of the sūtra; he must be able to penetrate its meaning. He must himself be in touch with the golden light, even at one with it. The golden light must shine through him. When he speaks, it must be the golden light speaking – otherwise the *Sūtra of Golden Light* is not truly preached. So the goddess promises to bestow great illumination and knowledge. At this point it becomes clear that she does not represent any merely external agency, because no external agency can give illumination and knowledge. Sarasvatī really represents the monk's own cultured, cultivated consciousness, and the refined, powerful emotions associated with that consciousness, emotions which have now become integrated with the spiritual life and which therefore contribute to the realization of the transcendental.

Fifthly and lastly, Sarasvatī promises to bestow a *dhāraṇī*. A *dhāraṇī* is a sort of magical spell. It is something to be borne in mind, something to be recited. The word comes from the same root as the word Dharma, from the root *dhṛ*, which means 'that which supports or upholds'. The *Sūtra of Golden Light*, as we have already seen, is a late sūtra. It was written down in the fourth to eighth centuries CE, and at that time the Mahāyāna was being superseded as it were by the Vajrayāna, or rather by the Mantra-yāna, which was the early phase of the Vajrayāna.[63] The goddess's prom-ise of a *dhāraṇī* therefore represents the irruption of the Vajrayāna into the Mahāyāna, or the Mantrayāna into the Pāramitāyāna. It suggests that the preacher of the Dharma needs in his work the special quality associated with the Vajrayāna. He needs something magical, something transcend-entally charismatic. He needs to be a kind of Padmasambhava figure; otherwise it is very difficult for him to succeed in his task.

Immediately after Sarasvatī's promises there comes a very curious, indeed a very ethnic passage, which is concerned, believe it or not, with popular magic. Sarasvatī explains how the monk who preaches the Dharma should take a kind of ritual herb bath. The preparation of the bath involves grinding more than thirty different herbs and resins into powder – when a certain constellation is in the ascendant – and then consecrating them one hundred times with a magic spell. Brahminical ideas of ritual purification are clearly reflected here. What we have in this passage, in fact, it seems to me, is a lump of ethnic culture that the sūtra has not been able fully to digest.

Examples like this one give us evidence of the way the Mahāyāna absorbed elements of ethnic culture as a skilful means to help communi-cate the Dharma. A lot of our emotions, including our more refined emotions, are bound up with ethnic culture. As a teacher of Buddhism, one wants to encourage people to integrate these emotions into their practice of the Dharma, and one can do this by absorbing into one's presentation of the Dharma those elements with which people's emo-tions are tied up. The instance of the herb bath is clearly a case in which the attempt at skilful means doesn't quite work, to the extent that it becomes an unskilful avenue for the infiltration of Hinduism into Buddhism. In such 'undigested lumps' of ethnic culture we can perhaps see the beginning of the end of the Mahāyāna in India. But the principle, or the rationale, behind the incorporation of culture into the Dharma is still valid. It is to engage the emotions fully so that one can live the spiritual life wholeheartedly.

It is not possible, however, to incorporate *all* the emotions in this way. Some emotions are already quite refined, whilst others, although positive, are very crude. When, for instance, one appreciates a work of fine art, refined emotions are brought into play; whereas if one goes to watch a football match, although the emotions involved are positive ones, they will definitely be of a cruder nature. Only the more refined emotions can be absorbed into one's spiritual life, because only they have been developed to a point where it is possible for them to be absorbed. You can't really, therefore, absorb into the Dharma ethnic elements with which quite crude emotions are associated.

Take, for example, a social event like a party, say a birthday party. People may be very merry – especially if the wine is flowing – and all sorts of emotions will arise. Such an occasion is a sort of ethnic celebration, and it might be quite a positive one, but one can hardly imagine having a party of that sort as an integral part of, say, Wesak, the festival at which we celebrate the Enlightenment of the Buddha. It would be spiritually indigestible, so to speak. Even if it was nominally a part of the Wesak celebration, it would really disrupt things. But an art exhibition or a concert of music could certainly be absorbed into a Wesak celebration if it was in harmony with the spirit of the occasion.

Of course, in absorbing elements of ethnic culture to help communicate the Dharma, at the same time one subtly transforms them. The problem with the ritual herb bath prescribed in the *Sūtra of Golden Light* is that this transformation has somehow not happened. Perhaps it was incorporated in too much of a hurry for it to be properly absorbed.

Sarasvatī goes on to describe how she herself should be worshipped. First of all, one should make a magic circle with cow-dung. A very Indian thing, this cow-dung. Their associations as far as cow-dung is concerned are very different from ours. In India cow-dung is a very holy, sacred thing. So then, having made the magic circle, one should strew it with flowers, and place within it a gold vessel and a silver vessel filled with sweet juice. One should also place within the mandala – for this is what it is, virtually – four men clad in armour. This is all the text says: four men clad in armour. It may be a reference to the four great kings, but the text isn't giving us any clues. We hear little more about the four beautifully adorned maidens who are also, according to the text, to be placed within the circle – except that they are bearing pots. They may perhaps be reminiscent of the offering goddesses, but the text doesn't say so. Various other directions are also given – for example, that the image of Sarasvatī is to be decorated with umbrellas. Again Indian associations as far as umbrellas are concerned are different from Western ones, suggesting royalty, supremacy, triumph, victory – not just a rainy day. Flags and banners are to be raised; more spells are to be recited. Finally the goddess promises that she herself will be present at the ritual herb bath, and will remove diseases, quarrels, bad dreams, and evil spirits.

All this may seem rather a long way from the golden light. However, Sarasvatī concludes by saying that all that she has said is for the sake of the monks and nuns, laymen and laywomen who preserve and perpetuate the chief sūtras, so that they may gain Enlightenment. The Buddha congratulates Sarasvatī and praises her for her words concerning spells and medicaments.

Then it is the turn to speak of the brahmin Kaundinya, whom we have already met in chapter 2. He says:

> Sarasvatī, the great goddess, is worthy of worship, possesses great asceticism, famous in all worlds, a giver of boons, of great virtues.

He then goes on to describe what seems to be a very archaic form of the goddess.

> Dwelling on a peak, beautiful, clad in a grass garment, wearing grass clothing, she stands on one foot.[64]

After this, Kaundinya goes on to give us another, rather different description of her. First he tells us of an occasion on which all the gods assembled and asked the goddess to speak. In reply, she recited a long spell followed by a prayer that one's knowledge might prosper 'in such as textbooks, verses, magic books, doctrinal books, poems'. Then, when he has recounted the goddess's words, Kaundinya goes on to praise Sarasvatī in a beautiful hymn which closes the chapter. Here is the prose translation of the Sanskrit verse hymn, which gives a good description of Sarasvatī in a fully developed Puranic form.

> May all the hordes of Bhūtas hear me. I will praise the goddess, whose face is supremely, extremely beautiful, who among women in

the world of gods, Gandharvas, and lords of Asuras, is the supreme, chief, excellent goddess. Sarasvatī by name has members that have piles of adornments of various virtues. Her eyes are broad. She is brilliant in merit. She is full of the virtues of pure knowledge. She is beautiful like a variety of jewels. I will praise her by reason of her distinguished virtues of excellent speech, because she causes excellent, supreme success, because of her famous teaching, because she is a mine of virtues, because she is pure and supreme, because she is brilliant as a lotus, because her eyes are fair and excellent, because her residence is beautiful, because her appearance is beautiful, because she is thoroughly adorned with inconceivable virtues, because she resembles the moon, because her splendour is pure, because she is a mine of knowledge, because of the superiority of her mindfulness, because she is the best of lionesses, because she is a vehicle for men, because she is adorned with eight arms, because her appearance is like that of the full moon, because of her heartening speech, because of her soft voice, because she is endowed with profound wisdom, because she causes the accomplishment of the best deeds, because she is an excellent being, because she is honoured by the lords of gods and Asuras, because she is praised in all the dwellings of a multitude of gods and Asuras, because she is continually worshipped in the abode of a multitude of Bhūtas.[65]

So if this is Sarasvatī in a fully developed Puranic form, what are we to make of the preceding, clearly more archaic, description? Let's return to the first description of the goddess – that she stands on a peak, on one foot, clad in grass clothing. What can all this possibly mean? Clearly there is some connection with the sacrificial system, or at least with the culture that grew out of that system. But why is the goddess said to dwell on a peak? What is the meaning of her standing on one foot? No doubt there is a meaning, but I must confess that I haven't been able to find it out. I suspect it would require a good deal of research into ancient Indian symbolism, especially Vedic symbolism. Meanwhile, your guess is as good as mine.

The wearing of grass clothing is more explicable. Grass, especially kuśa grass and dūrvā grass, plays an important part in Brahminical ritual, and it is still widely used in India for religious purposes. Sarasvatī's grass clothing thus shows that there is a definite connection between, on the one hand, this very archaic form of the goddess and, on the other, the brahminical sacrificial system, the culture associated with it, and all that represents. Indeed, the mere mention of these sacred grasses sparks off all sorts of associations in the Indian, especially the orthodox Hindu, mind. Not being familiar with that cultural language, however, the thought of kuśa grass is going to leave us cold. So let's consider a parallel example from our own culture.

Take, say, mistletoe. What association does mistletoe spark off in our minds? First of all, of course, we are likely to think of Christmas, and what tradition dictates should happen under the mistletoe! But then we may think of the ancient Druids, of oak trees, golden sickles, human sacrifice. We may think of Stonehenge – wrongly, as it happens, because Stonehenge had nothing to do with the Druids. We may think of eisteddfods, Wales, devolution, Welsh dragons, bards, Thomas Gray's ode 'The Bard', Edward I.... For us mistletoe may have all these associations, and many more.

For Indian people it is just the same with kuśa grass and dūrvā grass. These sacred grasses spark off associations with sacrifices, brahmins, ancient sages, rishis with long white beards and sacred threads, asceticism, the hermit life, getting away from it all, Vālmīki, the Ramayāna, the gods, the Vedas, the Sanskrit language. For the orthodox Hindu, sacred grass will spark off all these associations, and many more. And all these associations are bound up with certain very deep emotions. So the fact that Sarasvatī is described as wearing grass clothing not only sparks off associations. It also brings into the sūtra the emotions bound up with those associations, and places them at the service of the spiritual development of the individual – at the service, that is, of the golden light. It is therefore of great importance to find what we may call cultural equivalence, to find symbols and images that really speak to us. It is vital that Buddhism should speak the cultural language of the people it is trying to reach.

This brings us back to our questions about the relation between Buddhism and culture, especially Buddhism and Western culture. First, can Buddhism be separated from Eastern culture? Well, not only can it be separated; it *must* be separated, or at least distinguished. Buddhism is not Eastern culture, however beautiful Eastern culture may be. Buddhism is not culture at all. The Dharma is not culture. The golden light is not culture. Culture is only the medium. Unfortunately, many Eastern Buddhists, including those who come to the West hoping to teach, do not understand this. Sometimes they think they are preaching the Dharma when they are only propagating their own national culture, and this causes great confusion in the minds of at least some Western Buddhists.

Second question: Is an acquaintance with Eastern culture necessary to the understanding of Buddhism? Yes and no. Historically Buddhism has found expression in terms of Eastern culture, and if we want to approach the Dharma we therefore need to have some acquaintance with Eastern culture, at least to begin with. In the *Sūtra of Golden Light*, for example, the Dharma is expressed very much in terms of Indian culture, so that unless one has some understanding of Indian culture, the message of the sūtra remains more or less inaccessible. An acquaintance with Eastern culture can be dispensed with only if one is in personal contact with a spiritual teacher who does not have to rely on Eastern culture as a medium of communication.

There is, I think, very little purely 'Buddhist' culture. In my view there are very few cultural forms or artefacts which can be said purely to express the spirit of Buddhism. Just because something is labelled 'Buddhist' does not mean that you can call it an expression or even a part of Buddhist culture. At the same time you need, generally speaking, a cultural context of some kind for the practice of Buddhism. So, although a Western Buddhist practising in the West does not have to adopt Eastern culture in principle, until Western Buddhist cultural equivalents have emerged we shall have to use or adapt some elements of Eastern Buddhist culture, for instance in such matters as robes, style of chanting, and iconography. In the East it is probably best for the Western Buddhist to conform completely to the local Buddhist culture – whilst being careful not to mistake that culture for the Dharma. However, it is becoming less and less necessary for the Western Buddhist to go East at all. Now we have everything we need at home.

Third question – and this is quite a complex one: how can Western culture place itself at the service of Buddhism? Western Buddhists can at least make a start by establishing points of contact with great artists, and other great Western creative figures, who, at least at times and to a limited extent, have made some approach to the Dharma: people like Goethe, Schopenhauer, Nietzsche, Blake, Wordsworth, and even D.H. Lawrence. I certainly hope that one day a Western Buddhist culture will be developed, and there are signs that beginnings are being made. But you can only really hope to create a Western Buddhist culture if you are deeply imbued with the spirit of Buddhism. In a sense, Buddhism comes first and Buddhist culture follows. However, it can work the other way round as well. Involvement with culture in the best sense helps to refine the emotions, and the refinement of the emotions is important, even essential, for one's spiritual development as an individual. The practice of Buddhism and the development of Buddhist culture must go together.

It is possible for the Dharma to be taught without the medium of culture, but only within the context of a close and intense spiritual relationship between teacher and disciple. This whole question of Buddhism and culture is therefore a very important one. Culture occupies a very important place in our lives, even a very important place in our spiritual development. I can't help wishing that we could have a celebration that would symbolize for us the integration of cultural activity into spiritual life – a Sarasvatī puja of our own, or, even better, a Mañjughoṣa puja.[66] Sarasvatī, after all, represents ethnic culture, but Mañjughoṣa is more universal. He is found all over the Mahāyāna Buddhist world – he was very popular in China and Tibet – and he could perhaps become just as popular in the West. Mañjughoṣa symbolizes the profoundest Wisdom expressed in terms of the most highly developed, most refined culture. He is usually depicted as a beautiful young prince, golden yellow in colour. He sits cross-legged on a blue lotus throne, and wears a head-dress of five full-blown blue lotus flowers. In his right hand, which is raised aloft, he wields a flaming sword, the sword of Wisdom, and in his left hand is a book which he holds against his heart. His expression is compassionate and smiling, and the whole figure radiates brilliant golden light.

In popular Tantric Buddhism, certain branches of which had at one time a mania for finding consorts for all archetypal figures, even the Buddha, an effort was made to regard Sarasvatī as the consort of Mañjughoṣa. Of course, in some ways it would be very natural and appropriate to regard Sarasvatī as the consort of Mañjughoṣa: the symbolism would refer to ethnic culture (represented by Sarasvatī) as being receptive to universal culture (represented by Mañjughoṣa). It ties up very neatly. But I am rather unwilling to give any prominence to *yab-yum* forms – these conjoint male-female Buddha or Bodhisattva forms – because people in the West have a tendency to take them as justifying a romanticization, not to say glorification, of the ordinary sexual couple, the neurotically dependent male and female human being. To most people, an image of male and female Bodhisattvas together communicates the message that it is not just OK but even of spiritual benefit to have a spouse. They may think that as husband and wife, or boyfriend and girlfriend, they somehow exemplify the wisdom and compassion of the Buddhas – which is not, to put it mildly, usually the case. It would definitely not be skilful means to encourage that sort of fatuous inflation.

As it happens, despite the best efforts of the Tantra, the *yab-yum* form of Mañjughoṣa has never been popularized, perhaps because he was so firmly established iconographically as a single, solitary male Bodhisattva figure. Mañjughoṣa remains eternally without a consort: single, celibate, perfect. There's no need, therefore, to have a personification of culture as a separate being. In the person of Mañjughoṣa, culture has been fully assimilated, fully absorbed. Culture is, if you like, represented by the ornaments that sparkle on the golden body of Mañjughoṣa. Ultimately, in other words, the golden light transcends culture.

5

NATURE, MAN, AND ENLIGHTENMENT

IN THE LAST TWO CHAPTERS we have been particularly concerned with the theme of protection. First the four great kings came forward and promised to protect the sūtra, and then the great goddess Sarasvatī promised to protect the monk who preached the sūtra. In this chapter we are still concerned with the theme of protection; indeed, we are concerned with the promise of another goddess to protect the sūtra. The goddess who *should* now come forward is Śrī, the goddess of wealth and prosperity, because in the sūtra, the chapter on Śrī follows immediately after the chapter on Sarasvatī. However, in this chapter, for the purposes of explication, we are introducing Dṛḍhā, the earth goddess, and keeping back Śrī for our next chapter, when we deal with Buddhist economics. No disrespect to the sūtra is intended, of course.

The last chapter was concerned with the great goddess Sarasvatī and her promise to protect the monk who preaches the sūtra, but said nothing at all about the monk himself. He remained simply an anonymous figure whom the goddess promised to protect. In this chapter I want to give quite a full introduction to Dṛḍhā, the earth goddess, but also to say something about the monk who preaches the sūtra, the monk who is the medium for the transmission of the golden light. I will also say just a little about the golden light itself.

So we shall be concerned in the first place with Dṛḍhā, the earth goddess; secondly, with the monk who preaches the sūtra; and thirdly, with the golden light. Or, in the terms of the chapter's title, we will be concerned with nature, man, and Enlightenment; but we won't deal with them in that order. We will look first at Dṛḍhā, the earth goddess or Mother Nature, then at the golden light or Enlightenment, and finally at the monk who preaches the sūtra – that is, we will look at man.

To begin with, we need to take a look at the opening words of the chapter on Dṛḍhā. It is an abrupt beginning: 'Then indeed the earth goddess Dṛḍhā spoke thus to the Lord' – that is to say, to the Buddha. In fact, chapter 8, the chapter on Śrī, begins in exactly the same way. But chapter 7, the chapter on Sarasvatī, opens in a noticeably different manner. It begins

> Then indeed Sarasvatī, the great goddess, covered one shoulder with her robe, placed her right knee on the ground, made the gesture of reverence in the direction of the Lord and spoke thus to the Lord.[67]

The difference is that Śrī, the goddess of wealth, and Dṛḍhā, the earth goddess, do not salute the Buddha before speaking, but Sarasvatī does, as do the four great kings and Saṃjñāya, the great general of the yakṣas who appears in chapter 11. This difference perhaps signifies that Śrī and Dṛḍhā are naturally less amenable to the influence of the golden light than is Sarasvatī: in other words, that it is more difficult to transform the world of economics and the world of nature than it is to transform the world of culture. This may sound rather far-fetched; but there is surely meaning to be discovered in many of the minor details of the sūtra.

Although she dispenses with the salutation, Dṛḍhā none the less makes her promise, and it is a long and beautiful one. First of all she promises to be present wherever the sūtra is expounded. Not only that; she says she will go up to the Dharma seat – the seat on which the monk who is preaching the sūtra is sitting – with her invisible subtle body, and lean with her head upon the soles of the feet of the monk who is preaching the Dharma. We are not told this, but the monk is presumably seated cross-legged on one of those rather high, throne-like Dharma seats, very nearly the height of a man, such as are still used today, or were at least used until very recently, in Tibet. We are apparently to imagine the goddess going up to this throne, bowing her head slightly, and placing it against the soles of the monk's feet. It could be, of course, that the monk is to be imagined sitting in European fashion as though in a chair, in which case the goddess would stand placing her head directly beneath his feet. She's not present in her gross physical body, so she doesn't have to stand on the surface of the earth.

In either case, this scene is reminiscent of a well-known episode from the life of the Buddha, an episode that occurred shortly before he gained full Enlightenment. The Buddha-to-be – Siddhartha as he still was then – had seated himself on the *vajrāsana*, the diamond throne, which is the seat on which all Buddhas sit when they gain Enlightenment, and which is regarded in Buddhist tradition as the symbolic centre of the universe. There Siddhartha seated himself. He knew that his hour had come, that he was going to attain Enlightenment that very night, so he seated himself on that spot, at the centre of the universe, on the diamond seat. And no sooner had he done so than Māra, the evil one, appeared. Māra had been dogging Siddhartha from the very moment that he left home, trying to find a way into his mind. On this occasion he challenged him, saying 'What right have you got to sit where all the Buddhas of the past have sat?' – as if to say 'Why are you so sure that you are going to gain Enlightenment?' Siddhartha replied that he had the right to sit there because he had practised the pāramitās, the perfections – generosity, ethics, patience, energy, meditation, wisdom – not in just one lifetime, but in many; not even in hundreds but in thousands, in tens of thousands of lives. He was now ready, he said, to gain Enlightenment. He had the right to take his seat on the diamond throne.

So Māra said 'It's all very well to talk like that. It's all very well to make these claims that you've practised the pāramitās, but who saw you? Who saw you doing all these wonderful things? Who is your witness?' And Siddhartha said 'The earth is my witness. All these deeds of mine have been performed on the face of the earth, so the earth goddess has witnessed them.' And Siddhartha tapped the earth with the tips of the fingers of his right hand, and at once the earth goddess rose up out of the depths of the earth. And she said 'Yes, I have seen it all. I have seen him practising all these pāramitās. He is truly worthy to take his seat on the diamond throne.'

This scene is often depicted in Buddhist art. The earth goddess, as she rises up, is usually depicted as a beautiful woman of mature appearance, not particularly young without being actually old. She is golden brown or dark green in colour, and she is usually represented with only the upper half of her body emerged from the earth, just like Mother Erda in Wagner's *Ring*. Her hands are clasped in salutation. Just occasionally she is depicted as standing beside or beneath the *vajrāsana*, with her head placed against the soles of the Buddha's feet, just as the earth goddess is

166 / TRANSFORMING SELF AND WORLD

described in the *Sūtra of Golden Light* in relation to the monk who preaches the sūtra. But however she is depicted or described, the significance is clear: the earth goddess is subordinated to the Buddha, and subordinated to the monk who preaches the sūtra.

This point is emphasized further by the symbolism of head and feet. According to the ancient Indians, including the ancient Indian Buddhists, the head was the noblest, most worthy part of the whole body. The Sanskrit for 'head' is *uttama aṅga*, which means the superior limb or superior member. The feet, on the other hand, are the most ignoble and unworthy part, because in ancient India people went barefoot, and their feet were often very dirty. If you wanted to show respect for someone, you placed your head in contact with their feet; in other words, you subordinated what was highest in you to what was lowest in them. If they were truly superior to you this would be the only way in which real contact between you could be established, the only way in which you could make yourself truly receptive to whatever they had to give.

We find the same kind of symbolism in the meditation practices in which one visualizes the Bodhisattva or Buddha Vajrasattva seated above one's head; or when one visualizes the lineage of gurus seated, one on top of another, above one's head. One makes oneself receptive to their spiritual influence by aligning oneself with them vertically. It is still the custom in India to touch the feet of holy men with one's fingers and then touch one's own head; the idea is that you take dust from their feet and place it on your head. Many Indians show respect not only to holy men but to parents, elders, and even secular teachers in the same way. In the Buddhist countries of the East we find much the same custom, the only difference being that in the Theravāda countries there is no physical contact. What happens is that the lay people salute the monks, and the monks salute the senior monks, their own teachers, by kneeling down and touching the ground in front of their feet with their own forehead. The principle is just the same.

In India and the Buddhist countries of the East there are a number of other customs connected with heads and feet. For instance, you should never touch the head of someone whom you regard as superior to yourself, and above all, of course, you should never touch his head with your feet. This would be regarded as a reversal of the natural order of things. In the same way, you should never sit with your feet stretched out pointing in the direction of anyone whom you consider superior – not in the direction, for instance, of a Buddha image, especially in the shrine-room. Such behaviour would be considered grossly disrespectful and insensitive.

Having promised to lean with her head against the soles of the feet of the monk who is preaching the Dharma, the earth goddess goes on to make further promises. She promises that she will feed on the nectar juice of the Dharma – that is to say, she will derive spiritual nourishment from the Dharma, from the golden light. She promises that she will do homage, that she will rejoice, that she will increase the savour of the earth. She will make the earth stronger so that trees, flowers, fruits, and crops will be made stronger – not only stronger but tastier, more beautiful, and more abundant. Not only that – the fact that the fruits that the earth produces are tastier, more beautiful, and more abundant will affect the people who live on them. Their longevity, their strength, their complexion, and the power of their senses will be increased, and they will then perform the numerous hundreds of thousands of activities appropriate to the earth. They will be devoted; they will be thorough; they will do acts that have to be done with power. Thus the whole of Jambudvīpa will become peaceful and prosperous. People will be happy and their thoughts will then turn to the *Sūtra of Golden Light*. They will approach members of the spiritual community with a pure mind, and ask them to expound the sūtra.

When the sūtra is being expounded, Dṛḍhā herself, together with her retinue, will become stronger and more powerful. The words she uses are almost the same as those used by the four great kings. She says 'In our body there will be produced great power, fortitude and strength. Brilliance, glory and fortune will enter our body.' She will be satisfied, she says, with the nectar juice of the Dharma, and the earth will increase its savour, will become stronger. People who are dependent on the earth will increase and grow, and they will experience various pleasures and enjoyments. For all these reasons, says Dṛḍhā, everybody should be grateful to the earth, and to the earth goddess who has made all these things possible. She wishes that they may listen to the sūtra respectfully, and then talk about it, rejoicing that they have heard the Dharma, that they have acquired merit, that they have pleased the Buddhas. They will also rejoice that they have escaped rebirth in lower states. They will not be reborn in hell, in the world of Yāma, nor as an animal, nor among the hungry ghosts. They will rejoice, Dṛḍhā says, that they are assured of rebirth among gods and men. Not only that; the goddess hopes that, after hearing the sūtra, people will tell their friends and neighbours whatever they remember of its teaching. When they do this, the earth will become stronger; people will become stronger. They will be blessed. They will have great wealth and enjoyment, but they will be devoted to liberality, to *dāna*, and they will have faith in the Three Jewels.

The goddess's promise makes a sort of circular movement. First the *Sūtra of Golden Light* is preached, and this nourishes the earth goddess. So nourished, she increases the savour and strength of the earth, and the people who live on the earth therefore become stronger and more prosperous. Because they are stronger and more prosperous, they become happy; because they are happy, they want to hear the sūtra preached. When the sūtra is preached, the goddess is nourished; when the goddess is nourished, she makes the earth stronger; and the whole process is repeated once again.

It is not surprising that the goddess's promise should follow this circular pattern. After all, she is the earth goddess. She is nature; she is even Mother Nature – and nature's activity is essentially cyclical. The earth goddess therefore represents change, mutability, especially cyclical change. She represents the cyclical process of action and reaction between opposites. She is conditioned existence. She is the saṁsāra. She is the Wheel of Life.

However, we are going a little too fast. We are not yet finished with Dṛḍhā's promise. You will probably have noticed that in the course of her promise the goddess repeats the circular pattern three times, each time on a slightly higher level. At the end of the first repetition, people listen to the *Sūtra of Golden Light*, at the end of the second, they tell others about it, and at the end of the third, they develop faith in the Three Jewels. In other words, the circular movement is not completely circular: the circle is trying to become a spiral. In a sense, it *is* a spiral, but it is not a true spiral. On the true spiral, the true Spiral Path, when we pass the Point of No Return, when we achieve Stream Entry, progress is irreversible. On the circle, the Wheel of Life, there is no progress; that is, no permanent spiritual progress, no transcendental progress. But in between the circle and the spiral comes the section of the path with which we are now concerned. On that section, spiritual progress does take place, but that progress is not irreversible. We can still fall back into the circle, into a state in which we simply go round and round without making any progress at all.

In chapter 7 Sarasvatī promises that the monks, nuns, laymen, and laywomen who hold the chief sūtras, including the *Sūtra of Golden Light*, will escape from the cycle of existence, but here the goddess Dṛḍhā makes no such promise. She can only promise that beings will escape rebirth in the lower realms, that they will be reborn among gods and men, that they will have faith in the Three Jewels. She can't even promise that they will go for Refuge. The earth goddess, in other words, has her limitations. Nature can only take us so far.

This is borne out by the remainder of the chapter. After Dṛḍhā has made her promise, the Buddha speaks. He says that those who hear even a single verse of the *Sūtra of Golden Light* will be reborn among the group of the thirty-three gods, and other groups of gods. Those who show honour to the sūtra will be reborn in heavenly palaces made of the seven jewels. They will be reborn seven times in each palace, and they will experience inconceivable heavenly blessings.

Dṛḍhā then speaks again. She repeats her promise, she prays that beings may continue to hear the sūtra and experience inconceivable divine and human pleasures. Finally she prays that they may awaken to supreme perfect Enlightenment. But this is only a prayer; it is not a promise. It is a prayer which she sees as being fulfilled in the infinitely remote future. From the standpoint of the natural order, Enlightenment is seen as a far-off divine event, not a practicable possibility here and now. With this prayer, the chapter on the earth goddess Dṛḍhā concludes.

The earth goddess in the sūtra is rather a shadowy figure. There is no description of Dṛḍhā, there is no hymn of praise to her as there is to the great goddess Sarasvatī – and indeed the great goddess Śrī in the previous chapter. She remains shadowy, amorphous, unrecognized. In modern Hindu India it is much the same. Sarasvatī is a highly popular goddess, worshipped all over India, especially by scholars, writers, and students. Śrī or Lakshmī is if anything even more popular, and even more widely worshipped – by all householders, and especially by shopkeepers, businessmen, financiers, and speculators in stocks and shares. Other goddesses are also worshipped. There is Durgā, the ten-armed slayer of the buffalo demon. There's Kālī, the Black One, she who dances on the prostrate corpse of her husband, she who wears a garland of freshly-severed heads, whose red tongue hangs out, and whose mouth drips with blood. There is also Sitala, the dreaded goddess of smallpox. All these goddesses are worshipped by millions of people in India; they all have their shrines, their images, and their priests. But Dṛḍhā is not worshipped. She has no shrine, no image, no priests.

The omission, however, is more apparent than real. In a simple sense, all goddesses are earth goddesses, just as all gods are sky gods. If you step down from Unity, so to speak, and taking that as the ultimate principle, you have a primordial dualism – which is to be found in all ancient philosophies, religions, and systems of mythology. Reducing this dualism to its simplest terms – as in, for example, ancient Egyptian mythology – you have the earth and the sky. The earth is represented by various goddesses, the sky by various gods.

One can, of course, think of individual figures who seem to be exceptions to this basic rule. Pluto, for instance, is the god of the underworld – but I don't think he can be seen as a god of the earth in the same way that Dṛḍhā is a goddess of the earth. He is a god, and he lives underground and rules over Hades, but that doesn't make him the masculine equivalent of an earth goddess. Demeter is an earth goddess, but she lives on the surface of the earth. In other words, living underground is not synonymous with being an earth god or goddess. As for Neptune, the god of the sea, he doesn't give the impression of being a masculine counterpart of an earth goddess. He is much more akin to his brother Jupiter, who rules the kingdom of the air.

One could say of Pallas Athene that she is not an earth mother figure because of her close association with Zeus. She was born from the head of Zeus, according to Greek mythology (she had no mother at all) so in a way she is an extension of Zeus's own personality, and she has a number of masculine attributes. A scholar once compared her to Mañjuśrī, the Bodhisattva of Wisdom, saying that, like Pallas Athene, Mañjuśrī was all intellect and chastity – hardly characteristics of the earth goddess. But if Athene is an exception, she is the exception that proves the rule; although technically feminine, she doesn't have any of the usual attributes of the earth goddesses.

Dṛḍhā is perhaps the original Indian earth goddess, not to say earth mother, before her various functions became differentiated. She is paralleled to some extent at least by similar figures in other cultures: by Rhea and Demeter in ancient Greece, by Isis and Hathor in Egypt, by Ishtar in Babylonia, by Diana of the Ephesians, and by Erda or Hertha in northern Europe. But we can find a closer parallel, perhaps, in the various anonymous neolithic figures, the so-called neolithic Venuses, figures with enormous breasts, buttocks, and wombs, but only rudimentary heads. Like them, perhaps, Dṛḍhā represents the primitive reality behind the more sophisticated appearance represented by some of the other goddesses.

Be that as it may, Dṛḍhā is not only a more shadowy figure than Sarasvatī or Śrī; she is also much less human. I have said that the three goddesses represent three different areas of human activity, and that their promises to protect the sūtra represent transformations of these areas achieved through placing them at the service of the golden light. In the case of Dṛḍhā, however, this is only partly true. Her promise to protect the preacher of the sūtra therefore has a somewhat different and more complex significance. Those human energies which are part of nature can be placed at the service of the golden light – they can be transformed. But nature herself cannot be placed at the service of the golden light. Nature herself cannot be transformed. All that we can transform is our attitude to nature, and that is sufficient.

I am going to look at our attitude to nature under three headings. First of all, our use of nature – that is to say, of natural resources and the environment – secondly, the appreciation of nature or enjoyment of nature, and thirdly the understanding of nature.

'Use of nature' means use of natural resources; nowadays we hear a great deal about this. We are being warned that certain natural resources are finite, and that we are using them up at an alarming rate and in a most wasteful fashion. As Buddhists, those who try to follow the Dharma, we should be very aware of this. We should try to use everything of natural origin very carefully indeed, and, moreover, use as little of it as is possible, and in the best possible way – that is to say, for the benefit, the true benefit, of self and others. The same principle applies to our use of the natural environment. We shouldn't destroy it or spoil it in any way, as, for instance, through pollution; and above all, we should think carefully before bringing about irreversible changes.

All this has become the commonplace of informed and responsible thinking, and there is no need for me to elaborate. I am only concerned to underline the general principle involved: that the right use of nature is part of the spiritual life. I would, however, like to make specific mention of one particular misuse of nature that is of special interest to all Buddhists: the pollution, the desecration even, of the environment by noise. Nowadays there is far too much noise. This is especially the case in big cities, but even little villages are not exempt. Even there, jet planes rip through the air overhead and thirty-tonne articulated lorries thunder through the tiny main streets. Under such circumstances, life becomes very difficult, and in particular meditation becomes very difficult. So Buddhists should be particularly aware of such problems, and should do whatever they can to reduce noise, even giving active support to organizations working to this end.

The second aspect of our attitude to nature I want to consider is the appreciation or enjoyment of nature in an aesthetic, even contemplative, sense. Here there is no question of using nature, or doing anything with it. You simply look at nature, simply appreciate it for its own sake – whether you are looking at a mountain or the vast expanse of the sea, a tiny flower or even just a grain of sand. This sort of appreciation of nature is comparatively new in the West. In England, for instance, it became general only with the romantic poets, especially with Wordsworth and Coleridge. Their time, of course, was the time of the industrial revolution, when there was a great upsurge of utilitarianism, when nature began to be used – and misused – more than ever before in history. Perhaps the emphasis the romantic poets gave to the appreciation of natural beauty was necessary to restore the balance – and that emphasis is still needed, especially by those who are trying to develop spiritually. There is no need to idealize or romanticize nature, much less to sentimentalize it as even Wordsworth sometimes did, but there is no doubt that the appreciation of nature, especially of great natural beauty, can play an important part in the spiritual life. It can have a very soothing, tranquillizing effect, even a restorative effect, as we find when we go away on retreat in the country, or even just for a walk in the park on a fine afternoon.

The third area I want to mention is the understanding of nature. The kind of understanding I mean is not scientific or even philosophical, but essentially a spiritual understanding which consists in seeing nature as she really is. Nature is seasonal, nature is cyclic, and nature is therefore saṁsāra.[68] Nature is the Wheel of Life: not as a static picture painted on a wall, but as a living, perpetually recurring process.

In the West we are accustomed to thinking of everything as having a definite beginning. Even nature itself, even mundane existence itself, we think, must have a beginning in time, or at least a beginning with time. Christians, for instance, have believed for centuries that the universe had a definite beginning, when God created it out of nothing. In fact they have pinned this event down to a definite date. They used to assert with some confidence that the world was created in 4004BC, although this date has since been revised.

But this idea that there was a beginning, that the world was created at a certain time, is not the Buddhist view. It is axiomatic to Buddhism that saṁsāra has no beginning, or rather, no perceptible beginning – the operative word here being perceptible. Where there is a perceiving subject there is an object – that is, there is a world. The subject, therefore, cannot perceive the beginning of the world. It can only go back and back in time indefinitely. It can perceive a relative beginning and a relative end, but not an absolute beginning or an absolute end. It can perceive the beginning of a particular universe, but before that it will perceive another universe; before that, another, and so on. According to Buddhist teaching, universes evolve over a period of many, many millions of years, from a subtle state to a gross state, and when they reach the height of their development the opposite process sets in – that is to say, involution from a gross state to a subtle state – and this also takes many, many millions of years. Thus there are periods of expansion and periods of contraction. There are breathings in and breathings out of the cosmos, just like the breathing in and out of the human body, except that these cosmic inhalations and expirations take millions of years. The saṃsāra is cyclic; conditioned existence is cyclic.

But we must be careful not to become too abstract or remote. After all, we are still dealing with nature. In fact, we are dealing with the earth goddess. The earth is not only cyclic, or seasonal. It is also cold and dark; it has no heat or light of its own. It receives them from outside itself, from the principle which is not only opposite to the earth, but higher than the earth. In terms of the earth, this higher principle is heaven. In terms of nature, it is Enlightenment. In terms of the changing, it is the unchanging. In terms of the conditioned, it is the Unconditioned. In terms of the mundane, it is the transcendental. In terms of saṃsāra, it is nirvāṇa. In terms of darkness, it is light. And in terms of Dṛḍhā, the earth goddess, it is the golden light, the light of Truth, the light of Reality, the light of the Buddha, the light which *is* the Truth, *is* Reality, *is* the Buddha. It is this principle that the Buddha refers to in the *Udāna* when he says: 'There is, monks, an unborn, an unbecome, an unmade, an uncompounded. If, monks, there were not here this unborn, unbecome, unmade, uncompounded, there would not here be an escape from the born, the become, the made, the compounded. But because there is an unborn, an unbecome, an unmade, an uncompounded, therefore there is an escape from the born, the become, the made, the compounded.'[69]

We thus have two principles: the compounded and the uncompounded, the conditioned and the Unconditioned, saṃsāra and nirvāṇa; or, in the terms of this chapter of the sūtra, nature and Enlightenment, Dṛḍhā the earth goddess and the golden light. These two principles are separate and independent, at least within the subject–object framework. The one cannot be derived from the other, or reduced to the other. Saṃsāra is without perceptible beginning in time. There is no point, therefore, at which it is connected with nirvāṇa as its effect. Nirvāṇa is beyond time altogether, just as it is beyond space, so there is no point in time at which it is connected with saṃsāra as its cause. Spiritual life consists in making the transition from one principle to the other, from saṁsāra to nirvāṇa, from nature to Enlightenment, from the conditioned to the Unconditioned. It consists in abandoning the ignoble quest for the noble quest, *anariyapariyesana* for *ariyapariyesana*. To quote the words of the historical Buddha, Śākyamuni, again, it consists in the conditioned pursuing the Unconditioned, not the conditioned pursuing the conditioned.

But who is it that makes the transition? Who is it that achieves the noble quest? It is man. It is the monk who is the preacher of the *Sūtra of Golden Light*. As we have seen, this monk is an anonymous figure. In three chapters of the sūtra a goddess comes forward and promises to protect him, but nothing whatever is said about him – at least, not in these chapters. It's as though he is simply a hook on which the goddesses hang their promises. However, something is said about him in chapter 13, the chapter on Susaṁbhava – or rather, something is said about *a* preacher of the sūtra, a monk called Ratnoccaya. (Ratnoccaya, incidentally, means 'jewel heap' or 'precious accumulation'.) In this chapter, the Buddha himself is speaking, and he tells the story of one of his previous lives. He says that there was once a king called Susaṁbhava, which means 'happily born' or 'born of happiness', and he was the ruler of all four continents. And one night Susaṁbhava had a dream in which he saw the monk Ratnoccaya shining in the midst of the sun. Apparently he was brighter even than the sun, and he was expounding the *Sūtra of Golden Light*. On waking up from his dream, feeling extremely happy, the king went to see the Buddha's disciples and enquired after Ratnoccaya. Ratnoccaya, at that time, was elsewhere, sitting in a cave, studying and reflecting on the *Sūtra of Golden Light*. So the disciples took King Susaṁbhava to Ratnoccaya. The king fell down and worshipped Ratnoccaya's feet, and invited him to expound the sūtra; and Ratnoccaya agreed to do so. The king very joyfully made all the appropriate preparations and Ratnoccaya expounded the sūtra. The king, needless to say, was greatly impressed, greatly moved – so much so that he shed tears of joy. Indeed, he was so moved that he presented all his possessions – which included, we are told, the four continents filled with jewels – to the Order of Ratnasikhin, who was the Buddha at that time. Having told the story, the Buddha, Śākyamuni, then reveals that he himself was Susaṁbhava, and that the Buddha Akṣobhya was Ratnoccaya.

So here something at least is said about the preacher of the sūtra, or at least *a* preacher of the sūtra, and what is said underlines one particular point. The preacher of the sūtra is always a monk, a bhikṣu. And all three goddesses promise to protect the monk who preaches the sūtra. This raises two questions. What is a monk? And why should a monk in particular be the preacher of the sūtra?

We must remember that the *Sūtra of Golden Light* is a Mahāyāna sūtra, and the Mahāyāna invariably attaches more importance to the spirit than the letter of the Buddha's teaching (although this does not mean that it ignores or neglects the letter). In the same spirit, it attaches more importance to the realities of the spiritual life than to the appearances. For the Mahāyāna, therefore, the monk is not just one who observes certain minor disciplinary precepts, who shaves his head and wears a yellow robe, although he may of course do these things. The monk, according to the Mahāyāna, is one who is totally committed to the spiritual life, to the noble quest for the Unconditioned, not just for his own sake but for the sake of all living beings. The Mahāyāna monk is therefore a Bodhisattva, at least in intention, even if the bodhicitta has not actually arisen.

Now only a free man can commit himself. You cannot be totally committed unless you are free from all mundane ties and responsibilities. And the two biggest mundane responsibilities, so far as a man at least is concerned, are, first, a wife and family, and second, wage-earning work; the two, of course, usually go together. The monk, therefore, is celibate, unmarried; he has no wife, no children, no family responsibilities. The English word 'monk' means one who is on his own, one who is single, solitary, alone. But this does not necessarily mean that the monk is a hermit. He may in fact live as a member of a spiritual community, even a monastic community. The idea that as a monk he is alone refers to the fact that he does not belong to any group that is held together by purely mundane ties of blood, emotional dependence, or common worldly interests. Within the spiritual community, one can be alone and one can be with others. Within the group, however, one is neither alone nor with others.

Also, the monk has no worldly occupation. He doesn't work for a living. He doesn't make anything, he doesn't produce anything, he doesn't earn anything. Economically speaking, he is a parasite. He is a glorious spiritual parasite, because he depends for food and clothing on others, as we shall be seeing in the next chapter.

I am, of course, using the word 'parasite' here ironically, and you may be wondering how realistic it might be to think of being a 'glorious spiritual parasite' in modern Western society. These days it is not actually possible to think in terms of being a parasite in the sense of living off the State; even when you are on the dole you are obliged to 'work' at looking for work. It is even more difficult to be a spiritual parasite, let alone a glorious spiritual parasite. A spiritual parasite, glorious or otherwise, is someone who is not making any direct economic contribution to society, but who is none the less supported by society.

This brings in the whole question of wages and payment and exchange. The Buddhist spiritual ideal is to give what you can on whatever level, without thinking in terms of *quid pro quo*, of payment of any kind, of taking what you need 'in return', but giving whatever you can, whether your gifts are material, cultural, or spiritual. It isn't a Buddhist ideal literally to be a spiritual parasite if by that one means someone who only takes and never gives. But there is certainly no taking and giving in terms of a sort of bartering – i.e. if you give me so much material support, I'll give you so much spiritual guidance. A spiritual parasite in a Buddhist sense would be someone who takes from society what he needs for his material support without necessarily giving anything material in return, but none the less quite genuinely giving what he can in other ways, and not simply as a rationalization for allowing himself to be supported.

The monk is one who leads a purely spiritual life, who is totally committed to a spiritual life, who has no worldly ties or responsibilities. The monk therefore lives what some of the old Christian writers called the angelic life. Monks live as it were in heaven. They live like angels. In heaven there is neither marriage nor giving in marriage, neither ploughing nor sowing nor reaping. The monastic life is therefore the happy life. I can testify to this from my own experience and observation, at least so far as Buddhist monks are concerned (I can't answer for the others). In fact, I have no hesitation in saying that the monastic life is the best and happiest of all lives. In India I not only lived as a monk myself; I had contact with monks of many different schools and many different nationalities – Theravādin monks and Mahāyāna monks, Zen monks, Nichiren monks, Gelugpa monks, Nyingmapa monks. Some were Sinhalese, some were Burmese; there were Thais, Vietnamese, Cambodians, Laotians, Chinese, Tibetans, and Nepalese. And they were all noticeably happier than the lay people, even than the Buddhist lay people. The lay people were happy enough, but the Buddhist monks were even happier.

Now this may seem odd. After all, the lay people had wives, children, jobs, money, motor cars, all conceivable pleasures and enjoyments. But it is true to say that more often than not they looked relatively miserable. The monks, on the other hand, usually had none of these things. Most monks that I knew owned little more than their robes, their begging-bowl, and a few books; maybe a fountain pen or the odd camera. Many of them took no solid food after midday at all, contenting themselves with a cup of tea. Some of them were so strict that they didn't even take milk in their tea. Yet they were all remarkably happy, contented, and friendly. It was really a joy to be with them.

So this is what a monk is – a real monk, not just someone who has formally received monastic ordination. A monk is one who is totally committed to the spiritual life, who has no worldly ties or responsibilities, who is celibate, that is to say unmarried, without wife and children, who does not work for a living, who is supported by others, who receives food and clothing and so on from others. Moreover, the monk is one who leads an angelic life, who is happy. In other words, the monk is one who has made the transition from the conditioned to the Unconditioned, from saṁsāra to nirvāṇa, from nature to Enlightenment, or one who is very definitely in the process of making that transition. The monk is one who has at least set out on the noble quest.

I may seem to be presenting an idealized picture of the monastic life. In fact, because in my interpretation of the sūtra the monk stands for man, just as Dṛḍhā stands for nature, and the golden light for Enlightenment, what I am really presenting is an idealized picture of man. The monk only happens to be a monk. He is primarily man, man as committed to the spiritual life, man as going for Refuge.

And, of course, I have taken 'monk' in the true sense, not just as someone who has formally received a certain ordination and is therefore a monk in the technical sense. There are many monks in the East who do not come up to the ideal because although they have been formally ordained, they are not really committed to the Three Jewels, to the ideal of Enlightenment. Perhaps it is rather misleading that the monk in the sūtra is called a monk, and the people who are wearing yellow robes but not living up to the ideals of Buddhism are also called monks. This is just an accident of history.

Having said all that, it is not easy to make the transition from the conditioned to the Unconditioned. It is not easy to leave saṁsāra behind, however miserable it is. It is not easy to give up the world. After all, saṁsāra is not only outside us; the world is not only outside us; it is also within us. Man is a being with a dual nature. On the one hand, he is the child of earth; on the other, he is the offspring of heaven. He is part of nature, but at the same time he transcends nature. He feels the gravitational pull of the conditioned; he also feels the gravitational pull of the Unconditioned. So man is a being in conflict, in conflict with himself, in conflict within himself. We may even go so far as to say that man is a battleground of opposing forces. There is a great battle taking place in

every human being, the forces of nature fighting with the forces of
Enlightenment, Dṛḍhā the earth goddess with the golden light.

The monk is one in whom the conflict has been resolved, the battle has
been won. His natural energies have submitted to the golden light, are
completely at the service of the golden light. In Christian phraseology, he
has overcome the world. It should be obvious now why the monk is the
preacher of the *Sūtra of Golden Light*, and why the earth goddess places
her head against the soles of his feet. Only one who has identified himself
with the golden light can be the preacher of the *Sūtra of Golden Light*. The
monk has made the transition from the conditioned to the Unconditioned, from saṁsāra to nirvāṇa, from nature to Enlightenment, or is in
the process of making it. He has identified himself with the golden light,
become as it were one with the golden light, at least to some extent, so he
is able to be the preacher of the sūtra. Ultimately, of course, it is the
Buddha himself who is the preacher of the sūtra, and therefore the
Buddha himself who is protected.

Nowadays, unfortunately, the earth goddess has got out of control.
Nature has got out of control; and by this I mean not nature outside man,
except in so far as this has been disturbed by man himself, but nature
inside man, the natural human energies. Today the conditioned pursues
the conditioned relentlessly. Hardly anyone pursues the Unconditioned;
the emphasis is almost exclusively on material values. But if civilization
is not to collapse, if mankind is not to destroy itself, there must be a much
stronger emphasis on spiritual values. There must be a revival of spiritual
life, and by 'spiritual life' I mean real spiritual life, not just the old
conventional religiosity, which we have, or should have, outgrown. What
we need, in fact, is an uncompromising assertion of the monastic ideal in
the truest and best sense.

6

Buddhist Economics

THE CHAPTER ON ŚRĪ, chapter 8, is quite short, consisting of less then three pages in the English translation, and Śrī's promise takes up only a part of it. But the length of her promise is no indication of its impact. She doesn't promise simply to protect the monk who is the preacher of the sūtra; she is much more specific, and promises much more, than that. As we have seen, she doesn't even begin by saluting the Buddha. She comes straight out with her promises. She says that she will give the monk first, zeal; second, garments; third, begging-bowl; fourth, bed and seat; and fifth, medicines – plus, she says, other excellent equipment. She also makes it clear why she is going to give these gifts. She will give them, she says, so that the preacher of the Dharma may be provided with every equipment, so that he may have no lack, so that he may be sound in mind, so that he may pass night and day with a happy mind, so that he may examine the words and letters of the sūtra, so that he may perpetuate them for the sake of all living beings, and so that all living beings may eventually awaken to full, perfect Enlightenment.

So, first of all, who is the great goddess Śrī? We have seen that the goddess Sarasvatī is widely worshipped by modern Hindus, especially by scholars, writers, students, and anybody who has anything to do with learning. In the same way, the goddess Śrī is still worshipped in India today; in fact, she is worshipped even more widely than Sarasvatī. Śrī is worshipped in practically every Hindu home, usually under the name of Lakshmī. It is easy enough to understand what she represents. The word Śrī means 'prosperity', and Lakshmī means 'luck' or 'good fortune'. The prosperity which is meant here, of course, is material prosperity, and the good fortune is good fortune in the worldly sense – the kind of good fortune that causes you to win the National Lottery, not the kind that causes you to find a copy of *Buddhism for Today* lying on a seat in the bus.

So the goddess represents material prosperity, material success. The modern Hindu Lakshmī is depicted more or less like the modern Hindu Sarasvatī: in other words, as a beautiful young woman with long, flowing, glossy black hair, dressed in a crimson sari with a golden border. Lakshmī, however, is more definitely represented as a young married woman. She wears the red *tilaka* of the married woman on her forehead, and perhaps also the red powder called *kum-kum* in the parting of her hair, as well as various items of jewellery: necklaces, bracelets, anklets, earrings, and, of course, nose ring or nose stud. The South Indian Lakshmī especially is adorned in this sort of way. Sarasvatī is generally dressed much more simply, as befits a goddess of learning. Lakshmī is seated not on a goose, as Sarasvatī is, but on an enormous lotus flower, usually pink or white, and sometimes she holds a lotus flower in her hand.

There are many images of Lakshmī in the temples, and often they have more than one pair of arms. Usually Lakshmī stands beside her consort, who is the god Vishnu, the second member of the Hindu *trimurti*. It is clearly appropriate for Vishnu the preserver and Lakshmī the goddess of wealth and prosperity to be regarded as being 'married' to each other, and sometimes they are jointly referred to as Lakshmī Narayan – Narayan being another name for Vishnu. In New Delhi there is a famous and colossal Lakshmī Narayan temple. It was built by a modern Hindu multi-millionaire, in fact a multi-multi-multi-millionaire, one of the wealthiest men that India has produced in modern times (so he had good reason to be devoted to Lakshmī). He was a well-known businessman who was the principal financial supporter of Mahatma Gandhi and the Congress Party in the days before Indian independence. It was he who made the famous remark: 'It costs me two thousand rupees a day to keep Bapu (that is, Mahatma Gandhi) living in poverty.'

As one might expect, the goddess Lakshmī is much worshipped by members of the business fraternity in India. Every Hindu shopkeeper has a brightly coloured image or picture of the goddess in his shop, as well as an image of Ganesha, the elephant-headed god who removes obstacles. The orthodox Hindu businessman worships these images every day – in the sense that he lights sticks of incense and waves lights in front of their pictures or images. Every Hindu shop has a safe in the corner, or at least a big, strong iron box; and you will find the image or picture of Lakshmī placed immediately above the safe, or sometimes even inside it. You see Hindu shopkeepers opening the safe first thing in the morning, and as they do so they worship the image or picture of Lakshmī inside the safe, so that you could say that they are quite literally worshipping riches; they really do worship money. Even the account books are bound in a traditional red because that is the colour of Lakshmī's sari.

Images or pictures of Lakshmī are also found in the home, for obvious reasons; Lakshmī is probably the most popular household deity in India. There is not much religious feeling attached to her; she is just generally believed to bring good luck and prosperity. A good wife, incidentally, is called a 'Lakshmī'. If a woman is cheerful and industrious, if she is a good cook, housekeeper, and mother, and if her husband's affairs prosper, then his friends will say to him 'Your wife is a real Lakshmī,' or 'The goddess of fortune has surely come to your house' – in other words, your wife has brought you good luck. But I'm sorry to say that there is a darker side to the picture. If the husband's affairs go wrong, or if he dies prematurely, then his relations will say that it was his wife's fault, that she brought him bad luck. Generally speaking, however, the married woman, especially the young married woman with children, is regarded as a bringer of good luck. If, when you are leaving house in the morning, whether to go to work or do something else, the first person that you see is a married woman – and in India you always know if a woman is married or not, because married women wear the red mark on the forehead – you will have good luck during the day. But if the first person you see is a monk, you will have bad luck, because the monk represents the negation of worldly prosperity and success. This belief prevails so strongly that there are some Hindus, especially some orthodox brahmins, who, on meeting a monk of any kind first thing in the morning, just turn back and go home again. They don't even attempt to do anything that day; they say they know it won't be successful. They have met that monk, and he has completely destroyed their good luck for the whole day.

This is, of course, the Hindu point of view, and Hinduism, being an ethnic religion, stresses group values and worldly prosperity. The Buddhist point of view is quite different. I won't go so far as to say that according to the Buddhist point of view it is unlucky to meet a married woman in

the morning, but it is certainly regarded as auspicious to meet a monk –
auspicious, that is, from a spiritual point of view.

There are many legends concerning the goddess Lakshmī, one of which
concerns her birth. It is said that the gods one day decided to churn the
great cosmic ocean of milk. So they uprooted Mount Meru to use as their
churning stick, and took Ananta the cosmic serpent as a rope to wind
round Mount Meru, and then some of the gods and goddesses pulled one
end of the rope, some pulled the other, and as they pulled back and forth,
they churned this cosmic ocean of milk. And out of it all sorts of marvellous things were produced, just like butter. First of all, up came the cow
of plenty. Next to appear was the wish-fulfilling tree, the tree that fulfils
all desires; you have only to touch it and wish, and at once your wish is
granted. Then there came the heavenly elephant, the elephant that goes
as fast as the wind and has six tusks. And then there came up the goddess
Lakshmī; this is how she was born. But after her there came up a pot full
of poison, poison strong enough to kill all the beings in the universe.

Of course, everybody wanted to take the good things that had come up
– the gods especially wanted to take the goddess Lakshmī – but nobody
wanted the poison. In the end Vishṇu took Lakshmī and married her, and
as for the poison, it was swallowed by the god Shiva. That, at least, is
what happened according to the Hindus. According to the Buddhists, it
was the Bodhisattva Avalokiteśvara who swallowed the poison. But
whether it was Shiva or Avalokiteśvara who swallowed it, it did neither
of them any harm because it went no further than their throat. But each
of their throats turned deep blue – which is why they are both known as
Nilakaṇṭha, 'the Blue-throated One'.

The poison here represents the suffering of the world, *duḥkha*, which
Avalokiteśvara swallows out of wisdom and compassion. The emphasis
in the Buddhist version, and probably in the Hindu one too, is on the
Bodhisattva or the god intervening to take upon himself the sufferings of
the world. But of course that can't be taken literally. He can only show
you – out of wisdom and compassion – how to swallow the poison
yourself, how to deal with suffering yourself. It is not that he literally
swallows the pain which you would otherwise have experienced. As we
churn the ocean of saṁsāra – and this is what most of us are doing most
of the time – all sorts of beautiful and delightful things come up which
everybody wants, but sooner or later the pot of poison comes up. Nobody
else, strictly speaking, can swallow the poison for us, but they can show
us how to swallow it, in other words, how to face our own suffering, and

eventually transcend it. In a sense we each have to be our own Avalokiteśvara.

It is sometimes said that the myth of the blue-throated Avalokiteśvara came from the Hindu myth about Shiva, but it is not impossible that it might be the other way round. There is no doubt that in ancient India – we are not even sure exactly when – there was a whole floating mass of myth and legend and folklore which wasn't really the property of any particular religion. All the religions which we now call Hinduism, Buddhism, Jainism, and so on, dipped into this pool, as it were, and drew upon these stories, myths, parables, proverbs, and sayings, adapting them to their own purposes.

However, to leave these old stories and turn back to chapter 8 of the sūtra, we probably now have a fairly clear idea of what the modern Hindu goddess Lakshmī represents. She is worldly prosperity, she is wealth and riches, especially in their more domestic aspect. We could perhaps say that she is affluence or even that she is economics. In the sūtra she promises to give the monk who preaches the Dharma zeal, garments, begging-bowl, bed, seat and medicines, and other excellent equipment. And she does this, as we have seen, so that he can preach the sūtra properly and so that all beings can benefit.

This means that wealth and riches are placed at the service of the monk who is the preacher of the sūtra, and thus at the service of the Dharma, the golden light. So Śrī represents wealth and riches devoted to spiritual ends. The difference between the Hindu goddess Lakshmī and the Buddhist goddess Śrī is that Lakshmī represents wealth and riches devoted to worldly ends, and Śrī represents wealth and riches devoted to spiritual ends. Lakshmī is economics in general, but Śrī is Buddhist economics, which is of course the title of this chapter.

Before I go any further, I have a confession to make. This title is not original. As you may have guessed, I borrowed it from Dr E.F. Schumacher, the author of *Small is Beautiful*, a book which all Buddhists should read. In the chapter of this book called 'Buddhist Economics', Dr Schumacher's point of departure is exactly the same as my own. The chapter opens with the following statement:

'Right livelihood is one of the requirements of the Buddha's Noble Eightfold Path. It is clear, therefore, that there must be such a thing as Buddhist economics.'

Dr Schumacher goes on to explore the implications of this statement within a predominantly modern, non-traditional context, whereas in this book we are concerned with Buddhist economics within a predominantly traditional, spiritual context, within the context of the *Sūtra of Golden Light*. Nevertheless, I find myself fundamentally in agreement with Dr Schumacher's approach; his thinking, it seems to me, is very much along the right lines. I am glad that his book has received so much attention, and I hope it will continue to receive it. I hope also that more and more people will act on his recommendations. In short, to put it in Buddhist terms, I rejoice in Dr Schumacher's merits.

I also rejoice in the great goddess Śrī's merits, and in the promise that she makes. The fundamental nature of her promise is really very simple – so simple that we might easily overlook it. Fundamentally, the great goddess Śrī's promise is a promise to give. And what does she promise to give? Virtually everything – everything, that is, that is necessary to support the spiritual life: food, clothing, residence, and medicine. You don't really need anything more than that. So we can say that Buddhist economics is the economics of giving. We can even go further than that and say that the Buddhist life is the life of giving. To the extent that we possess, to that extent we must give – material things, at least, if we can't give anything more than that. If there is no giving, there is no spiritual life.

We can see this very clearly in the case of the Bodhisattva, the ideal Buddhist of the Mahāyāna, the one who is committed to the attainment of *bodhi* – Enlightenment – not just for his own sake but for that of all sentient beings. A Bodhisattva practises six pāramitās or transcendental virtues; and the first of these is *dāna* or giving. *Dāna* can be of many different kinds, because there are all sorts of things that can be given to all sorts of people in all sorts of ways.

The practice of *dāna* is widespread in all Buddhist countries, whether they practise according to the Theravāda, the Mahāyāna, or any other school. In those countries, the Dharma and those practising and preaching it are supported on a scale that we in the West can hardly imagine. And nowhere is this more so – or rather *was* this more so – than in Tibet as it existed until 1950, or to some extent even until 1959.

I remember in this connection a conversation I had in Kalimpong many years ago – it must have been in the early 1950s – with a Tibetan student called Aggen Chototsang who was learning English with me. He was about thirty years old, and he was a native of eastern Tibet; in fact, he was a Khamba. The Khambas have a reputation for being fierce and warlike to the point of being both aggressive and undisciplined, but also for being very good Buddhists. Aggen was one of five brothers, and they were all traders. He was short and stocky, and very straightforward, very direct.

I am sorry to say that he was killed about ten years later fighting the Chinese in eastern Tibet. I hope he had a good rebirth, even though he died fighting. Anyway, Aggen once told me how he and his brothers spent their income. They divided whatever money they had made by the end of the year into three parts. Then they gave one third for Dharma purposes: for repairing monasteries, providing food and clothing for monks, printing copies of sacred texts, sponsoring religious ceremonies, commissioning images and paintings of Buddhas and Bodhisattvas, and so on. They spent another third on pleasure: this consisted, regrettably, mainly of drinking and gambling, especially gambling – though not smoking. The old-fashioned Tibetans regarded smoking as much worse than drinking. And the third part was devoted to household expenses, as well as being reinvested in the business. According to Aggen, this was the general practice in Kham; every family gave one third of their income for the Dharma – which is really something for Buddhists everywhere to live up to. We generally think that we are giving quite a lot if we give a tenth of our income, but by Khamba standards this would be comparative meanness.

The goddess Śrī promises to give the monk who is the preacher of the sūtra such things as food, clothing, bed, and seat; in other words, what she gives, she gives in kind, not cash. This is the traditional practice which is still widespread in some parts of the Buddhist world, though less so now than it used to be. I lived in this way myself for a couple of years – not in a Buddhist country but in India. I didn't keep any money at all, not even in the bank. I didn't handle money, didn't touch it, and I didn't accept money if it was offered to me. And I found that this arrangement simplified life greatly. There were lots of things that I simply did not have to think about, because I didn't have any money.

I later discovered, however, that it was only possible to live like this while I was concerned exclusively with my personal spiritual practice. I couldn't sustain that life-style when I started to engage in organizing Buddhist activities. For that I needed money, even in India. And if this was the position even in India, it is much more the position here in the West. It is still possible even here to invite the monk who is the preacher of the sūtra for a meal; it is still possible to present him with a pair of socks or a small country house. But if you want to support the Dharma to any great extent, it means giving money; in fact, it means giving quite a lot of money.

People's attitude to money is rather strange. This is perhaps not surprising: money itself is a strange, protean thing. One could almost say that money is everything except money. Money is life, money is power, money is prestige, money is success, money is security, money is pleasure, money is love. After all, with money we can buy love, or anything we want – or at least we think we can. The strangest thing about people's attitude to money is perhaps their reluctance to part with it. In the West this is true even of some Buddhists. They seem to think that there is somehow something wrong in giving money for Dharma work. This reluctance probably has something to do with our basic attitude towards money. We tend to think of it as something dirty and disgusting, something that decent people have as little to do with as possible, at least in public. The expression 'filthy lucre' probably reflects our basic attitude towards money – and some Western Buddhists tend to share this attitude. They think of the Dharma as something that is very pure, and has to be kept pure. And how do you keep the Dharma pure? Well, one way is to keep your dirty, disgusting money as far away from it as possible.

But this is certainly not the traditional attitude. The traditional attitude is that money – money that you've acquired by ethical means, in accordance with the principles of Right Livelihood – is good, wholesome stuff, and the best thing you can do with it is to give it for Dharma work. You could say that money is like manure: it smells a bit sometimes, but it's good, clean, wholesome stuff really. We need not be squeamish about handling it, or about giving it away. As Sir Francis Bacon said four centuries ago: 'Money is like muck, no good except it be spread.'

So if you have any of this muck, you want to spread it around, especially in the direction of the Dharma. As the Buddha himself said, 'Don't be afraid of giving.' The Salvation Army used to have a slogan: 'Give until it hurts.' But surely this is quite wrong; surely this reflects a typically Christian attitude. It makes us think of the spiritual life as something essentially painful, and prompts an attitude to giving like the one most of us have towards going to the dentist. We put it off for as long as possible because we think it is going to hurt. (It is an attitude that requires the recipient of one's giving to be truly miserable as well.) But in fact giving doesn't hurt at all. In fact, the more you give, the happier, lighter, and freer you will feel. So we should leave others to work their way up to giving in whatever way they can. As Buddhists we should say 'Give till you swoon with joy.'

Giving, I should add, does not mean paying. When I first began to run Buddhist activities in England, I found that people were very reluctant to give for the sake of the Dharma, even though they assured me that they were benefiting from it. They were, however, quite ready to pay – for lectures, yoga classes, retreats, and so on. I used to wonder why this was so, and eventually came to certain tentative conclusions which seemed to shed at least some light on the matter.

When you pay, you buy. What you buy, you own. And when you own something, it's yours, it's for you, so you don't mind paying – even paying for the Dharma. When you give, however, you give away. Money given is money lost. What you give away is no longer yours, it's not for you, so you are reluctant to give, even for the sake of the Dharma. This whole mental attitude is quite a miserable one, and I have noticed that people who can get rid of it are decidedly happier.

Now for the things that the great goddess Śrī promises to give the monk who is the preacher of the sūtra. First of all, she promises to give him zeal, which implies both enthusiasm and energy. But how does this goddess come to be giving zeal? Surely she is essentially a goddess of wealth and riches. How does she come to be giving a psychological or even spiritual quality like zeal? Has she not stepped a little out of line? Has she not gone beyond her proper jurisdiction?

Not really. She gives zeal not directly but indirectly, by giving the other things: garments, begging-bowl, bed, and so on. The monk needs to be able to devote all his energies to the spiritual life, to preaching the *Sūtra of Golden Light*. If he had to bother about food and clothing, that would take up some of his energy, so food and clothing have to be provided, and this is what the great goddess Śrī does. By giving the monk food and clothing, she enables him to devote all his energies to preaching the sūtra. After all, the monk has not only given up the responsibility of supporting a wife and family; he has also given up the responsibility of supporting himself, and this is widely recognized in most Buddhist countries. This is especially the case in Theravāda countries, where, as I know from my own experience, a monk is not permitted to cook for himself, or even to make himself a cup of tea. Everything is provided for him, everything is done for him.

There is, though, another side to the coin. The monk has to devote all his energies to the Dharma, and all means *all* – not an easy thing for anybody to do. He may devote himself to Buddhist activities such as preaching the *Sūtra of Golden Light*, or to meditation, or to a combination of the two, but in one way or another all his energies are devoted to the Dharma. And it is the goddess Śrī who makes this possible. In other words, it is Buddhist economics – the economics of giving – that makes this possible.

188 / TRANSFORMING SELF AND WORLD

Secondly, Śrī gives the monk the gift of garments. It is interesting – and very much in accordance with the original spirit of Buddhism – that the translator renders it 'garments', not 'robes'. In the Buddha's day, monks (as we call them now) wore ordinary dress: one piece of cloth round the waist, another piece draped under the right arm and over the left shoulder, and a third cloth of double or treble thickness which served several purposes – it could be worn as a shawl during the day, used as a blanket at night, and folded to make a sort of cushion. Some monks stitched a number of small pieces of cloth together to make one large piece, and this later became general practice.

The only real difference between the monk's dress and that of the layman was in the colour. The layman's dress was white; the monk's dress was dyed – or rather discoloured – a sort of yellowish-brown, a bit like khaki. The reason for this discoloration was twofold. If the cloth looked rather dirty rather than clean and white, it would be much less likely to be stolen; and it also made the monk easy to recognize. If people saw someone wearing this discoloured cloth, they knew that here was someone who needed to be supported. The monk's dress was not a robe, if by robe we mean something gorgeous and ceremonial, not to say theatrical, though in the course of time it tended to become so. So the goddess Śrī gives the monk who is the preacher of the sūtra garments, in other words, ordinary clothes.

Thirdly, Śrī gives the monk a begging-bowl. The Sanskrit word for monk is *bhikṣu*, and a *bhikṣu* is usually explained as one who lives upon *bhikṣā* or almsfood – food that has been begged. *Pātra* means bowl – or rather, 'bowl' is used to translate *pātra* – and it can be of earthenware or wood or iron, so the *bhikṣāpātra* is the bowl in which almsfood is collected and out of which it is eaten. The begging-bowl is one of the traditional eight requisites of the monk, the eight things that you are given when you are ordained as a monk. (The others are the three garments – the inner, the outer, and the upper, one girdle or belt, one water strainer, one razor, and one needle and thread.)

The general practice was that the monk went out early in the morning, and went from door to door without missing out any house – that is, without picking and choosing where he would be best received and fed. At each house he received a small quantity of cooked food, and when his bowl was full, or when he had collected enough, he stopped and returned to his monastery or wherever he happened to be staying. When he got back he would offer some of the food to his teacher, and perhaps also share it with fellow disciples. The rest of the day he spent meditating, studying, teaching, and so on. If he happened to be travelling, after collecting his food he would retire to a secluded spot, perhaps to a grove of trees, where he would eat the food, rest, and meditate, before resuming his journey.

Monks are also allowed to accept invitations to eat food at the houses of the laity, and the laity can bring food to the monastery, but in either case the food is deposited in the bowl and the monk eats from it. The bowl is also used for fetching water, and for drinking from, so it is clearly a very useful piece of equipment. A well-known ancient text says that the monk with his bowl and his three garments is like a bird with its two wings; equipped with them, he can go freely wherever he pleases.

It is interesting to note that the goddess does not promise to supply the monk with food, but with a begging-bowl. We could, of course, say that the begging-bowl stands for food, and this is true, but perhaps there is another explanation. The monk begs food, or at least collects it. He is dependent for food on others. But not only that: he is dependent on others even for the very means by which he begs food – the begging-bowl. He doesn't even provide his own bowl. Even that has to be given to him. In other words, he is totally dependent on others for his worldly require- ments, and left totally free to devote all his energies to the Dharma, in this case to preaching the sūtra.

Fourthly, Śrī gives a bed or seat. The word used is *sayanāsana*: not so much bed or seat in the sense of big, heavy items of furniture, but something more like a place to sleep, a place to sit, or somewhere to stand. We mustn't forget that the monk was originally a wanderer. There was no question of his being permanently settled in the monastery; that came later. And in the course of his wanderings, all that he needed was a place to stay, either just for a single night or for a few days. It could be at the foot of a shady tree, or in a summer house in somebody's private park, or in a cave. In the last chapter we found the monk Ratnoccaya sitting in a cave, studying and reflecting on the *Sūtra of Golden Light*. And this is what the goddess promises to supply, whether in the form of a tree, a hut, or a cave: she promises to supply somewhere to stay.

Fifthly and lastly, the goddess promises to give medicines. In the Buddha's time these were comparatively simple. A medicine that is frequently mentioned in Pāli texts is gallnuts dissolved in cow's urine, which was regarded as a sort of panacea for the sick monk. I have never tried it myself, but I have known monks who had great faith in it. There was one Sinhalese monk in particular who strongly recommended it to me in my early days as a monk, saying that it would cure me of all my complaints. This was the monk who – as I have recorded in my volume of memoirs, *The Thousand-Petalled Lotus* – urged me to stop writing poetry and turn out more articles on Buddhist philosophy.[70] I'm afraid I have not been able to follow his advice: I haven't yet tried gallnuts dissolved in cow's urine, and I still occasionally write poetry. He must be turning in his stupa.

However, to return to the medicines, whether it is gallnuts in cow's urine or the latest miracle drug, the principle is the same: there is no objection to the monk's receiving medical treatment. There is, in fact, a chapter on healing illness in the sūtra itself. Medical treatment, whether of the monk or anybody else, should, however, be in accordance with spiritual principles, and with the laws of nature. To tell whether or not treatment is 'in accordance with spiritual principles' one has to look at both the purpose of the treatment and its nature. The purpose of medical treatment is ultimately to restore one's health so that one can use that health and energy to lead a spiritual life. And the nature of the treatment shouldn't be unethical or violate any spiritual principle. I have serious doubts, for example, about experimenting with animals. It is not in accordance with spiritual principles to have recourse to medical treatment which is dependent upon the suffering of other living beings.

Another issue is whether or not some treatments take away pain at the expense of mental clarity. Obviously mental clarity isn't something to be sacrificed lightly, but there is no point in suffering if you don't really need to. One should only refuse pain-killers if their use has implications that are worse than the pain itself. We experience enough pain anyway from time to time – toothache, stomach-ache, and so on. We don't need to be reminded of what that kind of suffering is like.

The general point here is that you are not necessarily any nearer to insight into the truth of suffering because you are experiencing suffering. You can even have insight into the truth of suffering while you are in a state of happiness. Experiencing suffering as such doesn't teach you anything. People who have suffered quite a lot can very quickly forget it, if they have had no insight into the truth of suffering.

Often when people are dying, they are given increasing doses of morphine, and this might seem to be at odds with the Tibetan teachings about dying with mental clarity. But if the pain is clouding your awareness as much as the drug is, it's really six of one and half-a-dozen of the other. You have to try to find the fine point of balance where you are not taking so much of the drug that you have no mindfulness left, but not taking so little that the pain is clouding your mind just as much as the drug would have done. That may be a very fine point of balance, and in some sad cases it may not be possible to find it. You have no choice, really. The pain clouds your awareness and so does the drug. For most people it is just not possible to bear the pain and remain mindful, still less turn their thoughts to the Buddha, Dharma, and Sangha.

Some people say that if you are in pain it is the result of your karma, and you shouldn't really interfere with that process. But you don't *know* whether it's the result of your karma. It may be, but it may not – you normally don't know unless you have some very special insight. The practical test is usually said to be that if all means of relieving your condition fail, you can fall back on the explanation of karma; but if your pain can be relieved by drugs, presumably it isn't due to karma, because drugs would not defeat karma. And even if the illness was due to karma, you could argue that it was due to subsequent good karma that drugs were available to treat it.

In saying that medical treatment should also be in accordance with the laws of nature, I mean that it should not be merely palliative. It should do more than just patch people up. Some people lead unhealthy lives and as a result suffer from all sorts of ailments which they expect the doctor to cure while they continue to live in an unhealthy way. If you lead a healthy life, you will be healthy; the way to be healthy is to lead a healthy life. So medical treatment should not simply enable you to carry on leading an unhealthy life; it should encourage you to live a healthy life.

I am not just advocating naturopathy or nature cures here. If an ordinary doctor says to a patient 'You've just got to cut down on the meat and eat fewer eggs. It's no use my just giving you pills. You should take more exercise and cut down on alcohol' – *that* is giving medical treatment in accordance with the laws of life and nature.

So these are the five things that Śrī promises to give the monk who is the preacher of the sūtra: zeal, garments, begging-bowl, bed and seat, and medicines. The last four correspond to a well-known list which is to be found in many ancient Buddhist texts, a list of four things that the monk has the right to expect from the Buddhist laity: food, clothing, shelter, and medicine. These four represent the indispensable minimum required to support life; in other words, the monk has the right to expect from the laity only what is necessary, no more.

This brings us to the question of the relation between the monk and the laity. In the Buddhist East the lay people accept full responsibility for supplying all the material needs of the monk, and they do this very happily. They are very happy to be able to make it possible for the monk to devote all his time and energy to the spiritual life because they believe that this is for everybody's benefit. In fact, they believe that by supporting the monk they are laying up for themselves a stock of merit which will help them to have a better rebirth, and even contribute to their material prosperity in this life. Some lay people, it must be admitted, support the monk simply for the sake of the merit. But even though they may not have much understanding of the spiritual life, they do have a firm belief in the superior virtue of the monk and in the meritoriousness of supporting him.

In the modern West the monk cannot expect to be supported in this way or for this kind of reason, certainly not by the general public; perhaps not even by the lay Buddhist public. It is becoming difficult for monks to be supported in this way even in the East. Some other way must be found to provide for the material needs of the full-timer – that is to say, one who is devoting all his or her time and energy to the Dharma. This is why the development of Right Livelihood businesses is such a crucial aspect of the establishment of Buddhism in the West.[71]

After the great goddess Śrī has made her promise, the chapter continues with, evidently, the Buddha Śākyamuni speaking, although we are not actually told so. He tells of a previous Buddha, a Buddha under whom the goddess Śrī planted, as the text says, a merit root – in other words, under whom she performed skilful actions, actions which have presumably led to her being reborn as the goddess Śrī. He says that this Buddha should be ceremonially worshipped with perfumes, flowers, and incense, and that he should be worshipped by the power of the great goddess Śrī. Śrī herself, he says, should also be worshipped with perfumes, flowers, and incense, as well as by the sprinkling of various juices. In this way one will acquire 'a great heap of corn'.

The Buddha then quotes a rather interesting verse (at least, we can still assume it is the Buddha speaking).

> The earth's savour grows in the earth. The deities rejoice continually.
> The deities of the fruits, crops, shrubs, bushes, trees make the crops
> grow in brilliant condition.[72]

There are two things to notice here. According to the verse, fruits, crops, and so on do not grow as a result only of material factors. Psychical factors – referred to here as *devas* or deities – are also involved. Only a few years ago, people in the West would have dismissed such a notion as utter nonsense, a relic of ancient pre-scientific, animistic superstition. But now

Western people, even scientists, are not so sure. They are now considering the matter rather more carefully.

The second thing to notice is that in this passage the great goddess Śrī becomes a sort of goddess of agriculture, even a goddess of corn. This illustrates something I said in the last chapter – that in a sense all goddesses are earth goddesses. In Śrī's case, the connection is particularly clear. After all, the most primitive form of wealth, next to cattle, is corn or grain. The Sanskrit word for riches (*dhana*) and for corn or grain (*dhānā*) is almost the same, because a wealthy man was a man who had a lot of grain in his storehouse.

The remainder of this chapter of the sūtra consists mainly in directions for the ceremonial worship of Śrī as the goddess of riches, even as the goddess of corn or grain – and various magic spells are provided for the purpose as well. The worship is to be carried out mainly by lay people. They should perform meritorious actions, repeat magic spells over a period of seven years, observe the full moon and new moon days – by keeping the eight moral precepts – and worship all the Buddhas in the morning and in the evening with flowers, perfumes, and incense. And they should do this for the sake of their own Enlightenment and that of all beings. If one does all this, all one's wishes will be fulfilled, the great goddess Śrī will appear, and one's abode will be replete with gold, jewels, and wealth. One will – in short – be blessed with a supply of every blessing.

Clearly this kind of practice is more appropriate for lay people than for monks. Nevertheless, it seems that monks also worshipped the great goddess Śrī. The text says that one who performs worship makes his house – or his monastery or forest retreat – pure. And later the text says:

> In that house, village, city, settlement, monastery or forest retreat, no one at all will cause deficiency.[73]

So it appears that monks were worshipping the great goddess Śrī at the time that the sūtra was committed to writing – that is to say, monks performed magical ceremonies for the acquisition of wealth. This would seem inconsistent with the first part of the chapter, in which the great goddess Śrī promises to supply the monk with everything that he needs anyway. We could regard this passage as evidence of some degeneration, as evidence of the fact that some of the monks, at least, hankered after worldly things. This is one interpretation. Alternatively, we could perhaps regard it as pointing in the direction of the future, to a time when monks would no longer be able to rely for support on the laity in the traditional way.

Be that as it may, the chapter on Śrī clearly falls into two parts. In the first part, the great goddess Śrī promises to give the monk who is the preacher of the sūtra everything he needs. Here we have Buddhist economics in its purest form, the economics of giving. Worldly wealth, worldly riches, are dedicated to purely spiritual ends, placed at the service of the golden light. In the second part of the chapter we are more concerned with the great goddess Śrī herself – more concerned, indeed, with wealth itself. Despite the reference to Enlightenment in this part of the chapter, it seems that wealth and riches are tending to become ends in themselves. In the first part of the chapter we encounter the Buddhist goddess Śrī, but in the second part we really encounter the Hindu goddess Lakshmī. Śrī represents Buddhist economics; Lakshmī represents economics in general. Śrī represents wealth devoted to spiritual ends; Lakshmī represents wealth simply collected and accumulated. Śrī is the bare necessities of life; Lakshmī is abundance, even opulence.

This ceremonial worship of Śrī, or Lakshmī, does raise one topic of fundamental importance: the subject of the production of wealth. It is all very well to talk about giving money, but where is it going to come from? Before you can give it away you've got to have it, and before you can have it you've got to produce it. So how is this to be done? How is wealth to be produced?

The second part of the chapter on Śrī tells us this quite clearly. It says wealth is produced by worship of the great goddess Śrī, or rather of Lakshmī. But can we really accept this? We may need money for our Buddhist activities, but do we really believe that it will come if we perform the ceremonial worship of Lakshmī, even if we perform it for seven years? I don't wish to deny the importance of the psychological factor in the creation of wealth, even the psychic factor; it might help – it certainly wouldn't do any harm – but I don't think it would be the really decisive factor. Hindus, of course, believe very much in worship – not so much in the sense of devotion for the sake of purely spiritual ends, but in magical worship, worship for the sake of bringing about some worldly objective. If you want to pass your examinations, the Hindu would say, worship Sarasvatī; if you want to remove obstacles, worship Ganesh; if you want success in battle, worship Kārttikeya; if you want wealth, worship Lakshmī. We also find this attitude reflected in this chapter of the sūtra. But it does not really belong to Buddhism. It belongs more to

Indian culture, and we need not therefore consider ourselves to be bound by it.

So if wealth is not produced by worship, what is it produced by? It is produced by work, by the application of human energy – your energy and my energy. Of course, there is work and work. There is work which is not in accordance with the principles of Right Livelihood, and there is work which is. Most people are only too familiar with the first kind: work which is concerned with the production of harmful or frivolous things, work which is boring, repetitive, and non-creative, work which is done under conditions that are unfavourable to personal development, and in the company of people who are indifferent or even hostile to spiritual life. But there is an alternative: work done for the sake of the Dharma, not for the sake of a wage or one's own creature comforts. It is done so that the wealth produced or acquired can be given to the Dharma. And it is ideally done with others similarly committed to the spiritual life.

Of course, efforts are being made in the direction of more ethical work practices even within the capitalist system. There is now some ethical stockbroking: companies that advertise themselves as guaranteeing that any money you invest won't go into arms dealing, tobacco, or any other unethical enterprise. This would suggest that some non-capitalist ideology must have got a toehold; usually capitalists want to make money at any price, regardless of ethical considerations. So ethical investment is at least a step in the right direction, even though it is a modification of the system rather than a replacement of it by something more ethical and idealistic.

But I am doubtful as to whether there is an alternative economic system that can supply us with consumer goods in the way and to the extent that the capitalist system does. People tend to assume that we could change from the capitalist system to some other ethically more desirable one and still have the consumer goodies coming in just as before. I personally rather doubt that. I don't even know that one could come up with a viable alternative, but if there *was* an alternative, I think it would be at the expense of at least some of the consumer goodies. It would therefore be an alternative that most people would not be prepared to contemplate – at least, not without a great deal of education, perhaps over a period of centuries.

To give a crude example, suppose everybody did go back to the land and grow their own food. To do that they would probably have to give up their cars and televisions, and most people simply wouldn't be prepared to do that. There is a price to be paid if you want to introduce a more ethical system, and I doubt whether most people would be prepared to pay that price. So we have to be prepared to live in a capitalist world without partaking in capitalist values, practices, and objectives.

I regard the co-operative structure as being opposed to the capitalist one, and that is one reason I favour it. But it is not at all easy to apply. In a team-based Right Livelihood situation, as distinct from a business of the ordinary capitalist type, there is an equal sharing of responsibility – or rather, everybody has responsibility to the measure of their understanding and experience of the business. This principle gives rise to a lot of difficulty, because for various reasons people don't find it easy to co-operate with each other in the way that is essential if the business is to work. Some people *want* to be bosses, although the co-op structure doesn't really allow for that, and others *want* to be told what to do rather than taking a share of the responsibility. These opposite tendencies both detract from the application of the co-operative principle. It is important, therefore, to be realistic about what setting up a Right Livelihood business involves. People sometimes get starry-eyed about how easy and lovely it will be just because you are all working together, but it isn't really as simple as that. However, it is well worth making the effort and having faith in the co-operative principles – that you take what you need and give what you can.

A Buddhist team-based Right Livelihood project has three aims. First, it aims to provide its workers with a means of support – that is, it aims to provide for their needs: not just their need for food, clothing, and shelter, but also their need to go on retreat, buy Dharma books, and so on. Second, it aims to provide a working situation that is conducive to spiritual progress. This means that it functions, within that particular economic context, as a sort of spiritual community, inasmuch as its workers are friends with one another and share the ideals of the project. In short, it should provide the people working within it with an experience of *kalyāna mitratā*, spiritual friendship. And the third aim is to help finance Buddhist activities: Buddhist centres, publications, and so on. To be considered fully successful, the Right Livelihood business needs to fulfil all these three objectives.

If it does so, Right Livelihood becomes a spiritual practice in itself. It becomes what the Hindus call *niṣkāma-karma yoga*, unselfish action practised as a means of self-development. Buddhist economics is not only an economics of giving; it is also an economics of the right acquisition of wealth, the right creation of wealth. And it is this that will help us transform the world.

7

The Moral Order and its Upholders

In the course of this commentary I have not been able to deal exhaustively with the theme of transformation of self and world in the *Sūtra of Golden Light*. I have only been able to draw a rough sketch – and the sketch is not complete. There are quite a few areas of human life and activity still untransformed. And it is with one of these that we will be concerned in this concluding chapter, in which I propose to examine chapter 12 of the sūtra, 'On Instruction concerning Divine Kings'.

The chapter opens with a salutation to a Buddha who has already appeared in the chapter on Śrī. The Buddha Śākyamuni is also saluted, as well as the goddesses Śrī and Sarasvatī. We are then introduced to two kings, King Balendraketu and his son King Ruciraketu. (We are not told whether this Ruciraketu is the same as the Bodhisattva Ruciraketu whom we encountered in chapters 2 and 3.)

At the beginning of chapter 12, King Ruciraketu has just been consecrated or, as we would say, crowned. In other words, he has just been installed as king, presumably by his father. This was apparently the custom in ancient India: each king consecrated his successor and then retired. More often than not he went off into the woods and mountains and became a hermit, passing the rest of his days in contemplation. But before he left, the old king would naturally give the new, young king, some good advice, and this is what we find King Balendraketu doing. He tells his son, King Ruciraketu, that there is a textbook for kings called 'Instruction concerning Divine Kings'. He further says that his father, King Varendraketu, explained it to him when he himself was consecrated, and he adds that for twenty thousand years he has exercised sovereignty according to its teaching (in those days they lived much longer, apparently). It is now his intention to explain that textbook to Ruciraketu.

But first he relates how the textbook came into existence. Once upon a time, he says, the divine kings held a meeting. They met on a great mountain called Vajrākara. Brahma, the teacher of the gods, was present, and so were the four world-protectors, the four great kings. Now we have already met the four great kings – but do we recognize Brahma, the teacher of the gods?

In the sūtra as a whole there are, as we have seen, many examples of Hindu mythology being incorporated into the structure of Buddhist thought and spiritual practice. We have noticed, for instance, that Sarasvatī and Śrī have very definite 'Hindu' features – ethnic, Indian features, we might say. It is much the same here. Here it is Brahma in his originally Vedic or semi-Vedic character who is introduced, not a Brahma such as we encounter in, say, the Pāli scriptures.

In Buddhist cosmology, as we saw in chapter 4, *brahmas* occupy the heavens of the *rūpaloka*, which correspond to the four dhyānas, so they are more or less spiritual beings; but the Brahma of Hindu mythology is a rather different kind of figure. He is conceived of, especially within the Vedic context, as a sort of chaplain or spiritual adviser (the term is *purohit*) to the gods. It is in this capacity that he appears in this chapter. One must therefore dissociate him from the more refined and spiritual Buddhist associations of the term 'Brahma'. Neither should he be confused with the Brahma of Puranic Hindu mythology, who is a creator god. In the earlier Vedic mythology with which we are involved here, Brahma is often conceived of as the brahmin *par excellence*. If the gods, especially Indra, are archetypal rulers, then Brahma is a sort of archetypal brahmin adviser to them. So it is quite appropriate that Brahma gives the instructions concerning divine kings.

Again the question arises as to whether the emergence of these Hindu mythological figures represents a sign of corruption – the Hindu world encroaching on the Buddhist world – or a brave attempt to go out into the Hindu world on behalf of the Buddhists. There is a thin dividing line, really. Yes, you can go out into the world and speak the world's language, and try to express through it your particular spiritual message. But you have to be careful that the world doesn't overcome you, that the medium doesn't become the message. Perhaps one could argue that there was a point at which Buddhism overbalanced and incorporated so much of popular Hindu belief and practice that the spiritual message of Buddhism was eventually swamped and lost sight of. It is perhaps not really possible to say whether this happened in the case of the *Sūtra of Golden Light*, and for us in the West it is an abstract question; there is little danger of our being overwhelmed by Hindu mythology, although modern Indian Buddhists might be very suspicious of any attempt to express Buddhist truths in this sort of language. In the West it is much more the attitudes, beliefs, myths, and legends of Christianity against which we have to be on our guard.

Anyway, it is definitely the Brahma of the Vedic tradition who advises the four great kings on this occasion. They begin by asking him a series of questions:

> You, Brahma, are a venerable teacher among the gods, you are lord of the gods. Solve our problems. Remove our doubt. Why is a king, though born among men, called 'divine'? And for what reason is a king called a 'divine son'? If he is born here in the world of men, he should become king, but how will a god exercise kingship among men?[74]

Apparently it was the ancient Indian custom to address kings as 'deva', much as we say 'Your Majesty'. *Deva*, of course, means god with a small G – a divine being, a divine one – and this is the usage we find in the Pāli Buddhist texts. The Buddha himself, for instance, addresses King Bimbisāra as 'deva', though translators usually render this as 'your majesty', which rather obscures the point. So the four great kings are asking why the king is addressed in this fashion. After all, he is to all appearances a man. Why is he addressed as a divine being? The rest of the chapter consists of Brahma's reply to this question, which is very interesting, not only for what he says but also for the terms in which he says it.

In the course of his reply he uses, in fact, two kinds of terms, even two languages, which we can call the mythic and the conceptual, or the mythic and the rational. This serves as a reminder of the general situation in the midst of which Buddhism arose. Very broadly speaking, the age in which the Buddha lived was an age of transition from old values to new values, from the ethnic to the universal, from the group to the individual. The group spoke, as it were, the language of myth, while the individual spoke the language of concepts, the language of reason. As far as the existing records show, the Buddha himself spoke the language of reason. Later, individuals in the Buddhist tradition learned to speak the language of myth and adapt it to their own higher spiritual purposes, but that is another story. As a literary document, Brahma's speech, or the chapter in which Brahma's speech is embedded, belongs to a period one thousand years later than that of the Buddha, but it reflects very clearly the process of transition from the old to the new, from Vedic Hinduism to Buddhism. Brahma therefore gives, in effect, two replies to the four great kings, or rather, he gives the same reply twice in two different languages: firstly the language of myth, and secondly the language of concepts, or even the language of doctrine.

Brahma says first of all that, having been asked, he will speak, for the good and the welfare of all beings, of the origin of kings born in the abode of men, and explain how they become kings in their regions. So first we have the more mythic explanation. Brahma says:

> Under the blessing of the divine kings, he will enter the womb of his mother. Having first been blessed by the gods, he afterwards enters her womb. Although as king he is born and dies in the world of men, yet since he comes from the gods he is called a divine son. The Thirty-three divine kings have given a portion to the king. Hence his sonship to all the gods, for the lord of men has been magically created.[75]

So here Brahma makes four statements. They are not logically consistent, but this doesn't really matter, because we are concerned here with myth. The first statement is that the king comes to this earth from the world of the gods. He is, as it were, a god incarnate. Second statement: before entering the womb of his future mother, he is blessed by the divine kings, and by the gods. Third statement: the thirty-three divine kings have each given a portion of themselves to the king; in other words, the king is fashioned, as it were, from their substance. And, fourth statement: the king has been magically created; presumably this means that the king possesses what is called an illusory body, a body that, like a mirage, is perceived by people but does not really exist in the sense of having any real empirical existence.

Inconsistent though they may be, these four statements all clearly convey one thing, which is that the king is not an ordinary man. There is something divine about him; he is indeed a divinity. This belief, strange as it may sound to us, was widespread at a certain period of ancient history, and indeed traces of it are found even in modern times, even in England. The belief that the king was a sort of divine being was particularly strong in ancient Egypt, in Sumeria, and, in a somewhat different form, in China; it was certainly strong at one time in India. But by the Buddha's day it had already begun to decline. A more rational justification of the nature and function of kingship was needed, and it is this that Brahma now proceeds to offer.

Continuing his speech, Brahma says:

> For the sake of suppressing what is unlawful, a destroyer of evil deeds, he would establish beings in good activity in order to send them to the abode of the gods. Whether a man or a god, a Gandharva, a lord of men, a Rākṣasa, an untouchable, he removes evil deeds. The king is the parent of those who do good deeds. The king has been blessed by the gods in order to show their fruition and fruit. The king has been blessed by the gods as belonging to the present world to show the fruition and fruit of deeds well done and of deeds ill done. For when a king overlooks an evil deed in his region and does not inflict appropriate punishment on the evil person, in the neglect of evil deeds lawlessness grows greatly, wicked acts and quarrels arise in great number in the realm.[76]

Before going on we need to be sure we know who these gods or devas really are in this context. In the Vedas, the most ancient Hindu sacred books (or what were later written down as books), the devas are on the whole personifications of natural phenomena. There is, for instance, Sūrya the sun god; there is Indra the god of rain and violent thunderstorm. There is Uṣas, the goddess of the dawn, and Agni, the god of fire, particularly the sacrificial fire. There are the Maruts, the wind gods. All these are personifications of natural phenomena. Later on, there arose gods of a different kind, gods that personified ethical and spiritual qualities, gods like Mitra and Varuṇa; even deities that personified human activities and functions, like the goddess Vāc, speech, whom we met in the chapter on Buddhism and Culture.

When we meet some of these gods a few hundred years later, in the Buddhist scriptures, we find that a great change has taken place. The gods are no longer personifications of natural phenomena, no longer to be feared or propitiated. They are beings like ourselves, only happier, more powerful, and much longer-lived. So what has happened? What has brought about this change? What has in fact happened is that a new idea has been introduced: the law of karma, or, if you like, an extension of the law of karma. It is not always realized that the law of karma was not known to the most ancient Aryans. It is briefly referred to in one of the most ancient pre-Buddhist Upanishads, but only as an esoteric teaching. It is with Buddhism, and perhaps Jainism too, that karma is placed in the forefront of the teaching and described in a full and detailed manner.

The law of karma is the operation on one level of the still more comprehensive law of conditionality, which applies to all conditioned existence whatsoever. The law of karma applies to all sentient existence. It applies wherever there is consciousness, wherever there is mind and will. Briefly stated, it says that skilful action produces happiness and unskilful action produces suffering. Skilful actions are those that are free from greed, hatred, and delusion; and which are, on the contrary, accompanied by contentment, friendliness, and wisdom. Unskilful actions are those that are accompanied by, and spring from, greed, hatred, and delusion.

Traditionally, the law of karma is envisaged as operating not just within the context of the present life, but over a whole series of lives; in other words, the law of karma, traditionally speaking, is bound up with the fact of rebirth. Because the law of karma operates at all levels of conditioned existence, a human being can be reborn as a god as a result of performing skilful actions while on earth; and conversely a god can be reborn as a human being. We can also be reborn as asuras, infernal beings, hungry ghosts, and so on. According to the popular version of the teaching, human beings can even be reborn as animals as a result of performing unskilful actions. All this is depicted in the well-known Tibetan Wheel of Life.

We are now in a better position to understand Brahma's second, more rational, explanation of why kings are addressed as 'deva'. We'll take it sentence by sentence. First of all, Brahma says:

> For the sake of suppressing what is unlawful, a destroyer of evil deeds, he would establish beings in good activity in order to send them to the abode of the gods.

As we have already seen, the king has come from heaven; the king is a god reborn on earth as a man. This is common ground to both of Brahma's explanations, the mythical and the rational. In the mythical account, however, there is no explanation of how the god became a god. No explanation, in fact, is needed. A god is a personification of natural phenomena.

In the rational account, however, an explanation is needed, and this explanation is given within the framework provided by the law of karma. A god has become what he is as a result of skilful actions. Originally he was a man, but having performed an extraordinary number of skilful actions, he was reborn after death in a higher heavenly world as what we call a deva, a god. In that higher heavenly world he enjoys great happiness and power, and he lives for a very long time, even for thousands of years. But eventually the karma that caused him to be reborn as a god is exhausted, and he is reborn again on earth. However, as a secondary result of all his skilful actions, he is not reborn as an ordinary man. He is reborn as a very prominent man, a leading man, a king.

All this is common ground to all forms of Buddhism; there is no school that would not accept it, although they might place varying degrees of emphasis upon it. But the whole idea suggests a rather idealized view of kingship; it suggests that the institution of kingship is such that it has a definite moral basis, and is an extremely happy state. It would have to be so in order to be the reward, as it were, of skilful deeds. So kings could be said to be gods reborn only where the institution of kingship exists in an ideal form.

Put it this way. Suppose you were to be reborn in the family of one of the Caesars, say Caligula or Nero. That would hardly be a blessing – it would be more of a disaster. So kingship as such cannot be the reward of virtuous deeds, and therefore it is not necessarily the case that kings have been devas in their previous existences. It would seem to depend upon the nature of kingship at the time into which they were born. If one happened to be born into a royal family that represented or embodied an ideal conception of kingship, in a time of peace and prosperity, that could conceivably be the result of skilful actions performed in the past, and you could conceivably have been a deva in your previous existence. But if you were born into a royal family that simply exercised power, that had no moral basis or standards, in a time of war and conflict, even conflict within that royal family itself, with the possibility of being murdered or assassinated at an early age, or living in terror for decade after decade – well, clearly that would not be the result of any skilful actions you had performed.

So it would seem that Brahma is speaking of quite an ideal state of affairs, of kingship in the ideal sense, and of what one might describe as cosmically normal conditions. It also appears that, at the time of which Brahma is speaking, and presumably at the time the sūtra was composed or written down, kingship was hereditary, whereas in modern times rulers are often elected, or even seize power in the case of military dictators. Brahma's statement cannot be taken as implying that present-day rulers are gods reborn. They could well be asuras reborn, or – even worse – pretas.

Of course, one cannot infer from this that rulers born into unfavourable circumstances have done so necessarily because they have committed unskilful deeds in former lives. This raises a general question: can the innocent suffer? Take the case, say, of the Dalai Lamas. The ninth, tenth, and eleventh Dalai Lamas died, or were murdered, very young. It could be that the particular being who was identified as the Dalai Lama in each of these cases was not in fact the incarnation of the Bodhisattva Avalokiteśvara, but some other unfortunate being whose unskilful actions had caused him to be born into that particular family and selected in that particular way. On the other hand, it could be that he was indeed the real Dalai Lama, but that Avalokiteśvara's efforts on behalf of the Tibetan people were simply cut short by people who were hungry for power themselves. There are those two possibilities – but which of them applies to the case of any particular Dalai Lama we probably have no way of knowing. The popular Indian Buddhist attitude seems to be that the good man is always successful, because he has so much *puṇya* to his credit that no real misfortune can happen to him, but one has to question that.[77] A Bodhisattva, after all, is willing to take risks.

The Indian attitude, including the Indian Buddhist attitude, can be one of rather superficial optimism. Traditional Buddhism sometimes doesn't give sufficient weight to the fact that a person who is genuinely innocent and doesn't have a lot of unskilful karma to his credit – or rather debit – can suffer as the result of other people's unskilful actions. Perhaps there is too great a tendency – not so much in Buddhism, but in Indian thought in general – to assume that if anything unpleasant befalls you, you must have deserved it. This would seem to reduce everything that befalls you to your karma, to your own previous skilful or unskilful actions. But that is not really the Buddhist teaching.

To the best of my knowledge the teaching of the five *niyamas* – which shows that there are four other levels on which conditionality operates besides the karmic level – doesn't appear in Buddhism outside the Theravāda.[78] Even in the Theravāda itself it appears not in the canon but in the commentarial literature, as a sort of systematization of the teaching contained in the canon. One of the most important places in which it appears is Buddhaghoṣa's commentary on the *Dhamma-saṅgṇī*, the first book of the *Abhidhamma Piṭaka*. It doesn't seem to have reached Tibetan

Buddhism or the Sarvastivāda. The consequence is that in Tibetan Buddhism, and in the Mahāyāna generally, there is a tendency to think that everything that happens to you is a result of your own personal past karma, although the teaching of the five *niyamas* makes it clear that that is not the case.

No one school of Buddhism has got the whole Buddhist teaching, although there are useful teachings to be found in all the schools. So if you confine yourself to Tibetan Buddhist and Sarvastivādin sources, for example, you don't come across the teaching of the five *niyamas*, and that is a serious loss which can cause serious misunderstanding. Broadly speaking, no one school of Buddhism can concern itself with all possible aspects. Some things are bound to get left out, and others are bound to be emphasized. This makes it important to have as wide an acquaintance as one can with all the different forms of Buddhism. It may even be that relevant points are missed by the Buddhist tradition as a whole, for various perhaps historical reasons. Perhaps we can take a point from Plato or Schopenhauer or Shelley that is useful to us, but does not occur in the Buddhist tradition. It probably won't be a major point, but even minor points can be very useful at a comparatively early stage of one's spiritual development.

So we can say that Indian Buddhism didn't seem to be sufficiently aware that such a thing as tragedy was possible. It is perhaps an insight that has been contributed by the West. You might think that if someone was born with an accumulation of merit, he would be able to guide his life away from adverse events, and that is certainly the case – but there are limits. Sometimes other people, for unskilful reasons, are determined to do you some harm or injury. The fact that you yourself have always been skilful or are highly intelligent will not necessarily enable you to evade that. You may be able to maintain a positive mental or emotional attitude, but externally you may be defeated, or even killed, despite all the *puṇya* you have accumulated. Traditional Indian thought, including Buddhist thought to some extent, doesn't take that sufficiently into consideration. It always wants a happy ending. This attitude seems to be embedded in the Indian attitude to life, which is why in India they have got drama but not tragedy. There is always a happy ending, even if in order to produce it a god has to appear and restore all the dead bodies to life. It's a bit like the Book of Job, which comes very near to being a tragedy, but swerves away at the last minute. After all Job's sufferings God gives him back everything he has lost tenfold – as though having ten more sons and ten more daughters could compensate you for the sons and daughters that you have lost, as though the tragedy, the suffering, could be wiped out.

King Bimbisāra in the Pāli Canon may have lost his kingdom – but his story is no real tragedy. After all, he was a Stream Entrant, possibly an *anāgāmi*, so being deprived of his kingdom was no great loss from his point of view. A man who has attained Stream Entry cannot possibly be regarded as having failed in life, regardless of what has happened to him externally. If Oedipus or King Lear had gained Stream Entry, there would have been no tragedy, whatever other disasters may have befallen them.

So when Brahma says that a king has been a deva in his previous life, we have to ask ourselves what he is really saying, what kind of conception of kingship he is referring to. In some ways it doesn't seem very much in accordance with the kind of Western conception of kingship implied by Shakespeare's idea that 'uneasy lies the head that wears a crown'. On the other hand, another of Shakespeare's characters says 'There's such divinity doth hedge a king.' Shakespeare's historical plays certainly seem to involve the assumption that there is something divine about kingship. In the British coronation ceremony, which goes back to medieval times, the sovereign is ordained as a clerk in holy orders, and anointed with consecrated oil. Especially in Stuart times, the king was regarded as God's representative on earth. King Charles I asserted this principle very strongly at the time of his trial – that he was responsible only to God, not to his subjects. That was his basic principle, and he never budged from it: 'A subject and a sovereign are clean different things.'

There was also the belief, right down to the time of Queen Anne, that the sovereign had healing power. There was a disease called scrofula which was known as the 'king's evil', because people believed that the king (or queen) could heal it by touching the afflicted person. Charles II, it is estimated, touched about 200,000 people in the course of his reign. As a child Dr Johnson was touched by Queen Anne for this purpose – one of the last people in England to be touched in that way. It was believed that this power – which is supposed to have descended from Edward the Confessor through all the English sovereigns – died out with the Stuarts, because the Hanoverians were a collateral branch and therefore hadn't inherited that power. There are even now some remnants of the belief in divine kingship in the case of the English monarchy. It is quite interesting how much fuss was made over Princess Diana's shaking hands with victims of AIDS.

Although it is a commonplace within Buddhist tradition that the king was a deva in his previous life, the *Sūtra of Golden Light* has a further point of its own to make. As a result of his past history – we could even say his previous positive conditioning – the king has a natural inclination towards skilful actions. He performs skilful actions himself, and he encourages others to perform them. Not only that; as king, he suppresses what is unlawful, what is against the moral order. He destroys evil deeds. He establishes beings in skilful, meritorious activities.

He does this, we are told, so that as a result of such activities beings may be reborn in the world of the gods: that is to say, in the world from which he himself has come. This brings to mind a parallel with the *Bhagavad Gītā* which no one seems to have remarked on before. The *Bhagavad Gītā* is a dialogue between Krishna and Arjuna which forms part of the great Hindu epic, the *Mahabharata*. The *Gītā* consists of eighteen chapters, and in chapter 4, Sri Krishna explains to Arjuna that both of them have been born many times before. The difference is that he, Krishna, remembers his previous lives, while Arjuna does not. Krishna then says 'When righteousness declines, when unrighteousness increases, then I appear for the protection of the good. For the destruction of the wicked, for the establishment of Dharma, I am born age after age.' This is perhaps, at least in India, the most famous verse in the entire *Bhagavad Gītā*. It is the foundation of Hindu *avatāravāda*, the belief in the successive descents, or, as we might say, incarnations, of God – God with a capital G.

But there are two important differences between this text and the *Sūtra of Golden Light*. In the *Bhagavad Gītā* it's the Supreme Being himself who descends as Rama, Krishna, and so on; and he descends of his own free will. But in Buddhism, of course, there is no supreme being. The descent takes place within the framework of conditioned existence – from a higher to a lower plane of conditioned existence, from heaven to earth – and it takes place under the law of karma. Brahma speaks of the king as the 'destroyer of evil deeds'. Sri Krishna, however, speaks of himself as coming 'for the destruction of the wicked'.

Continuing with his explanation of why kings are addressed as 'deva', Brahma says:

Whether a man or a god, a Gandharva, a lord of men, a Rākṣasa, an untouchable, he removes evil deeds.

The connection here is not quite clear; the grammar, in fact, is not quite clear. 'He' could refer to the king, because in the previous sentence, Brahma has been talking about the king – 'he [i.e. the king] would establish beings in good activity'. So the sentence might mean that the king discourages all classes of sentient beings from performing unskilful actions. However, it's more likely that the sentence is a sort of interjection, so that 'he removes evil deeds' is to be understood more as 'one removes evil deeds'. In other words, it doesn't matter what class of beings one belongs to, what position in society one occupies, whether one is a man or a god: one can still perform skilful actions and evil deeds, and one has the possibility of a higher heavenly rebirth. Understood in this way, the sentence is an affirmation of the basis upon which Brahma's rational explanation of the nature and function of kingship rests. In other words, it is an affirmation of the law of karma.

But it is also possible to understand the sentence in another way. We could take it that it doesn't matter what the king's origin is, what caste he belongs to by birth. The main thing is that he removes evil deeds. If he does that, he is a king. This, of course, is very much in accordance with the general spirit of Buddhism as a universal religion, and in direct contrast to orthodox Hinduism, according to which only one who belongs by birth to the Kṣatriya caste can be king, just as only one who belongs to the Brahmin caste by birth can teach.

The next sentence is very short:

The king is the parent of those who do good deeds.

This means that those who do good deeds have nothing to fear from the king; he will look after them and protect them. More than that: by encouraging people to perform good deeds, he stands in a parental relation to them, morally speaking. I will have something more to say about the parental function in a more literal sense later on.

The next two sentences say practically the same thing in different words, so we will take them together. Brahma says:

The king has been blessed by the gods in order to show their fruition and fruit. The king has been blessed by the gods as belonging to the present world to show the fruition and fruit of deeds well done and of deeds ill done.

These sentences comprise the essence of Brahma's whole speech, the essence of the 'Instruction concerning Divine Kings', the essence of King Balendraketu's advice to his son King Ruciraketu. The matter is expressed still more clearly later on in Brahma's speech, when he says:

He is called king because he acts in various ways in order to demonstrate the fruition and fruit of acts that are well done or ill-done.

This means that the social order should mirror the law of karma. Under the law of karma, skilful actions result in happiness, and unskilful actions result in suffering. It should be the same within the social order: skilful actions should be encouraged, and unskilful actions should be punished. In other words, the social order should be a moral order, and the upholder of that moral order is the king. Each king is responsible for upholding it in his own region.

The moral order works according to a very simple principle, one which is even more simple and fundamental in a sense than the law of karma. *Actions have consequences.* We often forget this. We tend to do things on the spur of the moment, without thinking. We don't realize that what we are doing will have consequences – perhaps even very serious consequences – both for ourselves and for others. To act without thinking of the consequences of one's actions is irresponsibility; to act bearing in mind the consequences of one's actions is responsibility. To the extent that one acts responsibly, one is an individual; to the extent that one acts without responsibility, one is not an individual. So if one wants to become an individual, one must learn to act responsibly. One must remember that actions have consequences; one must be mindful of the law of karma; one should understand why the social order should be a moral order.

But why *should* the social order be a moral order? I have already answered this question to some extent. If the social order is a moral order, then it is a training ground, as it were, in skilful actions. If we perform skilful actions we will accumulate merit, and if we accumulate merit we will be reborn in a happy heavenly state – that is, as a god. So if the social order really *is* a moral order, if the king does his duty – if, in other words, he does not overlook any evil deed – and if his subjects observe the moral order and perform skilful actions, the result will be that they will all be reborn as gods, and the ranks of the gods will be strengthened.

This is of great significance. There is a constant battle going on in the universe between the gods and the asuras, between the positive and the negative forces within the conditioned, within saṁsāra. Sometimes the gods are victorious, but sometimes the asuras win the day. The gods, therefore, have a vested interest, as it were, in human beings performing skilful actions, because such human beings will be reborn as gods and the ranks of the gods will be strengthened. They will be then more likely to overcome the asuras. So the traditional Buddhist point of view is that the maintenance of the moral order on earth is of cosmic significance, because it helps to keep the balance in favour of the positive, even the spiritual, forces in the universe.

As we saw in the chapter on 'The Spiritual Significance of Confession', the spiritual is not the same thing as the transcendental. We should not, therefore, confuse this battle between the gods and the asuras with the conflict between the golden light and the darkness, the conflict between Enlightenment and nature. The first is a battle within the conditioned, but the second is the much more serious and radical conflict between the Unconditioned and the conditioned; or rather, between the Unconditioned and the negative part of the conditioned. The positive part of the conditioned is on the side of the Unconditioned, as it were. The gods are on the side of the Buddha; skilful actions are on the side of Enlightenment; the ethical is on the side of the transcendental; *śīla* and *samādhi* are on the side of prajñā; the moral order is on the side of the spiritual community.

However, I am going too far too fast. Let's go back to the responsible individual, the individual who performs skilful actions; or rather, let us go back to individuals in the plural. The moral order can be described as a network of ethically responsible individuals, people who act responsibly towards themselves and towards one another; people, that is to say, who try to do what is truly best for themselves and others. This creates a society in which everyone acts in an ethically responsible manner, a society which is totally a moral order, which clearly, faithfully, and fully reflects the law of karma. Perhaps no human society – certainly no large human society – has ever been a completely moral order. But, large or small, all human societies are moral orders to some extent.

The moral order obliges us to act in an ethically responsible manner, to perform skilful actions, to pay some heed to the law of karma. In other words, it obliges us to develop as individuals. The social order should be a moral order because ultimately it helps people to develop spiritually. We cannot develop without becoming ethical individuals, without developing some sense of responsibility towards ourselves and others. But it is very difficult to be an ethical individual in an unethical society, so society must help the individual; society must be a moral order. In other words, it must reflect the operation of the law of karma.

Now the first human society with which we come into contact when we enter this world is, of course, the family. The family is not just a biological unit; it should also be a moral order. It should reflect the larger moral order of society, just as society itself should reflect the ideal moral order which is the law of karma. And the upholders of the moral order within the family are, obviously, the parents. Parents are divine kings on a small scale. They educate their children in the observance of moral norms. They teach them that actions have consequences. It's not just a question of socializing your children; you have to give them some understanding, however rudimentary, of the law of karma, some training, however elementary, in the performance of skilful action. This will help the child to become later on a true member of a society which is also a moral order, and will help him to develop as an individual.

In the Pāli scriptures we find the Buddha himself doing this very thing. We are told that one day when he was out walking, maybe going for alms, the Buddha passed a group of small boys. And – as small boys will, whether in India or England or anywhere else – they were tormenting something. They had found a crow that had broken its wing, and they were tormenting it. So the Buddha went up to them and asked them whether they would like to be treated like that. So they replied no, of course not. The Buddha then said, well, if they would not like to be treated like that themselves, why treat others like that? The crow doesn't like it any more than they would. Hearing it put like that, the boys understood, and let the crow go free.

It is well known that children need to know where they stand, what they can and cannot do, what actions will meet with approval and what actions will get them into trouble. If the parents laugh when the child is naughty one day, but get angry with him the next day for just the same kind of naughtiness, the child will become confused and even anxious, because he just doesn't know what to do. And it is much the same with adults. We need to feel that certain actions will definitely be followed by certain consequences. We need to exist within an order; best of all, to exist within a moral order, although, psychologically speaking at least, almost any order is probably better than no order at all.

So what happens when the moral order breaks down? What happens when 'the king overlooks an evil deed', when an evil deed is not followed by its appropriate result? To find this out, we must go back to chapter 12 of the sūtra, back to Brahma's speech. This is his picture of a society which is not a moral order, and which is therefore not a society at all. I will just quote enough to give an idea of what happens when the moral order of society collapses.

Brahma says:

When a king overlooks an evil deed in his region and does not inflict appropriate punishment on the evil person, in the neglect of evil deeds lawlessness grows greatly, wicked acts and quarrels arise in great numbers in the realm. The chief gods are wrathful in the dwellings of the Thirty-three when a king overlooks an evil deed in his region. His region is smitten with dreadful, most terrible acts of wickedness, and his realm is destroyed on the arrival of a foreign army, his enjoyments and houses. Whoever has accumulated wealth, by various evil acts they deprive one another of them. If he does not perform the duty on account of which he has kingship, he destroys his own realm, just as the lord of elephants tramples on a lotus-pool. Unfavourable winds will blow; unfavourable showers of rain will fall; unfavourable will be planets and asterisms, likewise moon and sun. Crop, flower, fruit and seed will not properly ripen. Famine will arise where the king is neglectful. Unhappy in mind will the gods be in their dwellings when the king overlooks an evil deed in his region. All the kings of the gods will say to one another: 'Unlawful is this king, for he supports the side of the lawless.' This king will ere long anger the gods. Through the anger of the gods his region will perish. There will be destruction by the weapon in the region where there is lawlessness. Wicked acts, quarrels, diseases will arise. The lords of the gods will be angry. The gods will ignore him. His realm will be ruined. The king will come to grief. He will find himself separated from his loved ones, from brother or son, separated from his beloved wife. Or his daughter will die. There will be showers of meteors, likewise mock suns. Fear of foreign armies and famine will increase greatly. His beloved minister will die and also his beloved elephant. As soon as they have died, his beloved horses and female camels will likewise die. They will carry off one another's house, enjoyments, wealth. In every district they will slay one another with arms. In the regions there will be disputes, quarrels, evil acts. An evil demon will enter the realm. There will be severe disease. After that the venerable will become lawless. His ministers and attendants will become lawless. After that there will be respect for the lawless person and there will be constantly oppression of law-abiding beings. Where there is honour for lawless people and oppression of the law-abiding, there three things go wild: asterisms, water, and winds. Three things perish when there is acceptance of lawless people: the savour and strength of the good Law, the strength of beings, and the savour of the earth. Where there is honour for untruthful people and dishonour for truthful people, there will be three things: famine, thunderbolt, and defilement. After that there will be no savour or strength in fruit or crop. Many beings will become ill in those regions. Large sweet fruits in those regions will become small, bitter and sharp. Play, laughter and pleasure, things previously enjoyable, will become feeble and unenjoyable, fraught with hundreds of troubles. The moist nature and the savour of crops and fruits will disappear. They will not satisfy the body, the senses, or the elements. Beings will become of bad complexion, of very little strength, and very weak. Having eaten much food they will not attain satiety. After that they will get no strength, prowess or energy. Beings in those regions will become without prowess. Beings will become disease-ridden, oppressed by various illnesses. There will arise evil demons, asterisms and various Rākṣasas. A king would be lawless if he stood on the side of lawlessness: the three spheres in the circle of the whole triple world are harmed. Numerous such evils arise in those regions when a king is partisan and overlooks an evil act. If he overlooks an evil act, a king does not exercise his kingship according to the duty for which he was consecrated by the lords of the gods.[79]

The picture that Brahma paints is a grim and terrible one. It is also a picture that is not entirely unfamiliar. Certain features of it we recognize only too well, because we ourselves are living today in a society that is not a moral order. The moral order has not broken down equally everywhere, but it has broken down to a great extent in many parts of the world, and in many areas of human life. This is not to say that large numbers of people have all at once become deliberately wicked. People are probably much the same as they always were, but the situation has changed.

To begin with, the spiritual values on which the moral order was traditionally based are no longer so widely accepted. Science and technology seem to have made them irrelevant. In some parts of the world, in some societies, those values have indeed been openly attacked and overtly rejected, and even where that has not happened, spiritual values are not really important to significant numbers of people. The moral order of society therefore has no real, solid foundation. It continues only out of force of habit, as it were, and that cannot go on for very long. Then, corporate life has become not only larger but also more impersonal. Sometimes it is very difficult to find out who is responsible for what, who has done what. Things just happen – even things that have a strong effect on us personally. We cannot trace them back to anyone in particular. Nobody accepts responsibility. They are nobody's actions. This is particularly true of government departments, as well as of large businesses.

Social life, life as a member of a human society, has become very complex, like an enormous Persian carpet, but one without a pattern – just thousands and thousands of threads running in all directions, making it impossible to see where any particular thread begins and ends. Thousands upon thousands of events are happening in society, but it is difficult to trace any one event through its entire course, to know what has caused what. Very often we don't even know whether a particular factor in the situation is cause or effect.

The result of all this is that we feel we are living in a world where actions do not have consequences; where certain causes are not invariably followed by certain effects – at least, not in the human world. We feel that we are living in a society that is not an intelligible moral order. We feel that there is not much point in performing skilful actions, that it doesn't matter what you do, because actions seem to have no real moral consequences, at least none that one can either experience or observe. We thus cease to be ethically responsible, and to that extent we cease to be individuals; not only cease to develop, but even deteriorate. Not only that; we feel that we do not count personally. We feel that society at large takes no notice of us, doesn't take us into account, doesn't listen to what we say even when we can say it. Consequently we feel frustrated, powerless, and resentful.

So how can the moral order of society be restored? We no longer have any kings in the old sense, so we cannot exhort them to uphold the moral order as Brahma does. What are we to do? Well, there is only one thing we can do. We ourselves have to become the upholders of the moral order, to the extent that we can within our own sphere of influence. We ourselves have to become divine kings. Those who are true individuals or who are trying to develop individuality have to get together, have to establish an ethical order on a small scale among themselves, a smaller moral order within the larger non-moral order. And within that smaller moral order we have to behave responsibly towards ourselves and one another, strengthen our sense of ethical responsibility, and increase our awareness of the law of karma. To the extent that we can do this, we will become individuals. And when we become individuals, we will be able to act more effectively in the larger world, to act with ethical responsibility. The moral order to which we belong will give us the strength to do this.

This moral order is what I call the positive group. It is not the spiritual community, but it is the basis on which the spiritual community can be established. It doesn't represent the transformation of the world any more than the development of a sense of ethical responsibility represents the transformation of the individual self, but it is the basis of that transformation, just as the development of a sense of ethical responsibility is the basis for the transformation of self.

Within a spiritual community, within a Buddhist order, there can be no question of law and punishment, because law and punishment are based at least to some extent on the power mode, and by its very nature a spiritual community is based on the love mode. One member of the order cannot punish another, because that would mean invoking the power mode. In any case, if a member of the order behaves in such a way that punishment is necessary, he or she is to that extent no longer a member of the order. Suppose, to take an extreme example, he or she commits a murder. Because they have broken a precept to such a disastrous extent, they cease to be a member of the order. There would no question of their being punished by the order; they would simply have placed themselves beyond the pale of the order. The order wouldn't even punish them by expelling them; they would automatically expel themselves, and the order would recognize that.

But suppose a member of the order somehow succeeded to political power. Then the question of law and punishment would arise. One would have to consider the extent to which an order member could exercise political power; in other words to what extent they could function in the power mode. I would suggest that one can operate in the power mode in the world so long as that power mode is based on and controlled by the love mode – as when, for example, you forcibly restrain a child from doing something that would be harmful for the child. What form punishment would take if a member of the spiritual community happened to be in a position of power it is difficult to say; it seems remote from the present reality, but it might have to be considered one day.

There are, of course, 'Buddhist states' that have laws and punishments, but these do not always spring from Buddhist principles. In Burma, for example, it seems that they base themselves on the laws of Manu to a great extent.[80] Usually what has happened is that the influence of Buddhism has modified laws and punishments to some extent, rather than introducing a system of laws and punishments based on Buddhist principles.

One has to regard the extent to which a spiritual community can exercise political power as an open question. Traditionally, except in Tibet, the view has been that the spiritual community, especially if it is in the form of a monastic order, should exercise influence rather than power – but one could argue that that is a shirking of responsibility.

Dr Ambedkar, the great Indian statesman who championed the cause of India's Untouchables and eventually led them in converting to Buddhism, has discussed the question of whether a society can be kept in order by force.[81] His conclusion is that obviously it can't. There needs to be some generally accepted moral principle which will hold society together and maintain order. You can perhaps keep an anti-social minority under control by force, but you can't keep the majority of people under control by force – at least not for long – so a moral basis is needed. Perhaps the spiritual community would be better occupied in trying to strengthen the moral basis of society than in taking on political power and having direct responsibility for dealing with the anti-social minority by methods that are in accordance with the power mode rather than the love mode.

The spiritually committed can never really give up hope on anyone. You can't think 'There are people who are simply not spiritual, and need a kind of law distinct from that which operates within the spiritual community.' On the other hand, you need to be open to the possibility that even those people who in the long run would be amenable to the love mode, can only be dealt with in the short term in accordance with the power mode. The fact that you forcibly prevent the child from running into the fire doesn't mean that you give up all hope that one day he will be a rational human being. But it seems to me that the law and order problems experienced by many countries today are mainly attributable to the fact that the moral order has broken down for many people, and there are certain moral sanctions which they no longer accept or recognize.

Despite his fearful warning of what happens when the king overlooks an evil deed in his region, when he fails to uphold the moral order, Brahma's reply to the questions of the four great kings ends on a positive note, with a description of what will happen if the king *does* uphold the moral order. He says that the gods will be joyful. Asterisms, moon, and sun will move properly, the winds blow at the proper time, rain fall at the proper time, and the abode of gods become full of immortals and sons of immortals. The realm will become full of plenty. The king will become famous, and he will easily protect his subjects.

I want to end this exploration of the *Sūtra of Golden Light* on a positive note too. The crucial thing is this: there is only one way of transforming one's own self and the world, and that is by making them receptive to the golden light, the light of the transcendental. It is only this light that can really transform. In the words of the sūtra itself:

> By the exposition of the Suvarṇaprabhāsa [the golden light] may the ocean of evil be dried up for me; may the ocean of acts be destroyed for me; may the ocean of impurities be destroyed for me; may the ocean of merit be filled for me; may the ocean of knowledge be purified for me. By the excellent splendour of flawless knowledge may I become the ocean of all virtues. Filled with jewel-like virtues, with the virtues of enlightenment, by the power of the Suvarṇaprabhāsa and its Confession, may there be for me splendour of merits; may the splendour of enlightenment be pure for me. By the excellent splendour of flawless knowledge may there be splendour of body for me. By the shining of the splendour of my merit may I become distinguished in the whole triple world. Continually endowed with the power of merit, a deliverer from the ocean of woe, and like a sea of all blessing, may I proceed to enlightenment in a future aeon.[82]

Both now and in the years to come, may this be the aspiration of us all.

•

Notes and References

1 *The Sūtra of Golden Light*, trans. R.E.Emmerick, Pali Text Society, London 1979. All references are to this edition.

2 For a fuller exposition of the Bodhisattva ideal, see Sangharakshita, *A Survey of Buddhism*, 7th ed., Windhorse, Glasgow 1993, pp.431ff.

3 For further reading on Buddhism and Western culture, see Subhuti, *Sangharakshita: A New Voice in the Buddhist Tradition*, Windhorse, Birmingham 1994, chapter 10.

4 *Dharma* is a word with numerous meanings. Among other things it can mean truth or reality. It also stands for all those teachings and methods that are conducive to gaining Enlightenment, and thereby seeing things as they really are, particularly the teachings of the Buddha.

5 See *The Jātaka or Stories of the Buddha's Former Births*, trans. Robert Chalmers, Pali Text Society, London 1981.

6 For a fuller exposition of the development of Buddhism, see Andrew Skilton, *A Concise History of Buddhism*, Windhorse, Birmingham 1994, and Sangharakshita, *A Survey of Buddhism*, op.cit.

7 Buddhists and other non-Christians do not use the terms AD – 'Year of our Lord' – and BC. They refer to years under this accepted dating convention as either CE (Common Era) or BCE (before Common Era).

8 Gnosticism is a religious movement of Eastern origin which penetrates early Christianity, giving rise to a variety of sects who claimed spiritual knowledge. They developed the figure of Sophia to explain how the divine principle of light came into contact with darkness. See Tobias Churton, *The Gnostics*, Weidenfeld and Nicholson, London 1987.

9 *Prajñā* is the direct intuitive apprehension of the real nature of things. This can be brought about, according to Buddhist tradition, by (1) listening to the Buddha's teachings, (2) reflecting upon them, (3) meditating upon them. For more information see Sangharakshita, *The Three Levels of Wisdom*, Windhorse, Glasgow 1988.

10 This sūtra is available in several translations. For a commentary on the sūtra, and a reading list, see Sangharakshita, *The Drama of Cosmic Enlightenment*, Windhorse, Glasgow 1993.

11 *The Perfection of Wisdom in Eight Thousand Lines and its Verse Summary*, trans. E.Conze, Four Seasons Foundation, San Francisco 1983.

12 *The Holy Teaching of Vimalakīrti: A Mahāyāna Scripture*, trans. R.A.F.Thurman, Pennsylvania State University Press, University Park and London 1976. For a commentary see Sangharakshita, *The Inconceivable Emancipation*, Windhorse, Birmingham 1995.

13 A major development of Mahāsaṅghika teaching, which dates from c.120BCE, was the doctrine of the *lokuttaravāda*, or 'supramundane' Buddha – *lokuttara* meaning literally 'beyond the world', in contrast to 'worldly or unliberated' (*laukika*).

14 *Tipiṭaka* (Pali) means 'the three baskets' and refers to the collections of the Buddha's words. These are the Vinaya Piṭaka, the Sutta Piṭaka, and the Abhidhamma Piṭaka. Together with the *tantras* they make up the four chief divisions of the canonical writings.

15 The five precepts are the most fundamental set of Buddhist ethical guidelines. Put in negative terms they involve working to refrain from (1) harming living beings, (2) taking the not-given, (3) sexual misconduct, (4) untruthfulness, and (5) dulling the mind with intoxicants. Positively they mean striving to develop (1) loving-kindness, (2) generosity, (3) contentment, (4) truthfulness, and (5) awareness.

16 From Keats, 'Ode on a Grecian Urn', 1820, st.5.

17 *Tathāgatha* is a title of the Buddha. It can mean 'one thus gone' or 'one thus come'. A Buddha goes from the world through wisdom – seeing its illusory nature. He comes into it through compassion – in order to teach living beings how to put an end to suffering.

18 The *dhyānas* are the different levels of higher consciousness experienced in meditation. There are the four 'dhyānas of the world of form' (*rūpa dhyānas*)

and four 'formless dhyānas' (*arūpa dhyānas*). For more see Kamalashila, *Meditation: The Buddhist Way of Tranquillity and Insight*, Windhorse, Glasgow 1992, pp.63–76.

19 The mandala of the five Buddhas consists of the four Buddhas mentioned here – Akṣobhya, Ratnasambhava, Amitābha, and Amoghasiddhi – plus a central Buddha, Vairocana. They embody the transcendent qualities of Enlightenment, the five Wisdoms of Buddhahood.

20 *Samādhi* (literally the state of being firmly fixed or established), is a state of deep and concentrated meditation usually conjoined with direct insight into the true nature of things.

21 This is a reference to that fundamental Buddhist teaching, the Noble Eightfold Path. According to the Buddha, one begins by traversing the mundane Eightfold Path – starting with Right View, which leads to the progressive development of the remaining seven stages: Right Resolve, Right Speech, Right Action, Right Livelihood, Right Effort, Right Awareness, and Right Samādhi. In the course of spiritual practice one gradually refines each area of one's life until transcendental insight is attained. It is then that one begins to tread the transcendental Eightfold Path, which is divided into the Path of Vision and the Path of Transformation. The Path of Vision corresponds to the arising of Perfect Vision, the transcendental counterpart of Right View, while the Path of Transformation comprises the perfection of each of the other seven stages of the path – Right Resolve becomes Perfect Emotion, Right Speech becomes Perfect Speech, and so on. When all eight stages have been perfected, full Enlightenment is attained. See Sangharakshita, *Vision and Transformation*, Windhorse, Glasgow 1990.

22 'Oh! the one life within us and abroad, / which meets all motion and becomes its soul, / A light in sound, a sound-like power in light, / Rhythm in all thought, and joyance everywhere.' Coleridge, 'The Eolian Harp', 1796, l.26.

23 Published as *A Guide to the Bodhisattva's Way of Life*, trans. StephenBatchelor, Library of Tibetan Works and Archives, Dharamsala 1979 (translated from the Tibetan).

24 *Puja* ('devotional worship') is a ceremony of recitation and chanting before the Buddha image. This is a demonstration of devotion in the sense of reverence for the ideal of Enlightenment. Regular practice of puja refines one's emotional positivity, breaking through habitual self-centredness and isolation, and leading to an empathy with all life. The sevenfold puja is a traditional Mahāyāna form.

25 *Bhikkhu* (Pali) means monk, or one who goes for alms. The Sanskrit is *bhikṣu*.

26 The monastic code is set out in the Vinaya Piṭaka of the Pali Canon. See *The Book of the Discipline, vol.iv*, trans. I.B. Horner, Pali Text Society, London 1982.

27 Dhardo Rimpoche was an eminent Tibetan lama of the Gelugpa tradition. Sangharakshita, who met Dhardo Rimpoche in Kalimpong in 1953, and received the Bodhisattva ordination from him, described him as 'perhaps embodying the Bodhisattva Ideal to a greater extent than anybody I had met' in *The History of My Going For Refuge*, Windhorse, London 1988, p.89.

28 See Emmerick, op.cit., p.9.

29 Ibid., p.9.

30 Ibid., p.9.

31 The *nidāna* chain is made up of the twelve links of conditioned co-production which represent the application of the general Buddhist principle of conditionality to the process of rebirth. See Sangharakshita, *A Guide to the Buddhist Path*, Windhorse, Glasgow 1990, pp.86ff.

32 Emmerick, op.cit., p.9.

33 The Four Noble Truths were set out by the Buddha in his first major pronouncement after his Enlightenment, in about 528BCE and are as follows:
(1) The truth of the existence of suffering.
(2) The truth of the cause of suffering, which is egotistical desire and craving.
(3) The truth of the cessation of suffering, which is the cessation of egotistical desire, and
(4) the truth of the way to the cessation of suffering which is the Noble Eightfold Path.

34 Emmerick, op.cit., p.9.

35 Ibid., p.9.

35 Ibid., p.10.

35 Ibid., p.10.

38 Ibid., p.10.

39 Ibid., p.10.

40 Ibid., p.10.

41 Ibid., p.14.

42 The Stream Entrant is someone who has developed a degree of insight sufficient to attain to the first stage of the transcendental path, thereby breaking the first three of the ten fetters, i.e. fixed self-view, doubt or lack of commitment, and dependence on mere morality and religious observances as ends in themselves. Traditionally, once one has gained Stream Entry, progress towards the goal of full Enlightenment is irreversible.

43 Emmerick, op.cit., pp.10–11.

44 There is no satisfactory equivalent for the Pali *mettā* in English, but it is usually translated 'loving-kindness'. This positive emotion is cultivated systematically in a specific meditation practice, the *mettā bhāvanā*, in the final stage of which the meditator develops *mettā* towards all living beings. For an

explanation of the practice, see Kamalashila, *Meditation: The Buddhist Way of Tranquillity and Insight*, Windhorse, Glasgow 1992, pp.25–27. Also *Metta: The Practice of Loving Kindness*, Windhorse, Glasgow 1992.

45 *Manu* in Hindu mythology is the forefather of the human race to whom the *Manusmriti* ('Lawbook of Manu') is attributed. This was the collection of works that finally gave institutional religious sanction to the caste system in India, the *Bhagavad Gītā* having already prepared the ground.

46 The *Sigālovāda Sutta* can be found in the *Dīgha Nikāya*. See *Dialogues of the Buddha, vol.iii*, trans. C.A.F. and T.W.Rhys Davids, Pali Text Society, London 1957, p.175.

47 In the widest sense, the sangha is the community of all those who are following the path to Buddhahood. As one of the three Refuges it refers to the Arya or Noble Sangha – those Buddhist practitioners who have gained insight into the true nature of things and whose progress towards Buddhahood is certain. In other contexts the term can refer to those who have taken ordination as Buddhist monks or nuns.

48 In Pali *lobha* means craving, *dveṣa* means hatred, and *moha* means delusion.

49 Emmerick, op.cit., p.12.

50 Ibid., p.12.

51 A *vajra* is a ritual sceptre which symbolically combines the qualities of both diamond and thunderbolt.

52 Emmerick, op.cit., p.13.

53 Ibid., p.14.

54 Ibid., p.12.

55 Ibid., p.16.

56 Ibid., pp.14–16.

57 'When one is aware of being aware, one is conscious of oneself as an individual, conscious of oneself as separate from the group. One is conscious of one's ability to think and feel and act differently from the group, even against the group. An individual of this type is a true individual. Such a person is not only self-aware but is emotionally positive, full of good will toward other living beings. He is also spontaneous and creative because he is not determined in his thinking, feeling, or acting, by previously existing mental, emotional, and psychological patterns – whether his own or those of other people. The true individual is also responsible, aware of his own needs, aware of others' needs, and prepared and willing to act accordingly.' From Sangharakshita, *New Currents in Western Buddhism*, Windhorse, Glasgow 1990, p.24. For a more detailed exposition of the significance of becoming a 'true individual', see Subhuti, *Sangharakshita: A New Voice in the Buddhist Tradition*, Windhorse, Birmingham 1994, pp.118ff.

58 The word *ḍākinī* is derived from a Sanskrit root meaning 'direction', 'space', 'sky'. The masculine form of the word is *ḍāka*. Empty space represents absence of obstruction, freedom of movement. A *ḍākinī* is a being who enjoys such freedom. 'Sky' also represents mind in its absolute aspect; the *ḍākinī* therefore represents that which moves about freely in the mind, the energies of the mind itself. In this sense the *ḍākinīs* symbolize powerful energies rising up from the depth of the mind.

59 The *devaloka* is the 'realm of the gods'. See page 130 for more information.

60 Some of the material in this section on the relative spiritual aptitudes of men and women is from a seminar Sangharakshita gave in New Zealand in 1979 on the *Sūtra of Forty-Two Sections*.

For a thorough exploration of this topic, and of the significance these teachings have for both men and women today, see Subhuti, *Women, Men, and Angels*, Windhorse, Birmingham 1995.

61 Emmerick, op.cit., pp.16–17.

62 Ibid., p.23

63 'The term Mantrayāna seems to have owed its origin to the necessity of distinguishing that branch of the Mahāyāna which advocated the repetition of the *mantras* as the principal means to Enlightenment from that which continued to emphasize the practice of the *pāramitās*.' Sangharakshita, *A Survey of Buddhism*, op cit., p.418.

64 Emmerick, op.cit., p.46.

65 Ibid., p.47.

66 For a fuller description of Mañjughoṣa, see Vessantara, *Meeting the Buddhas*, Windhorse, Glasgow 1993, chapter 13.

67 Emmerick, op.cit., p.43.

68 *Saṃsāra* is the cyclic round of birth and death, marked by suffering and frustration, which can only be brought to an end by the attainment of Enlightenment.

69 *Minor Anthologies vol.ii, Udāna*, trans. F.L. Woodward, Geoffrey Cumberlege, Oxford University Press, London 1948.

70 Sangharakshita, *The Thousand-Petalled Lotus*, Alan Sutton, Gloucester 1988.

71 Right Livelihood is the fifth limb of the Noble Eightfold Path. It is of crucial importance that those who wish to develop spiritually attend to their means of livelihood. See Subhuti, *Sangharakshita: A New Voice in the Buddhist Tradition*, Windhorse, Birmingham 1994, pp.242ff.

72 Emmerick, op.cit., p.49.

73 Ibid., p.50.

74 Ibid., p.58.

75 Ibid., p.58.

76 Ibid., p.59.

77 *Punya* is spiritual merit, as discussed on page 109.

78 The five *niyamas* are the different orders of cause–effect or conditionality obtaining in the universe. They are: physical inorganic order, (non-volitional) mental order, volitional order (karma as we usually understand it), and transcendental order. See Sangharakshita, *The Three Jewels*, Windhorse, Glasgow 1991, pp.69–71, and *Who is the Buddha?* Windhorse, Glasgow 1994, chapter 7.

79 Emmerick, op.cit., p.59.

80 See note 45.

81 Dr B.R.Ambedkar was independent India's first Law Minister and the first Untouchable to be educated in the West. Sangharakshita knew the champion of the Untouchables personally, and played an important part in the 'Mass Conversion Movement' that Ambedkar set in motion.

82 Emmerick, op.cit., p.19.

ILLUSTRATIONS

·

Recommended Reading

The Growth of a Mahāyāna Sūtra

Sangharakshita, *A Survey of Buddhism*, 7th edition, Windhorse, Glasgow 1993, pp.264ff.
Sangharakshita, *The Eternal Legacy*, Tharpa, London 1985, pp.93ff.
Andrew Skilton, *A Concise History of Buddhism*, Windhorse, Birmingham 1994, pp.93ff.
Paul Williams, *Mahayana Buddhism*, Routledge, London 1989.

The Bodhisattva's Dream

On Jātaka stories:
John Garrett Jones, *Tales and Teachings of the Buddha*, Allen & Unwin, London 1986.
On Zen koans:
Paul Reps, *Zen Flesh, Zen Bones*, Penguin, Harmondsworth 1971.
The Blue Cliff Record, trans. T. and J.C. Cleary, Shambhala, Boulder & London 1977.
On the Mandala of the Five Buddhas:
Vessantara, *Meeting the Buddhas*, Windhorse, Glasgow 1993.

The Spiritual Significance of Confession

Mahayana Purification, part 1, trans. Brian Beresford, Library of Tibetan Works and Archives, Dharamsala 1980.

The Protectors of the Dharma

On Buddhist cosmology:
W.M. McGovern, *A Manual of Buddhist Philosophy, vol. I – Cosmology*, Kegan Paul et al., London 1923.
Randy Kloetzli, *Buddhist Cosmology*, Motilal Banarsidass, Delhi 1983.
Shantideva, *A Guide to the Bodhisattva's Way of Life*, trans. Stephen Batchelor, Library of Tibetan Works and Archives, Dharamsala 1979, chapter 2, 'Disclosure of Evil'.

Buddhism and Culture

Raghunath Airi, *The Concept of Sarasvati (in Vedic literature)*, Munshiram Manoharlal, Rohtak 1977.
On the background to Hindu mythology:
A.L. Basham, *The Wonder that was India*, Sidgwick and Jackson, London 1954.
On Buddhism and art:
Sangharakshita, *The Religion of Art*, Windhorse, Glasgow 1988.
Sangharakshita, *In the Realm of the Lotus*, Windhorse, Birmingham 1995.

Nature, Man, and Enlightenment

Martine Batchelor, ed. *Buddhism and Ecology*, Cassel, 1992.
Maurice Ash, *The Fabric of the World*, Green Books, Devon 1992.

Buddhist Economics

E.F. Schumacher, *Small is Beautiful*, Vintage, London 1993.
On Right Livelihood:
Sangharakshita, *Vision and Transformation*, Windhorse, Glasgow 1990, chapter 5, 'The Ideal Society'.
Claude Whitmyer, ed. *Mindfulness and Meaningful Work: Explorations in Right Livelihood*, Parallax, Berkeley 1994.

The Moral Order and its Upholders

Greg Bailey, *The Mythology of Brahmā*, Oxford University Press, Delhi 1993.
On ethics:
Sangharakshita, *The Ten Pillars of Buddhism*, Windhorse, Glasgow 1989.
On karma and rebirth:
Sangharakshita, *Who is the Buddha?*, Windhorse, Glasgow 1994, chapter 7.

INDEX

The Windhorse symbolizes the energy of the enlightened mind carrying the Three Jewels – the Buddha, the Dharma, and the Sangha – to all sentient beings.

Buddhism is one of the fastest growing spiritual traditions in the Western world. Throughout its 2,500-year history, it has always succeeded in adapting its mode of expression to suit whatever culture it has encountered.

Windhorse Publications aims to continue this tradition as Buddhism comes to the West. Today's Westerners are heirs to the entire Buddhist tradition, free to draw instruction and inspiration from all the many schools and branches. Windhorse publishes works by authors who not only understand the Buddhist tradition but are also familiar with Western culture and the Western mind.

For orders and catalogues contact

WINDHORSE PUBLICATIONS
UNIT 1-316 THE CUSTARD FACTORY
GIBB STREET
BIRMINGHAM
B9 4AA
UK

WINDHORSE PUBLICATIONS (USA)
14 HEARTWOOD CIRCLE
NEWMARKET
NEW HAMPSHIRE
NH 03857
USA

Windhorse Publications is an arm of the Friends of the Western Buddhist Order, which has more than sixty centres on four continents. Through these centres, members of the Western Buddhist Order offer regular programmes of events for the general public and for more experienced students. These include meditation classes, public talks, study on Buddhist themes and texts, and 'bodywork' classes such as t'ai chi, yoga, and massage. The FWBO also runs several retreat centres and the Karuna Trust, a fundraising charity that supports social welfare projects in the slums and villages of India.

Many FWBO centres have residential spiritual communities and ethical businesses associated with them. Arts activities are encouraged too, as is the development of strong bonds of friendship between people who share the same ideals. In this way the FWBO is developing a unique approach to Buddhism, not simply as a set of techniques, less still as an exotic cultural interest, but as a creatively directed way of life for people living in the modern world.

If you would like more information about the FWBO please write to

LONDON BUDDHIST CENTRE ARYALOKA
51 ROMAN ROAD HEARTWOOD CIRCLE
LONDON NEWMARKET
E2 0HU NEW HAMPSHIRE
UK NH 03857
  USA